T0393886

# ARTS AND COMMUNITY CHANGE

*Arts and Community Change: Exploring Cultural Development Policies, Practices, and Dilemmas* addresses the growing number of communities adopting arts- and culture-based development methods to influence social change. Providing community workers and planners with strategies to develop arts policy that enriches communities and their residents, this collection critically examines the central tensions and complexities in arts policy, paying attention to issues of gentrification and stratification.

Including a variety of case studies from across the United States and Canada, these success stories and best-practice approaches cross many media and present strategies to design appropriate policy for unique populations.

Edited by Max O. Stephenson, Jr. and A. Scott Tate of Virginia Tech, *Arts and Community Change* presents 10 chapters from artistic and community leaders: essential reading for students and practitioners in economic development and arts management.

**Max O. Stephenson, Jr.** is Professor of Public and International Affairs, School of Public and International Affairs at Virginia Tech, USA, and director of the Virginia Tech Institute for Policy and Governance. His current research and teaching interests include the arts and community change processes, nongovernmental organizations, and international development and peacebuilding.

**A. Scott Tate** is an educator and community development practitioner. He currently serves as a senior economic development specialist in the Office of Economic Development at Virginia Tech, USA. His community work includes directing or co-directing the Engaging Communities and Campuses national demonstration project and the Virginia Entrepreneur Express Workshop Series.

# The Community Development Research and Practice Series

Series Editor: Rhonda G. Phillips, Purdue University, USA

As the series continues to grow with the seventh volume, it is our intent to continue to serve scholars, community developers, planners, public administrators, and others involved in research, practice, and policy making in the realm of community development. The series strives to provide both timely and applied information for researchers, students, and practitioners. Building on a long history since 1970 of publishing the Community Development Society's journal, *Community Development* (www.comm-dev.org), the book series contributes to a growing and rapidly changing knowledge base as a resource for practitioners and researchers alike. For additional information, please see the series page at http://www.routledge.com/books/series/CDRP/.

The evolution of the field of community development continues. As reflected in both theory and practice, community development is at the forefront of change, which comes as no surprise to our communities and regions that constantly face challenges and opportunities. As a practice-focused discipline, change often seems to be the only constant in the community development realm. The need to integrate theory, practice, research, teaching, and training is now even more pressing than ever, given rapidly transforming economic, social, environmental, political, and cultural climates locally and globally. Current and applicable information and insights about effective research and practice are needed.

The Community Development Society, a nonprofit association of those interested in pushing the discipline forward, is delighted to offer this book series in partnership with Routledge. The series is designed to integrate innovative thinking on tools, strategies, and experiences as a resource especially well suited for bridging the gaps between theory, research, and practice. The Community Development Society actively promotes continued advancement of the discipline and practice. Fundamental to this mission is adherence to the following core principles of good practice. This book series is a reflection of many of these principles:

- Promote active and representative participation toward enabling all community members to meaningfully influence the decisions that affect their lives.
- Engage community members in learning about and understanding community issues and the economic, social, environmental, political, psychological, and other impacts associated with alternative courses of action.
- Incorporate the diverse interest and cultures of the community in the community development process, and disengage from support of any effort that is likely to adversely affect the disadvantaged members of a community.
- Work actively to enhance the leadership capacity of community members, leaders, and groups within the community.
- Be open to using the full range of action strategies to work toward the long-term sustainability and well-being of the community.

We invite you to explore the series and continue to do so as new volumes are added. We hope you will find it a valuable resource for supporting community development research and practice.

*Other books in the series:*

**Community Visioning Programs**
Processes and Outcomes
*Norman Walzer and Gisele Hamm*

**Catalysts for Change**
Twenty-first Century Philanthropy and Community Development
*Maria Martinez-Cosio and Mirle Rabinowitz Bussell*

**Theory, Practice, and Community Development**
*Mark Brennan, Jeffrey Bridger, and Theodore Alter*

**Schools and Urban Revitalization**
Rethinking Institutions and Community Development
*Kelly L. Patterson and Robert Mark Silverman*

**Knowledge Partnering for Community Development**
*Robyn Eversole*

**Social Capital at the Community Level**
An Applied Interdisciplinary Perspective
*John M. Halstead and Steven C. Deller*

"*Arts and Community Change* is an excellent resource for serious students and practitioners in cultural policy and creative placemaking. Taken together, the diverse chapters provide a well-rounded view of issues and current practices. Readers can take away a lot from this book: critical insights about the challenges and consequences of current practices, a description of engagement tools, and examples of communities that succeeded to varying degrees. This is the kind of book that a scholar should read before embarking on a new research project; a student should read to get smart about cultural policy and creative placemaking; and a placemaking practitioner should read to hone his or her craft."

*Leonardo Vazquez, Executive Director,*
*The National Consortium for Creative Placemaking*

# ARTS AND COMMUNITY CHANGE

## Exploring Cultural Development Policies, Practices, and Dilemmas

*Edited by*
*Max O. Stephenson, Jr. and A. Scott Tate*

Routledge
Taylor & Francis Group

NEW YORK AND LONDON

First published 2015
by Routledge
711 Third Avenue, New York, NY 10017

and by Routledge
2 Park Square, Milton Park, Abingdon, Oxon OX14 4RN

*Routledge is an imprint of the Taylor & Francis Group, an informa business*

*Library of Congress Cataloging in Publication Data*
Arts and community change : exploring cultural development policies, practices and dilemmas / edited by Max O. Stephenson, Jr. and A. Scott Tate.
   pages cm – (The community development research and practice series ; volume 7)
   Includes index.
   1. Arts and society. 2. Art and state. 3. Cultural policy.
   4. Community arts projects. I. Stephenson, Max O. (Max Olin), Jr., 1955– editor. II. Tate, A. Scott, editor. III. Goldbard, Arlene. Making beauty, making meaning, making community.
   NX180.S6A758 2015
   700.1´03–dc23                                         2014045444

ISBN: 978-1-138-02433-5 (hbk)
ISBN: 978-1-138-02434-2 (pbk)
ISBN: 978-1-315-77581-4 (ebk)

Typeset in Bembo
by HWA Text and Data Management, London

For Jessica, whose life is daily an inspiration to me.

MOS Jr.

For Meighan and Toby.

AST

# CONTENTS

*List of Figures* — xi
*List of Contributors* — xii

Introduction: The Place of the Arts in Community Identity and Social Change — 1
*Max O. Stephenson, Jr. and A. Scott Tate*

1  Making Beauty, Making Meaning, Making Community — 11
*Arlene Goldbard*

2  Rivers and Bridges: Theater in Regional Planning — 28
*Jon Catherwood-Ginn and Robert H. Leonard*

3  One New York Rising Together? Arts and Culture in Neighborhood Ecosystems — 54
*Jan Cohen-Cruz*

4  Sustaining Emergent Culture in Montreal's Entertainment District — 77
*Anjali Mishra*

5  Digital Storytelling in Appalachia: Gathering and Sharing Community Voices and Values — 99
*Holly Lesko and Thenmozhi Soundararajan*

6  Shaping the Artful City: A Case Study of Urban Economic Reinvention — 108
*A. Scott Tate*

7  Community Cultural Development as a Site of Joy, Struggle, and Transformation                                                    136
   *Dudley Cocke*

8  A Dialogue on Dance and Community Practice                    166
   *Liz Lerman and Jawole Willa Jo Zollar*

9  Assessing Arts-Based Social Change Endeavors: Controversies and Complexities                                     186
   *Kate Preston Keeney and Pam Korza*

10 Theater as a Tool for Building Peace and Justice: DAH Teatar and Bond Street Theatre                              212
   *Lyusyena Kirakosyan and Max O. Stephenson, Jr.*

   *Index*                                                      *232*

# FIGURES

2.1    A moment of audience interaction during a performance of
Building Home's *behind a stranger's face*     31

4.1    Map of Montreal, showing the Quartier des spectacles in relation
to surrounding districts     81

6.1    The Roanoke, Virginia, city skyline, featuring the Taubman
Museum in the foreground     114

7.1    Roadside Theater artists perform a traditional Jack tale     137

7.2    Roadside Theater performs *Red Fox/Second Hangin'*     140

7.3    Roadside Theater conducts a story circle     148

7.4    Junebug Productions and Roadside Theater ensemble performs
*Junebug/Jack*     150

7.5    Roadside Theater's Community Cultural Development
Methodology     156

7.6    Roadside Theater performs *South of the Mountain*     162

8.1    Jowale Willa Jo Zollar and Liz Lerman at the Performative
Teach-In Event of *Blood, Muscle and Bone*     168

8.2    Urban Bush Women's *Hep Hep Sweet Sweet*     172

8.3    The company of Liz Lerman's *Healing Wars*     178

8.4    Paul Hurley and Keth A. Thompson in *Healing Wars*     178

8.5    Urban Bush Women's *Walking with 'Trane, Chapter 2*     184

# CONTRIBUTORS

**Jon Catherwood-Ginn** is partnerships and engagement manager for the Moss Center for the Arts at Virginia Tech. Catherwood-Ginn has also worked with the Lost Nation Theatre in Montpelier, Vermont; Hamilton-Gibson Productions in Pennsylvania; Extant Arts Company; and the Off-Broadway Aquila Theatre in New York City. He holds a master's degree from Virginia Tech.

**Dudley Cocke** is a writer, stage director, and media producer, and is the artistic director of Roadside Theater, the professional theater wing of the award-winning Appalachian arts and humanities institution Appalshop in Whitesburg, Kentucky. Cocke serves on the national boards of Appalshop; Bush Foundation; Imagining America: Artists and Scholars in Public Life; and the Rural Research Policy Institute. He received his bachelor's degree from Washington & Lee University; his graduate work was conducted at Harvard University.

**Jan Cohen-Cruz** began her work as a scholar and practitioner of engaged art co-facilitating a theatre workshop at Trenton State Prison as part of the NYC Street Theatre. She brought Augusto Boal to the United States and is a freelance practitioner and scholar of his work. Cohen-Cruz served on the faculty of New York University's Tisch School of the Arts for many years. She currently serves as university professor at Syracuse University and evaluator of a U.S. Department of State cultural diplomacy initiative involving community-based visual arts projects in fifteen countries. Cohen-Cruz previously was director of Imagining America and editor of its journal. She received her doctorate from New York University.

**Arlene Goldbard** is a writer, speaker, consultant, and cultural activist whose focus is the intersection of culture, politics, and spirituality. Her books include *Crossroads: Reflections on the Politics of Culture*; *New Creative Community: The Art* *of Cultural Development; Community, Culture and Globalization;* and *The Culture of Possibility: Art, Artists & the Future;* and her novels, *Clarity* and *The Wave.* Her essays have appeared in many leading magazines and journals. She has addressed academic and community audiences in the United States and Europe on topics ranging from the ethics of community arts practice to the development of integral organizations. She has provided advice and counsel to hundreds of community-based organizations.

**Kate Preston Keeney** has research interests which bridge arts management and public policy and management scholarship. Keeney earned her doctoral degree in public administration and public affairs from Virginia Tech and her master's degree in arts management from American University. She was the Americans for the Arts' Animating Democracy IMPACT graduate assistant in 2012, and has worked as an arts administrator at the John F. Kennedy Center for the Performing Arts in Washington, DC.

**Lyusyena Kirakosyan** serves as an affiliated faculty member of the Virginia Tech Institute for Policy and Governance. She has worked in several nongovernmental organizations in Sao Paulo, Brazil, two of which sought to ensure the rights of disabled individuals. Kirakosyan is currently engaged in collaborative research projects on digital storytelling and community change and the role of the arts in peacebuilding under the auspices of the Institute for Policy and Governance. She holds a doctoral degree from Virginia Tech.

**Pam Korza** is co-director of Animating Democracy, an Americans for the Arts program that fosters arts and humanities activity that encourages civic dialogue and engagement on contemporary issues. Korza provided research for and co-wrote the study *Animating Democracy: The Artistic Imagination as a Force in Civic Dialogue.* Her work includes organizational assessment, planning, program design and evaluation for cultural organizations, state arts agencies, and private foundations. She has directed the Boston-based New England Film and Video Festival; coordinated the New England Arts Biennial; co-authored *The Arts Festival Work Kit;* and co-edited and contributed to *Fundamentals of Local Arts Management.*

**Robert H. Leonard** teaches theatre arts at Virginia Tech, where he heads the master of fine arts degree program in directing and public dialogue. Leonard regularly directs plays at Virginia Tech and was the lead author of *Performing Communities: Grassroots Ensemble Theaters Deeply Rooted in Eight U.S. Communities* in 2006. Leonard is a trainer and facilitator with Alternate ROOTS' Resources for Social Change.

**Liz Lerman** is a choreographer, performer, writer, educator, and speaker and the recipient of numerous honors, including a 2002 MacArthur Fellowship and a 2011 United States Artists Ford Fellowship in Dance. She founded Liz Lerman Dance Exchange in 1976 and cultivated the company's unique multigenerational ensemble into a leading force in contemporary dance until 2011. She was an artist-in-residence and visiting lecturer at Harvard University in fall of 2011 and is creating collaborative works at Arena Stage, Center Stage, and Baltimore's Performance Kitchen, and continuing to teach nationally and internationally. Wesleyan University Press published her collection of essays, *Hiking the Horizontal: Field Notes from a Choreographer*.

**Holly Lesko** is a community engagement research faculty member with the Virginia Tech Institute for Policy and Governance, where she was the principal investigator for the New River Valley: Healthy by Design project in partnership with the New River Valley Planning District. Additionally, Lesko is the project coordinator for the Partners for Self-Sufficiency program, providing services to regional clients who currently receive public assistance and require more extensive employment and social service needs. Lesko earned her master's degree from Virginia Tech and was a resident fellow at the Massachusetts Institute of Technology Reflective Practitioner program.

**Anjali Mishra** is a professional planner who has overseen design competitions, infrastructure programming for large outdoor festivals, transportation, and urban design projects for major public institutions and neighborhood branding strategies. Work for small and/or alternative performance venues balances this experience with insight into Montreal's independent music scene. Mishra currently lives in Montreal, where she serves as a project manager for that city.

**Thenmozhi Soundararajan** is a transmedia artist and digital storytelling consultant who was featured in *Utne Reader* in 2003 as one of the top visionaries younger than thirty. She was also profiled in *The Source* as one of the top ten political forces in hip hop. Soundararajan also spent time in residence at the MIT Center for Reflective Community Practice, writing about storytelling, diversity, and future technology, and that research inspired her transition to narrative filmmaking and enrollment in the University of Southern California School of Cinematic Arts, where she earned her master's degree.

**Max O. Stephenson, Jr.** is professor of public and international affairs, School of Public and International Affairs at Virginia Tech, and director of the Virginia Tech Institute for Policy and Governance. His current research and teaching interests include the arts and community change processes, nongovernmental organizations, and international development, peacebuilding, humanitarian relief, and environmental justice. He has published several books and more than fifty refereed articles and book chapters. Stephenson earned his bachelor's, master's, and doctoral degrees from the University of Virginia.

**A. Scott Tate** is a researcher, educator, and community development practitioner. Tate currently serves as a senior economic development specialist in the Office of Economic Development at Virginia Tech. He has conducted ethnographic field studies of arts-based community change efforts in the United States and Northern Ireland. Past and current community work includes directing, or co-directing the Engaging Communities and Campuses national demonstration project and the Virginia Entrepreneur Express Workshop Series. He holds a PhD from Virginia Tech.

**Jawole Willa Jo Zollar** founded Urban Bush Women (UBW) in 1984 as a performance ensemble dedicated to exploring the use of cultural expression as a catalyst for social change. She has created works for UBW, Alvin Ailey American Dance Theater, Philadanco, University of Maryland, Virginia Commonwealth University, and others. Zollar's numerous awards include a New York Dance and Performance Award (Bessie) for her work as choreographer/creator of *Walking with Pearl … Southern Diaries* (2006); a United States Artists Wynn fellowship (2008); and a Guggenheim fellowship (2009). She serves as director of UBW's Summer Leadership Institute, is founding artistic director of UBW, and currently holds the position of the Nancy Smith Fichter Professor of Dance and Robert O. Lawton Distinguished Professor at Florida State University.

# INTRODUCTION

## The Place of the Arts in Community Identity and Social Change

*Max O. Stephenson, Jr. and A. Scott Tate*

The idea of the arts as a vehicle for community building is not new. Some version of this refrain has been present in development planning and policy making in communities throughout the United States and around the globe for some decades. This volume's editors have witnessed regions reshape economic activity around cultural heritage and neighborhoods torn by deep-seated racial, ethnic, and sectarian divisions use the arts in efforts to build a more peaceful post-conflict coexistence. We have also observed the many instances when the arts have been deployed less fruitfully, equated solely with tourism or economic development very narrowly understood, or have, consciously or not, contributed to neighborhood gentrification and increased inequality. This book emerged from our interest in the apparent paradoxes implicit in the question: What is the place of the arts in community change initiatives?

The question of art's role in community is important and timely. The number of localities adopting arts- and culture-based development strategies has grown rapidly in recent years as more towns and cities have embraced the view that these approaches will yield positive economic impacts, including increases in tourists/visitors and tourism-related taxes and expenditures; increased numbers of artists and arts studios; and new cadres of entrepreneurs and creative workers or revitalized spaces. Nonetheless, it is also well documented that arts-related development may foster or exacerbate gentrification, deepen class divisions, quicken and intensify neighborhood decay, and divert resources and attention from existing grass roots and cultural development organizations.

Sometimes as a part of these approaches, sometimes from outside these efforts, and in other instances in opposition to such activities, artists, activists, community groups, and civil society organizations are increasingly employing the arts to build civil society, secure democratization, and provide a share of the conditions necessary for social change. The nature and impacts of such initiatives vary widely and scholars, policy makers, cultural leaders, and community planners do not as yet fully understand all of the political, social, and economic dynamics associated with many arts-based social change strategies. Such endeavors go by many names including community arts, community-based arts, and community cultural development.

Sketching a discrete number of methods to art's role in community change would be an oversimplification. Indeed, the role of arts and culture in development is varied, complex, and multi-faceted. The widespread adoption of approaches based in some measure on growing the "experience economy" (Harvey, 1989; Pine and Gilmore, 1999) or to attract the "creative class" (Florida, 2002, 2005a 2005b) ultimately focus on attraction and consumption. Instead of economic development activities concentrated on efforts to lure branch plants of larger firms to particular locations, many development leaders now seek to attract visitors, investors, young "creative" professionals, artists, and hipster/bohemians.

These initiatives to strengthen an experience-based or creative economy have a feel-good, low-risk, high-reward appeal. Residents, even of the more activist stripe, rarely object to more art, more music, more festivals, and more artisanal food. Though slightly more controversial, many people also welcome many high-profile cultural facility development projects and urban design initiatives to promote walkability and mixed use. Still, some important questions persist, such as what kind of cities and neighborhoods are being designed and for whom are they being created?

Writing in *The Washington Post*, Joel Kotkin has raised a version of this question, emphasizing demographic and economic changes in many American cities in which the numbers of immigrants, families with children, and manufacturing and jobs related to science, technology, engineering, and math have all increased. By designing places for unmarried individuals and, more critically, for experience-based consumption, planners and development professionals are complicit in the rise of gentrification and "luxury cities" frequented most predominantly by upper-class whites (Kotkin, 2014).

Researchers have found that arts-based development often produces socioeconomic segregation and social distancing effects (Strom, 2003; Zukin, 1982). Cultural development as consumption can construct or reinforce cultural and class-based divisions. Examples are nearby in almost every community; think of the museum whose patrons and visitors are mostly from out of town or from particular socioeconomic segments or the performance venue whose average ticket price is $75 or more. The arts entity then may become a symbol of a divide—between those who are and are not able to access the arts due to affordability, content, or disparate levels of cultural capital (Bourdieu, 1986).

Arts-oriented development, even its more consumption-focused guises, has spurred positive change, job creation, downtown revitalization, and a stronger cultural industries sector. Charles Landry has argued that culture and creativity are tightly linked, that investment flows to those locales that demonstrate cultural vibrancy, and that the ability of such places to innovate and problem-solve yields economic benefits that are not easily quantifiable (Landry, 2000). In our view, however, it is insufficient to conclude that cultural vibrancy and creative development approaches are tangibly elusive and largely positive. Elizabeth Currid has framed the issue well:

> We must, however, be careful here. What do we mean by art and culture? Because art and culture are both businesses and, in that sense, tangible and quantifiable but also a zeitgeist of society and, in that sense, ephemeral and intangible, "developing" them becomes multilayered and their definition debatable.
>
> (Currid, 2009, p. 368)

In the broadest sense, all development efforts represent a kind of cultural intervention in the life of a place, as efforts where "someone (or some institution) consciously and programmatically takes action within a culture with the intent of affecting it in some specific way that the intervener thinks desirable" (Whisnant, 1983, p. 13). Such efforts may vary in scale and intensity and may have positive, negative, and/or mixed effects.

Thus, conceiving of the arts as economic engine has its limits. As noted above, art and culture serve other functions, such as the ability to illuminate these types of contradictions and to increase a community's stock of social capital and effect individual and civic change. In *The Aesthetic Dimension*, Herbert Marcuse described this innate and radical potential of art. Art, by taking reality and "re-presenting" it, is "committed to an emancipation of sensibility, imagination, and reason" and may "lead to the emergence of a new consciousness and a new perception" (1978, pp. 9, 41).

Community cultural development and community-based art are fields whose practitioners aspire to employ art to encourage such productive disruption and awareness-enhancing potential. Arlene Goldbard has described community cultural development as a form of community-artist collaboration to explore concerns and express identity in ways that build capacity and lead to positive social change (2006, p. 20). This conception of community-based art constitutes "a field in which artists, collaborating with people whose lives directly inform the subject matter, explore collective meaning" (Cohen-Cruz, 2005, p. 1). Examples of community cultural development efforts, both historical and contemporary, abound. Goldbard has provided a comprehensive historical sketch of the field in her book, *New Creative Community: The Art of Cultural Development* (2006, pp. 101–138).

Community-based arts approaches have also been tightly linked with democratic goals and embodied in terms such as cultural citizenship and cultural democracy (Graves, 2005). The Ford Foundation's Animating Democracy Project, undertaken from 2000 to 2004, supported thirty-six organizations utilizing arts and culture to enhance civic dialogue. That initiative, continued under the aegis of Americans for the Arts, found that arts-based civic dialogue "brought forward new voices, empowering disenfranchised groups and providing access to public dialogue and decision-making processes to people who had never before felt a welcoming entry point" (Korza, Schaffer Bacon, and Assaf, 2005, p. 83).

The distinction among cultural development approaches, however, is rarely clear. Arts activities rooted in creative or experience economy concerns are not always easily separated from community-based arts activities. An arts initiative may be conceived on largely instrumental motivations, such as attracting visitors, and yet may grow to include projects or exhibit characteristics associated with more intentional community-arts interventions. Larger cultural projects may include a host of projects and programs, each of which might differ in terms of purpose, principles, processes, and impacts. Community-based arts projects are also not without challenges in realizing specific impacts or in ensuring social equity and inclusivity.

The expanding number of cultural development efforts and their increasingly complex and heterogeneous elements prevent quick diagnoses or easy division into predetermined, dichotomous categories such as "community-based vs. market-based," "creative economy versus cultural ecosystem," or "intrinsically versus instrumentally motivated." Initiatives may include a blend of characteristics and features that elude ready-made labeling.

This said, the broad approaches to the roles of the arts in community sketched here do differ in intention and in how their adherents conceive of the arts. Those efforts focused on using the arts as instruments for economic growth typically commodify arts and artists and embrace them as a vehicle for the desired purpose of development. Cultural development approaches, meanwhile, typically view the arts as opportunities through which to catalyze citizen agency and secure individual and civic empowerment for change. Advocates of these roles for the arts see them as potentially emancipatory and as fruitful mechanisms to build individual and community social capital. In short, while these approaches each employ the arts, their intentions in so doing differ markedly, as do their desired ends. Nevertheless, as we observe above, while it is useful to imagine these strategies along a spectrum in terms of their intentions, it is often more difficult to divide them on the basis of their effects.

To summarize, arts-based development approaches have assumed a variety of guises, and their impacts are not always easily measured. The same is true of social capital and of supposed indirect economic external benefits of arts development. Likewise, museums can be struggling economically and succeeding programmatically, attracting far-flung visitors but simultaneously failing to engage a diversity of local residents. This volume's authors explore these dilemmas and complexities of culture-led development policy and practice.

Most authors of the chapters that follow examine the role of the arts and culture in community evolution. Collectively, they engage the difficult and perplexing challenges and paradoxes that arise in the various stages of a project or policy's development as a consequence of the coexistence of a number of competing values, norms, goals, and interests in a self-defined community, at a point-in-time.

The framework for this book draws on the concept of imaginaries used in somewhat different ways in the fields of philosophy, social theory, geography, planning, urban and cultural studies, and literature. We define imaginaries as the multiple and intersecting ideas, images, myths, and stories of place and community in various stages of development and coexistence. Our own definition is tightly linked to theories of space and place. In our view, imaginaries intersect in situated spaces in a kind of ideational struggle, manifested in processes of negotiation, with one typically dominant during a given period in a community and one or more others simultaneously vying for pride of place. Although a single imaginary may prevail, localities pursuing arts-based strategies typically encounter multiple and contrasting conceptions of art, development, and place among their citizens. These differing beliefs produce dilemmas revealed in alternate community frames. As such, as interventions are mapped and proceed, communities become sites of contestation regarding meaning; they emerge as loci of an ongoing tug-of-war concerning which values and norms will prevail and be accepted by the general population. Because of their peculiar power, the arts may play profound roles both in revealing the contradictions implicit in extant imaginaries and in assisting citizens in posing or catalyzing new possibilities.

Social theorist Henri Lefebvre has emphasized the non-neutrality of space (Merrifield, 2006, p. 105), which, he has argued, is produced by a complex and often under-analyzed and usually unrecognized set of processes. This "produced space" influences both the cognition and behavior of the individuals residing within it (Lefebvre, 1991). Every site is characterized, according to Lefebvre, by a preponderance of images arising from oversimplification, stereotyping, and labeling, and some of these coalesce into one or more myths underpinned by norms and values, helping to construct the "imagined geography" that residents and nonresidents alike associate with a particular locale. Thus, a community's imaginary is intricately linked to the material as residents experience it as "these spatial conceptual forms play a significant part in the rationale by which daily lives are lived and by which decisions, policies, and actions are rationalized and legitimized" (Shields, 1991, p. 47).

We asked each of our contributors to consider the difficulties and tensions in evidence among major groups contending to define or redefine their community's imagined geography in the cases they examined. By doing so, our authors investigated communities as multiple, fluid, evolving, and non-interchangeable. As a result, the chapters reflect a broad canvas of intersecting place images, stories, ideas, and interests in differing stages of development and recognition. Social constructs play a profound role in understanding place and in influencing the decisions that either enable or inhibit the creation and adoption of alternative possible futures for communities.

Arts- and culture-based development activities, then, are a form of spatial production, reflecting, influencing, and altering places and their meanings, depending on the forms adopted and pressed and the effects achieved. This volume explores the ways such initiatives take shape at specific sites as part of a localized constellation of place ideas and images, influenced and shaped by existing social and cultural claims and conditions and economic activities and governance actions.

So, what does such a theoretical lens portend for community leaders and development practitioners? As arts- and culture-based strategies have multiplied, it becomes ever more important to conceive and pursue effective place-specific policies and approaches. This necessity represents one reason why cultural planning has taken on new life in many localities and regions. Still, the quality, scope, and impact of such efforts vary widely, "Cultural planning at its worst can produce the best so-called cultural centre in the world surrounded by decaying neighbourhoods, deserted streets, minimal public transport, homeless families and bankrupt businesses" (Mercer, 2002, p. 171).

This book's authors engage the questions and controversies surrounding cultural development by drawing on grounded examples to generate observations and findings of relevance and accessibility to practitioners and academics. We suggest scholars, public officials, and private developers will benefit from applying a place-based, critically analytical approach to understand better the dynamics and import of arts-based change efforts irrespective of their form. Our authors, as artists, scholars, and development practitioners, offer contributions from multiple perspectives that today characterize the field of arts-based development. Contributors employ specific cases, critical assessments, and dialogic exchange to focus on the tensions and complexities of art as they relate to place identity and social change.

Most basically, this volume explores the paradoxical and multi-faceted dynamics of art in community change processes by addressing such questions as the following:

- Which arts- and culture-based approaches contribute to what kinds of changes?
- In what ways do such approaches hinder or complicate social change endeavors?
- How can artists, planners, and community development practitioners employ the arts to promote positive and inclusive change while honoring the agency of those they address?

Our contributors offer examples from their research and experiences that offer insights into these concerns. In Chapter 1, Arlene Goldbard explores the connections between culture and development, tracing the cultural policy discourse at the international level and assaying its implications for U.S. policy and for officials and arts professionals. Goldbard provides a wide-lens overview for the volume, underscoring the significance of policy while also suggesting the importance of core principles for cultural development practices. She describes development projects incorporating a "cultural lens" that are guided by concerns of widespread engagement, active citizen involvement, and equitable distribution. Such activities, she contends, tend to produce increased agency and community belonging among those for whom they are targeted. Viewed in this light, culture is not a particular type of development or a commodity, but an inherent element of every project aimed at securing community change.

In Chapter 2, Robert Leonard and Jon Catherwood-Ginn describe the Building Home project that brought performing artists and community planners together in a three-year regional planning project to employ the arts to encourage public participation, especially among traditionally disenfranchised and disadvantaged citizens. The initiative was funded by a national Sustainable Communities grant and sought to produce a plan for livability in the New River Valley (NRV), a mostly rural area in the Blue Ridge Mountains of western Virginia. The authors employed arts-based strategies to expand the depth and breadth of public involvement in the regional planning process. Leonard and Catherwood-Ginn describe a number of techniques that the project's principals developed or employed. As noted, the animating rationale for involving the artists in this effort was to assist public officials in addressing a common and recurring planning dilemma: how to attract and engage populations that are typically poorly represented in planning processes? Public input helps to shape plans, and such proposals inform policy and influence practice. The challenge of securing widespread and representative public participation is important.

Building Home not only helped engage groups of NRV residents who had traditionally not been involved in planning initiatives, but the effort also elicited their input in more varied and textured ways through the use of story circles and theater derived from their lived experience. This chapter provides rich detail on the genesis and implementation of the program and offers readers an in-depth examination of the benefits and challenges of involving the arts in such efforts.

In Chapter 3, Jan Cohen-Cruz, an internationally known cultural development scholar and arts practitioner, describes the arts ecosystem of New York City and the efforts of several cultural organizations there to establish deeper collaborative structures in the form of Naturally Occurring Cultural Districts. In contrast to the designation of arts-districts through legislation, a consortium of New York City arts and culture entities and neighborhood organizations formed to establish a more place-relevant, locally responsive cultural district. The partnership provided opportunities for enhanced collaboration, learning, and issue advocacy. The effort was partially motivated by the interest of several arts institution leaders to engage more deeply with neighborhood-based concerns and activities. As one example, Cohen-Cruz describes the New York Chinatown History Project that has sought to connect scholars, artists, and residents to help reclaim the history of the Chinese community in the city. Her chapter provides insight into the inter-organizational dynamics of arts entities and the challenges and promises of deeper partnerships. The Queens Museum, for example, has come to represent an approach that Cohen-Cruz dubs, "community embeddedness." Through a network of place-engaged cultural organization and neighborhood leaders, new projects and foci have emerged that are more responsive to and inclusive of the concerns and experiences of local residents.

In Chapter 4, Anjali Mishra continues the examination of urban arts ecosystems. Mishra, a professional planner in Montreal, Canada, surveys the independent and experimental arts scene in that city's Quartier des Spectacles. While the area has been a longtime hub for entertainment and nightlife in the city, the Quartier has experienced a number of changes and threats to its status as a cultural center. In 2004, officials and stakeholders crafted a culture-led revitalization plan for the area that has now become a premier tourist destination and epicenter for festivals and events. The growth in tourism, infrastructure investment, and commercial development has also been accompanied by challenges to the Quarter's historic mix of alternative artists, underground venues, and informal arts economy. Mishra's analysis reveals the fragility of arts-based ecosystems and how public policies may influence their capacity for sustainability.

Digital storytelling is a process that engages and equips residents to employ media to craft policy-relevant personal narratives. Holly Lesko and Thenmozhi Soundararajan recount their experiences with a digital storytelling initiative involving rural teenagers that addressed public health concerns that each youth had experienced first-hand. As the chapter relates, employing arts-related approaches to conduct both the process and to create its final product led to tangible products that could be shared with fellow residents and local policy makers and informed policy debates and illuminated public concerns in novel and meaningful ways.

In Chapter 6, Scott Tate examines one city's experiences in employing arts and culture as a central element of its economic re-identification effort. He describes the multi-pronged strategies employed by Roanoke, Virginia public officials and cultural leaders. In particular, the chapter outlines the development and evolution of three significant arts-based efforts in that community: the Taubman Museum of Art, the city's Arts and Cultural Plan, and its Marginal Arts Festival. Each of these initiatives has played a significant role in shaping the city's identity as an emerging arts center. The three examples also illustrate the nuanced, complex, and evolving nature of cultural regeneration activities and offer insights for officials and arts leaders in other localities whose leaders have elected to employ the arts as a part of their economic restructuring efforts.

Roadside Theater and its artistic director, Dudley Cocke, have a long history and a prominent place in the field of community arts. Headquartered in central Appalachia, Roadside is a small professional company that places community cultural development at the core of its mission. This commitment is demonstrated in a number of ways, perhaps none more significantly than the theater company's decision to perform only in communities that contractually commit to bring together an inclusive mix of the area's population for its performances and workshops. In Chapter 7, Cocke discusses how the arts may be especially powerful as a mechanism for engaging historically marginalized populations, wherever these may be located. Roadside Theater has also developed and tested a number of methods, especially story circles, that engage community members in workshop settings and through which formative stories of personal identity and community experience can be shared and common understanding forged.

Liz Lerman and Jawole Zollar are colleagues and long-standing community arts practitioners. Each gained prominence as the leaders of a dance company: Lerman with the Dance Exchange and Zollar with Urban Bush Women. In 2011, the two collaborated in a comprehensive multi-disciplinary project, *Blood, Muscle, Bone: The Anatomy of Wealth and Poverty*. Zollar and Lerman structured Chapter 8 as a dialogue, exploring jointly and individually their experiences and insights related to the practice of community-engaged art-making. Their introspective and interactive discussion offers a wealth of insight into the creative process and participatory practice of artists committed to socially and community-engaged work.

In Chapter 9, Kate Preston Keeney and Pam Korza discuss the challenges associated with assessing arts-based change endeavors. These analysts address a critical concern: What do arts practitioners and development professionals mean by change and how are they measuring it? Arts project leaders use various methods to gauge and convey project outcomes. In most instances, assessment is an organizational imperative driven by funding and sustainability considerations. Alternatively, some community arts practitioners have argued against focusing too narrowly on quantifiable metrics. Arts-based processes, as Keeeney and Korza emphasize, often proceed in unexpected ways, and their results may be neither immediately tangible nor readily assessed. They provide examples of more dynamic and reflexive assessment strategies as one response to this reality. Such processes allow greater flexibility and avoid a reduction of arts-based change impacts to over-simplistic reporting according to a-contextual and preestablished quantifiable measures.

In Chapter 10, Lyusyena Kirakosyan and Max O. Stephenson, Jr. explore two cases in which theater was used as a tool for peace building and social justice. The chapter describes the increased incorporation of arts-based approaches in efforts to ameliorate social conflicts or to build peace after war. Kirakosyan and Stephenson profile DAH Teatar and Bond Street Theatre. The two companies have long utilized theater to pursue positive social change within the conflict-stricken societies in which they have worked. The authors compare the approaches of the two arts groups to employing performance arts for social change, identifying a number of lessons relevant to use of the arts in conflict situations specifically and in social change efforts more generally.

This volume's chapters, taken together, offer a wide-ranging, nuanced, and multifaceted examination of art's role in community change. Viewed as a piece, these contributions illuminate a field in flux, offer promising models and strategies of different sorts reflecting disparate intentions while charting the multiple ways and means by which the arts may play roles in spurring social and economic change and in developing stronger, more democratic, and more socially just communities.

## References

Bourdieu, P. (1986). The forms of capital. In J. Richardson (Ed.) *Handbook of theory and research for the sociology of education* (pp. 241–258). New York, NY: Greenwood.

Cohen-Cruz, J. (2005). *Local acts: Community-based performance in the United States.* Piscataway, NJ: Rutgers University Press.

Currid, E. (2009). Bohemia as subculture; "Bohemia" as industry: Art, culture, and economic development. *Journal of Planning Literature*, 23 (4): 368–382.

Florida, R. (2002). *The rise of the creative class: And how it's transforming work, leisure, community and everyday life.* New York, NY: Perseus Books.

Florida, R. (2005a). *Cities and the creative class.* New York, NY: Routledge.

Florida, R. (2005b). *The flight of the creative class: The new global competition for talent.* New York, NY: HarperCollins.

Goldbard, A. (2006). *New creative community: The art of cultural development.* Oakland, CA: New Village Press.

Graves, J. B. (2005). *Cultural democracy: The arts, community, and public purpose.* Chicago, IL: University of Illinois Press.

Harvey, D. (1989). *The condition of postmodernity.* Oxford, UK: Blackwell.

Korza, P., Schaffer-Bacon, B., and Assaf, A. (2005). *Civic dialogue, arts & culture: Findings from Animating Democracy.* Washington, DC: Americans for the Arts.

Kotkin, J. (2014). The people designing your cities don't care what you want. They're planning for hipsters. *The Washington Post*, August 15. Retrieved August 25, 2014 from http://www.washingtonpost.com/posteverything/wp/2014/08/15/the-people-designing-your-cities-have-no-idea-what-you-or-the-rest-of-the-middle-class-want

Landry, C. (2000). A cultural approach to developing the creative city. *Culturelink* 11(32). Zagreb: Institute for International Relations.

Lefebvre, H. (1991). *The production of space.* Oxford, UK: Basil Blackwell.

Marcuse, H. (1978). *The aesthetic dimension.* Boston, MA: Beacon Press.

Mercer, C. (2002). Making it walk and talk: Cultural mapping and cultural planning. In C. Mercer, *Towards cultural citizenship: Tools for cultural policy and development* (pp. 165–177). Stockholm, Sweden: The Bank of Sweden Tercentenary Foundation; Gidlunds Förlag.

Merrifield, A. (2006). *Henri Lefebvre: A critical introduction.* New York, NY: Taylor & Francis.

Pine, J. and Gilmore, J. (1999). *The experience economy.* Boston, MA: Harvard Business School Press.

Shields, R. (1991). *Places on the margin: Alternative geographies of modernity.* New York, NY: Routledge.

Strom, E. (2003). Cultural policy as development policy: Evidence from the United States. *International Journal of Cultural Policy*, 9 (3): 247–263.

Whisnant, D. E. (1983). *All that is native and fine: The politics of culture in an American region.* Chapel Hill, NC: The University of North Carolina Press.

Zukin, S. (1982). *Loft living: Culture and capital in urban change.* Baltimore, MD: Johns Hopkins University Press.

# 1

# MAKING BEAUTY,
# MAKING MEANING,
# MAKING COMMUNITY

*Arlene Goldbard*

Reality is not shaped by official pronouncements. Rather, such declarations tend to cluster wherever lived experience has nurtured an underlying truth or principle into a ripeness that attracts official recognition. Just so, the process whereby culture and development have come to be seen as essential, integral partners has been gradual, international, and organic. Today, it is also official.

Increasingly, culture and development are understood as inseparable in the annals of development practice. Addressing a World Bank meeting in 2000, so towering a figure as the economist Amartya Sen began his speech on "Culture and Development" with what has since become a virtually inarguable point:

> [C]ultural issues can be critically important for development. The connections take many different forms related to the objectives as well as instruments of development. Cultural matters are integral parts of the lives we lead. If development can be seen as enhancement of our living standards, then efforts geared to development can hardly ignore the world of culture. Economic and social changes in pursuit of development can certainly influence—positively or negatively—the opportunities for cultural pursuits, and it would be appropriate to see that the effects on these opportunities receive serious attention. It can be argued that development is best seen as enhancement of freedom in a very broad sense. If this is more or less right, then surely cultural freedoms are among the liberties in terms of which development has to be assessed.
>
> (Sen, 2000, p. 1)

Indeed, it is a foundational principle of the United Nations Educational, Scientific, and Cultural Organization (UNESCO), the chief international authority concerned with community development, that culture drives development:

> Consideration of culture effectively *enables* development when projects acknowledge and respond to the local context and the particularities of a place and community through the careful use of cultural resources, as well as emphasis on local knowledge, skills and materials. Emphasizing culture means also giving members of the community an active role in directing their own destinies, restoring the agency for change to those whom the development efforts are intended to impact, which is crucial to sustainable and long-term progress. Respecting and promoting cultural diversity within a human right based approach, moreover, facilitates intercultural dialogue, prevents conflicts and protects the rights of marginalized groups, within and between nations, thus creating optimal *conditions* for achieving development goals.
>
> On the other hand, culture as a sector of activity—including tangible and intangible heritage and the creative industries—is in itself a powerful *driver* of development, with community-wide social, economic and environmental impacts.
>
> (UNESCO, 2012, Culture for Sustainable Development)

Economic impacts are often seen as primary. Since culture generates marketable products, places of significant historic and tourism value, and sought-after experiences of difference, development authorities are increasingly seeing cultural resources as parallel to natural resources, as raw material for economic development.

> Experience is showing how the cultural resources of a community can be converted into economic wealth by promoting the unique identity, traditions, and cultural products and services of a region, towards generating jobs and revenue. Investing in the conservation of cultural assets, promoting cultural activities and traditional knowledge and skills developed by humans over very long periods of adaptation to the environment, moreover, are also very effective means to strengthen environmental sustainability and the social capital of communities.
>
> (UNESCO, n.d., Theme)

UNESCO's portal on Culture for Sustainable Development opens this way:

> At a time when the international community is discussing future development goals beyond 2015, all efforts are focused on putting culture at the heart of the global development agenda.

Culture is who we are and what shapes our identity. Culture contributes to poverty reduction and paves the way for a human-centred, inclusive and equitable development. No development can be sustainable without it.

Placing culture at the heart of development policy constitutes an essential investment in the world's future and a pre-condition to successful globalization processes that take into account the principle of cultural diversity.

(UNESCO, n.d., Portal)

General statements such as these translate into principles and actions of considerably greater specificity. For example, in June 2012, the United Nations–sponsored Rio + 20, the UN Conference on Sustainable Development, included an International Conference of Indigenous Peoples on Self-Determination and Sustainable Development, which adopted a joint declaration. Consider just a single section of this document:

Within and among Indigenous communities, Peoples and Nations

1   We will define and implement our own priorities for economic, social and cultural development and environmental protection, based on our traditional cultures, knowledge and practices, and the implementation of our inherent right to Self-determination.

2   We will revitalize, strengthen and restore our institutions and methods for the transmission of our traditional knowledge and practices focusing on transmission by our women and men elders to the next generations.

3   We will restore knowledge and trade exchanges, including seed exchanges, among our communities and Peoples reinforcing the genetic integrity of our biodiversity.

4   We will stand in firm solidarity with each other's struggles to oppose projects that threaten our lands, forests, waters, cultural practices, food sovereignty, traditional livelihoods, ecosystems, rights and ways of life. We also stand in solidarity with others whose rights are being violated, including campesinos, fishers and pastoralists.

(Tebtebba, 2012, Within and among communities)

The deep meaning of each of these assertions will instantly be clear to anyone who works on the ground in culture and community development. Artists who place their gifts at the service of a community's aspirations, self-development, and concerns live out these understandings every day. Community organizers who have learned to draw on heritage for resilience and strength, who understand that images, metaphors, and stories are infinitely more affecting than dry documents, know their truth.

But what ground did they spring from? Behind every seemingly self-evident conclusion is a history of ideas in dialectical opposition fighting for possession of the spirit of the times. One could say that these debates started in the articulation of "cultural democracy" as a counter to anti-immigrant and Ku Klux Klan agitation in the early twentieth-century United States; (Kallen, 1915) or before the 1930s, when African intellectuals in France articulated the concept of Négritude as against colonial domination and the asserted superiority of colonizers. One might say that World War II brought them home, as people who had been denied full cultural citizenship were expected to fight and die for the nations that had consigned them to second- or third-tier status, survivors returning home with a new awareness of human and civil rights.[1]

Wherever they are rooted, they continue uninterrupted to this day in heated debates concerning immigration, voting rights, racial profiling, and other issues that place culture at the center of civil society. This chapter describes some aspects of that contest and its results so far, seeking to illuminate a larger context of ideas, discourses, and challenges affecting the many and diverse practices situated at the intersection of culture and development.

I have seldom met anyone outside academia as enamored as I am of the international cultural policy discourse quoted above. I can still remember my first galvanizing encounter with these ideas. I was introduced to the notion of cultural policy in the mid-1970s when I was handed a copy of *New Cultural Policy for Sweden*, a 1972 publication of the Swedish Ministry of Culture laying out that nation's values, plans, and apparatus for cultural development. I had never heard the phrase "cultural policy" before, nor had I been exposed to the term "cultural development." On first reading, however, both expressions seized my imagination, exciting that sense of recognition that flares when lived knowledge becomes named knowledge and sparking an appetite for more. For example, not just a few rubrics but the whole body of objectives and requirements set forth in Sweden's policy were described in a language I had never heard before but which I immediately understood. In them, culture was portrayed not as a special-interest area—which is how it is still commonly treated in the United States (U.S.)—but at once as the fabric binding disparate peoples into a whole and as a fit crucible for forging an inclusive, democratic, and equitable society. Cultural development was understood as necessarily countering the negative effects of the market economy, and decentralization was posited as a first principle. These thoughts quickly became my own:

> The general objective for cultural policy is to contribute to the creation of a better social environment and to contribute to equality.
>     For this objective to be possible to achieve it is required
> - that the activities and decision-making functions of the cultural area are decentralized to a higher degree (the Decentralization Objective);
> - that cultural policy measures are coordinated with society's involvement in other fields and are differentiated with consideration

to the conditions and needs of various groups (The Coordination and Differentiation Objective);

- that cultural policy measures are formulated in such a way as to improve communication between various groups in society and to give more people the opportunity to[for] cultural activity (The Community and Activity Objective);

- that cultural policy contributes to the protection of freedom of speech and to create real opportunities for this freedom to be exercised (The Freedom of Speech Objective);

- that artistic and cultural renewal are made possible (the Renewal Objective);

- that historical [äldre tiders] culture is preserved and reinvigorated [levandegörs] (The Preservation Objective); and

- that society has an overall responsibility for promoting pluralism [mångsidighet] and distributing the supply of culture and to decrease or prevent the negative consequences that the market economy can bring. (The Responsibility Objective).[2]

By the time I read Sweden's policy, I had been a cultural activist for several years. For example, I had worked as an organizer for the San Francisco Art Workers' Coalition, a group dedicated to pluralism, equity, and participation in that city's public cultural agencies and arts programs. For one project, we had published research documenting how the Board of Trustees of the city's publicly owned Fine Arts Museums had become an exclusive club. Our chart graphing interlocking relationships with the financial and political sectors showed how easily and often money and influence flowed to those who already possessed economic and social power. Our proposals focused on transparent and representative governance that would value and promote cultural diversity and support for living artists, as opposed to the actions the Fine Arts Museums' leadership had recently taken, such as allocating taxpayers' funds to establish a new American wing comprising works exclusively by dead white men. Our work was grounded in the understanding that everyone who made up San Francisco's neighborhoods had an equal place and entitlement to representation in community life and a share of cultural resources and that public institutions ought to be publicly accountable.

I was an autodidact whose study had been guided by curiosity, with no preset path. Everything I knew about culture, community, and organizing I had learned by doing. Through my experience in cultural organizing projects, I implicitly understood the principles underpinning the Swedish cultural policy's objectives and requirements. Until I saw them spelled out in so many words, however, it had never occurred to me that such values could be proclaimed as public policy and set in place to guide future actions and decisions. They resonated off the page, burning into my brain. Like just about everyone I knew, I had internalized a tacit consensus that the market ought to be culture's controlling mechanism: If you wanted to address the great disparities capitalism created, you were free to protest and hope for the best. It was a contest of wills, not rights, but Sweden's stance suggested to me that rights were at the heart of the matter.

The United Nations' Universal Declaration of Human Rights of 1948 contains Article 27: "Everyone has the right freely to participate in the cultural life of the community" (United Nations, 1948). It may sound innocuous, but from such a slender sprout a rather full understanding of social obligation has grown, as then UNESCO Director-General René Maheu pointed out in 1970:

> It is not certain that the full significance of this text, proclaiming a new human right, the right to culture, was entirely appreciated at the time. If everyone, as an essential part of his dignity as a man, has the right to share in the cultural heritage and cultural activities of the community—or rather of the different communities to which men belong (and that of course includes the ultimate community—mankind)—it follows that the authorities responsible for these communities have a duty, so far as their resources permit, to provide him with the means for such participation. ... Everyone, accordingly, has the right to culture, as he has the right to education and the right to work. ... This is the basis and first purpose of cultural policy.
>
> (Girard, 1983, pp. 182–183)

I discovered that there were libraries full of international cultural policy and cultural development documents, sharing examples from around the world and attempting to extract from these experiences principles that could guide future action. Reading this material had a huge influence on my work.

I began to inquire into the policies of my own country with respect to culture and development. There was abundant evidence of a passionate international cultural policy debate in the forty-odd years since World War II, but through the decades after creation of the National Endowments for the Arts (NEA) and National Endowments for the Humanities in 1965, the official American government line was that the United States had no cultural policy: Our national strategy was simply to follow the lead of private patrons. In fact, the NEA, our country's arts funding apparatus (and therefore the agency most emblematic of U.S. cultural policy), was based on something that an early 1960s Rockefeller Foundation panel on the performing arts called the "culture gap," which was the difference between red-carpet arts institutions' budgetary aspirations and their ability to raise money from private donors. The NEA was created to fill that gap, a very modest purpose in comparison with the broad scope of culture and the potential sweep of the public interest in its development as reflected in the Swedish policy published just a few years later and in many similar volumes from other world regions.

Just because the United States, however, disclaimed any official or explicit cultural policy did not mean the nation lacked one. I practiced reading between the lines to learn what virtually everyone committed to culture in the service of democracy and community has also learned: that some types of history and cultural heritage are routinely treated as superior to others; that the artifacts and past experience of some cultures are enshrined in museums as national treasures while others are treated merely as relics and specimens or ignored entirely; that neither broadcasting nor education nor any other cultural sector is commonly held to account for inclusion, equity, or any other broad cultural development goal.

I began to see that my own community (and many others across the U.S.) suffered from sharp imbalances that distorted cultural life, disparities that badly needed addressing. It quickly became clear that the U.S. had a long way to go in articulating and institutionalizing the principles of cultural democracy that could correct these damaging practices, replacing them with policies and instruments that could enable and support truly responsive and sustainable cultural development.

It is possible to carry out effective cultural development work without being familiar with the thematic universe (to borrow Paulo Freire's term for the dialectical interaction of ideas and themes that characterizes a particular culture, moment, or field) surrounding it (Freire, 1982), but I have no doubt that the work will be deeper, more conscious, and nuanced if policy makers and practitioners are acquainted with the territory. Even small choices and gestures can carry long tails of implication. Reflexive awareness of these enduring concerns increases the likelihood that their effects will ripple out in the direction of greater freedom, autonomy, harmony, and democracy.

Ideas about culture and development have a long, complicated, and diverse history, but it helps greatly to understand that certain themes have been primary in shaping this now decades-long conversation. I sketch a few of those key themes here.

## Decolonization and Cultural Equity

In Africa and other parts of the developing world, the cultural legacy of colonialism was as damaging as its economic and political impact. Colonial subjects were made to feel culturally inferior as each colonizing power installed a national theater that focused on classics of the relevant Western nation and an educational system that reinforced in every classroom that country's right to rule. As Ashish Nandy wrote in *The Intimate Enemy: Loss and Recovery of Self Under Colonialism*, this type of domination "colonizes minds in addition to bodies and … releases forces within the colonized societies that alter their cultural priorities once for all" (Nandy, 2010, p. 11).

Sometimes inspired by writers focusing on the colonization process in the developing world, such as Frantz Fanon and Amilcar Cabral (Fanon, 1968; Cabral 1969), and often guided by their own extrapolations from the domestic civil rights movement, cultural activists in the U.S. responded to a condition of internal colonization of minority ethnic and racial groups with the notion of "cultural equity" aimed at ensuring a fair share of resources for artists and organizations grounded in non-European cultures, redressing historic imbalances in favor of European-derived culture. The concept has been extended to other marginalized groups: cultural equity for rural communities, for instance, which long have suffered the effects of a distribution of resources that favors urban tastes, organizations, and centers.

The counterforce to decolonization is a continuing attachment to colonizers' entitlement to impose cultural norms and to limit freedom of expression for those under their rule or influence. Nowadays, the term *globalization* describes the ground of debate: on the one side, bringing progress to a benighted world; on the other, a transnational process that imposes the culture of multinational corporations on far-flung local communities, catalyzing rootlessness and social problems, including triggering a vast migration that has created unprecedented numbers of refugees and displaced persons.

## Self-Determination versus Expert Prescription

The discourse on culture and development has unfolded in parallel with an unprecedented rise in corporatization, commodification, mechanization, and a resultant polarization of wealth (Fuentes-Nieva and Galasso, 2014). The conflict is sharp: on the one side, growing understanding of the centrality of culture, an ever-renewing organic resource; and on the other, a passionate desire to reduce the human subject to whatever can be quantified, generalized, and dispatched with machinelike efficiency. Around the world, experts have been searching for "indicators"—benchmarks, often based on numeric factors such as the number of arts organizations—of cultural development or culture's impact on social change processes. The fear this evokes in artists and activists who understand that culture is too subtle, dynamic, and multifarious to be quantified—and which has already been justified in too many places—is that running the numbers will result in policies that impose a template of development on communities too diverse to fit any single model. Thus, this aspect of the debate pits lived local knowledge against expert formulations. Nonetheless, the lived knowledge of local residents must be the ground for all culture-based development work because that is where culture resides, in a community's direct experience.

## Democratization of High Culture versus Cultural Democracy

In both "popular front" culture of trade unions and left-wing parties of the 1930s and in European cultural authorities' post–World War II actions to rebuild their societies, the underlying principle that guided political leaders' efforts was "democratizing" elite culture. According to this way of thinking, everyone should be able to partake of what those in authority deem to be the best a national culture has to offer. These programs sought to democratize access to approved cultural products. Symphonies bused students to concerts, nonprofit theaters offered tickets at discount rates, art groups staged exhibits in nontraditional venues, and "blockbuster" museum shows used massive promotional campaigns to draw audiences that had not visited before.

Investment in this approach is still robust, (especially in the U.S. where overall public resources are small but the lion's share continues to go to red-carpet organizations), although studies have almost always found it to be a failure.[3] People who visit a museum to see an especially popular show find no reason to return; audience members who fill discounted concert and theater seats do not become season subscribers. Getting bused to a theater or museum does not have any demonstrable effect on the development of the community the passengers call home. To supplant this failed notion, the countervailing construct of "cultural democracy" (Girard, 1972) has gained credibility since the 1960s: that a society comprises many cultures, heritages, and publics that ought to be treated equally in terms of access, subsidy, and other forms of support. The core idea has to do with ends and means. Rather than prescribing some types of art and cultural experience as especially edifying—rather than focusing on the distribution of end products—this approach suggests that the means of cultural participation should be available to all, with an attendant public responsibility to support the ability to take part.

## Culture as Commodity or Dynamic Process

The logic of the market economy prefers many copies of a single consumable to participatory processes in which participants control the means of production. Hollywood—the home of the nation's massive commercial cultural industries (marketing mass-produced music, film, television, and much else)—prefers that you buy a ticket to a dance film (followed by another and another) rather than join a dance group with your friends. In the context of development, in contrast, active participation in community life is a recognized social good, a precursor to other forms of citizenship, and a path to both individual and social development. This makes active participation a universal aim of cultural development, clearly posited in contrast to the passive and isolating approach of the commercial cultural industries (Girard, 1972).

The dialectic is clear: On one side are our fundamental right and responsibility to act as makers of culture, engaging with our neighbors, valuing and learning about difference, ensuring that our official choices and our sites of public memory reflect the full texture and diversity of our collective creation. On the other side is massive corporatization with commensurate advertising that promises to cure any malaise with the right purchases, shrinking culture to a commodity. Their interaction generates our current cultural development challenge.

For an artist or organizer who works in community, these issues are almost certainly settled on the side of pluralism (engagement of diverse individuals and groups), participation (active involvement), and equity (fair distribution of access and resources). It is just that (especially in the U.S.) many funders and policy makers have not yet caught up with the efficacy of this approach, so resources for this work are neither commensurate with its impact nor with the level of need. This is a huge challenge for the field. It is perpetually underfunded and therefore perceived as perpetually emerging, rather than proven and ripe for major investment.

But when resource providers do catch up with reality, they will see that a cultural approach to community development is far more powerful than conventional approaches in several ways. A cultural approach to development recognizes and enlarges the agency of the communities and individuals involved, because it engages the whole person and the entire population. In contrast to an old style of imposed development, where how people feel is irrelevant to the design of new industrial capacity or the promulgation of agricultural protocols, in culture-based community development, actions, emotions, ideas, and the social fabric that binds them are all relevant, all simultaneously engaged. The work always starts with community members' own stories: Who are you? How did you get here? Where do you want to go? In contrast to imposed development, where a preset notion of success leads to fairly similar interventions in quite different contexts, with community cultural development, people's own answers to these questions shape what happens next in their community.

This is easy to see in the work of Roadside Theater in Appalachia (profiled in Chapter 7), which always begins with a story circle that engages community members in a situation of equal sharing and listening on a theme of their choice. Perhaps eight or ten individuals sit in a circle and, guided by protocols that prevent interruption or contradiction, in turn share stories of roughly equal length, then reflect together on whatever the entire body of narrative has revealed. This has been the basis for Roadside's work on domestic violence, the prison-industrial complex, and many other issues. Here is how the theater company describes this use of people's stories:

> Roadside's Story Circle methodology supports a basic principle of … community change work: those who directly experience a problem must make up the generative base for devising and enacting the solution. In this work, Roadside first uses its Story Circle methodology to help individuals discover their own truth of the issue, and then to test and develop that truth in dialog with other community members. By periodically collecting and organizing the knowledge about the issues generated by the stories, communities have an informed basis for recommending change, abetted by an enhanced sense of mutual trust. To sustain the momentum for change, the process of individual

and collective learning about the issue must continue to inspire and shape action.

(Roadside Theater, 2014, para. 4)

This approach applies equally to other modes, such as visual arts–driven work. Consider the ongoing Rwanda Healing Project facilitated by Barefoot Artists, (Barefoot Artists, Rwanda Healing Project), an organization founded by Lily Yeh, who also founded North Philadelphia's Village of the Arts and Humanities. Beginning in 2004, Yeh collaborated with international agencies and local residents on two complementary development projects: co-creating a Genocide Memorial Park on the site of a mass grave resulting from the 1994 massacre and developing the village occupied by survivors of the carnage. Through a gentle process of story sharing using artwork as a medium, villagers expressed their grief and began to articulate their aspirations for the future. The ongoing project has four goals that tie local experience to global questions, integrating cultural development and the work of artists with locally driven social and economic development:

1   Nurture the relationships established with residents and leaders of the host village to honor their grief and inspire hope, empowerment, vision, leadership, and means to continue the project throughout the year.
2   Provide opportunities for U.S. citizens, especially college students, to interact with people living in the third world to better understand our shared vision and global challenges.
3   Create a model of a sustainable village where local talents and creative energy are honored and international volunteers and experts find real situations to work to solve difficult global problems such as environmental deprivation, poverty, poor health care, lack of education, lack of hope, and the like.
4   Contribute to the prevention of violence and war through effective documentation of project methodology and benefits to educate a wider audience about the impact of genocide on individuals, local communities, and the larger world.

(Barefoot Artists, Genocide Memorial Park project goals section)

In addition to the memorial with its sculptures and murals, the project thus far has created a micro-lending program; a rain harvest water storage system producing potable water; clean energy, such as solar lighting and recycling corncobs into cooking fuel; new sanitation systems; and economic development initiatives focused on a sunflower seed oil cooperative, basket weaving, and a young women's Empowerment and Sewing Cooperative.

In this, as in other development projects approached through a cultural lens, artists work alongside engineers, medical professionals, teachers, and other skilled partners, aiming for a collaboration that generates beauty, meaning, and community simultaneously. In imposed development practice, where each specialty is seen to have a distinct area of expertise and therefore applicability, working relationships often become more of a competition than a collaboration. Here, as in art making, all aspects of the human subject are integral and central to the work; diverse practitioners come together with the intention of collaborating in a spirit of equality that recognizes different contributions without devaluing any.

A cultural approach to community development also recognizes that mastery means many things, not merely command of practical economic development-related tasks. Apart from the artistic skills that might be built through projects like these—storytelling, painting, sculpture, playmaking, and so on—artists working in community teach cultural citizenship: empathy, social imagination, resourcefulness, resilience, improvisation, communication. These capacities may be learned directly as explicit lessons or indirectly: When the members of a group share and explore individual visions of their community's future, they are practicing holding dual viewpoints simultaneously. The individual asks, "What do I want?" The member of a community asks, "What serves the greatest collective good?" Synthesizing both, they practice social imagination. When they join in portraying onstage or in a mural some of the challenges and experiences not directly their own, they learn how to put themselves in the place of another and feel something of the other's feelings. They learn to practice empathy.

Throughout this field, in countless ways, we see artists adept at making something beautiful and meaningful out of the broken pieces of an old order that can no longer contain the culture of possibility needed to face the future with courage. Resourcefulness and resilience can turn recycled trash into useful and beautiful structures or repurpose ancient wisdom of folktales into fresh guidance for new challenges.

Consider "Southeast by Southeast," a project of the City of Philadelphia Mural Arts Program in partnership with the city's Department of Behavioral Health and Intellectual disAbility Services. Together, they designed the project to provide a safe space for new refugees from Burma and Bhutan while also offering a way to preserve and share heritage culture while acknowledging and celebrating the resilience of refugee families. Working from a storefront, Mural Arts and partner organizations provide a range of social services, collaborating with artists to develop an immersive long-term residency and an ongoing multifaceted program that addresses the complex needs that attach to resettlement, including language and literacy classes, apprenticeships, mentorships, and traditional art therapy. The community's cultural fabric is strengthened through monthly workshops and other events in support of practicing traditional and contemporary cultural forms: a sari giveaway, a Bollywood versus Breakdance-off, a Burmese food night, and a workshop for silk-screening traditional Burmese and Bhutanese textile patterns onto T-shirts.

Teenagers are on the frontline in such transitions, living in the buffer zone between cultures and acting as bridges, as translators, for both sides. There is pressure to assimilate and also fear that young people will become disconnected from their cultural inheritance. In "Southeast by Southeast," teen participants chronicled their experiences growing up in refugee camps in Burma and Bhutan (including many from the Karen, Chin, and Shan tribes, persecuted in their homelands) and their journeys to the U.S., creating a bilingual book that serves as an exercise in sustaining the written and spoken Karen language while also making their stories available to readers in English.

The most public face of this two-year process has been a series of murals that reflect the artists' responses to the cultures of Southeast Asia: color, pattern, dress, landscape, and architecture intermingled with the local ways of Southeast Philadelphia, including a vibrant community garden—Growing Home—developed with the new residents by the Nationalities Service Center.

This multiplicity of project elements reflects the integral understanding that characterizes community development grounded in culture. It also reflects the key themes underlying culture and development discourse. These newcomers to Philadelphia are given resources and support to emerge with pride from a situation in which their own languages and customs were suppressed. They are provided an opportunity to declare their presence by adding beauty and meaning to their new neighborhood's sites of public memory. Lived local knowledge is the ground for cultural development work. The vernacular beliefs, norms, and forms of this community give rise to arts projects that engage all ages, starting where they are, drawing on existing interests rather than prescribing. The work takes place in community, rather than seeing neighborhoods as a place to apply the work of outside professionals. Community members are helped to make their own place, by their own lights, in their new homes.

I would like to be able to write that culture's centrality to development having been established, we can look forward to a period of deep, effective, self-guided, and empowering community work in the U.S. and beyond, but it is possible to recognize culture's importance without turning that perception into useful action. Even such recognition is open to misinterpretation. Since the turn of the millennium, we have seen approaches that effectively reduce the role of culture to a flourish on imposed development: The presence of art galleries, theaters, and artsy cafes becomes an indicator of vitality, and development specialists prescribe means of attracting artists to raise such indicators. Richard Florida has had a large influence on this way of thinking about development, positing a "creative class" whose presence aids economic growth (Florida, 2003). Cities have sought to implement his ideas with policies that are aimed at attracting such individuals by creating arts districts; providing incentives for creative industries, including high-tech, to relocate to their community; supporting initiatives in what is now called "creative placemaking" (ArtPlace America, n.d. Principles), for example, by animating urban neighborhoods with public performances or festivals that bring people into depressed sections of a city.

Practitioners of community cultural development can be the beneficiaries of the grant programs that support creative placemaking, which is all to the good; in a landscape with few funding options, they must seek support for good work wherever it may be found. The trouble is that with the increasing popularity of this way of thinking, the values embodied in the international culture and development declarations and dialogues I described above often get short shrift. What in the "creative class" context is seen as revitalization is otherwise called "gentrification," displacing local residents in favor of those able to pay higher rents, spend more discretionary cash in the neighborhood, and remodel both dwelling places and public spaces. The process can become a kind of colonization, exacerbating rather than addressing cultural inequities. The self-determination of local residents is seldom a focus; their displacement is often regarded as a kind of collateral damage in the march toward progress. Rather than a continuous, participatory process, culture is understood primarily as a form of commerce: ticket sales, the trade in artifacts and objects, and so on. And the performances and objects likely to provide the most short-term economic stimulus (albeit benefiting primarily those who already have means) are works that have some sort of external imprimatur rather than those deriving from individuals or a community rooted in the neighborhood.

The gap between theory and practice thus continues, but that fact does not prevent progress in the realm of ideas and policies. In May, 2013, for instance, international delegates to the UN Conference on Culture and Sustainability adopted "The Hangzhou Declaration: Placing Culture at the Heart of Sustainable Development Policies," offering nine recommended actions to implement the following core understanding of culture and development:

> We consider that in the face of mounting challenges such as population growth, urbanization, environmental degradation, disasters, climate change, increasing inequalities and persisting poverty, there is an urgent need for new approaches, to be defined and measured in a way which accounts for the broader picture of human progress and which emphasize harmony among peoples and between humans and nature, equity, dignity, well-being and sustainability.
>
> These new approaches should fully acknowledge the role of culture as a system of values and a resource and framework to build truly sustainable development, the need to draw from the experiences of past generations, and the recognition of culture as part of the global and local commons as well as a wellspring for creativity and renewal. ...
>
> We reaffirm that culture should be considered to be a fundamental enabler of sustainability, being a source of meaning and energy, a wellspring of creativity and innovation, and a resource to address challenges and find appropriate solutions. The extraordinary power of culture to foster and enable truly sustainable development is especially evident when a

people-centred and place-based approach is integrated into development programmes and peace-building initiatives.

We also reaffirm the potential of culture as a driver for sustainable development, through the specific contributions that it can make—as knowledge capital and a sector of activity—to inclusive social, cultural and economic development, harmony, environmental sustainability, peace and security. This has been confirmed by a wealth of studies and demonstrated by numerous concrete initiatives.

We recognize that one size does not fit all and that different cultural perspectives will result in different paths to development. At the same time, we embrace an understanding of culture that is open, evolving and strongly framed within a rights-based approach and the respect for diversity, the free access to which enables individuals "to live and be what they choose," thus enhancing their opportunities and human capabilities while promoting mutual understanding and exchange among peoples.

We believe that the time has come, building on these important statements of principle and lessons learnt, for the full integration of culture—through clear goals, targets and indicators—into agreed development strategies, programmes and practices at global, regional, national and local levels, to be defined in the post-2015 UN development agenda. Only such a concrete political and operational framework can ensure that all development initiatives lead to truly sustainable benefits for all, while securing the right of future generations to benefit from the wealth of cultural assets built up by previous generations.

(UNESCO, 2013, pp. 2–3)

Official pronouncements do not shape reality. I doubt that governmental and quasi-governmental bodies *make* things happen. Instead, they notice what is emergent and seize the moment when what is already becoming can finally be acknowledged—and if they are wise, can be helped into fuller realization. Around the world, artists and creative organizers who are practicing community development grounded in culture are living the vision outlined in the Hangzhou Declaration, co-creating the reality that such official documents now proclaim. In joining with community members to make meaning, to accord "to the laws of beauty even in times of greatest distress," as Milan Kundera has written (Kundera, 2004, p. 17), and thus to create community, a process that is always becoming, never complete. This discourse has been vital, generative, and continuous. Public intellectuals such as myself have shared what we have learned with the larger field, further extending the dialogue. Whether a particular artist or organizer takes an active part in this discourse, the underlying ideas permeate the cultural development field's thematic universe to the extent that all those who care about this work will be influenced by them and will also take part in their evolution. The more conscious this process becomes, the more the theory-practice gap is likely to narrow, but that remains to be seen.

## Notes

1 This document is out of print, and I no longer have a copy. It is referenced as a Swedish government document: *A New Cultural Policy* SOU:1972

2 See, for example, the original NEA enabling legislation. Its first point: "that the encouragement and support of national progress and scholarship in the humanities and the arts, while primarily a matter for private and local initiative, is also an appropriate matter of concern to the Federal Government." Retrieved June 2014 from http://www.gpo.gov/fdsys/pkg/STATUTE-79/pdf/STATUTE-79-Pg845.pdf

3 See, for example, National Endowment for The Arts (2012). *How A Nation Engages with Art*. This public participation survey shows no growth in attendance at such institutions and, in many cases, declines. Retrieved June 2014 from http://arts.gov/sites/default/files/highlights-from-2012-SPPA-rev.pdf

## References

ArtPlace America. (n.d.). *Principles of creative placemaking*. Retrieved June 2014 from http://www.artplaceamerica.org/articles/principles-of-creative-placemaking

Barefoot Artists (n.d.). The Rwanda healing project. Retrieved June 2014 from http://barefootartists.org/projects/the-rwanda-healing-project

Barefoot Artists (n.d.). Genocide Memorial Park. Retrieved June 2014 from http://barefootartists.org/projects/the-rwanda-healing-project/genocide-memorial-park

Cabral, A. (1969). *Revolution in Guinea*. New York, NY: Monthly Review Press.

Fanon, F. (1968). *The wretched of the earth*. New York, NY: Grove.

Florida, R. (2003). *The rise of the creative class: And how it's transforming work, leisure, community and everyday life*. New York, NY: Basic Books.

Freire, P. (1982). *Pedagogy of the oppressed*. New York, NY: Continuum.

Fuentes-Nieva, R. and Galasso, N. (2014). *Working for the few*. Oxford, UK: Oxfam. Retrieved June 2014 from http://www.oxfam.org/en/policy/working-for-the-few-economic-inequality

Girard, A. (1972). *Cultural development: Experience and policies*. Paris: UNESCO.

Girard, A. with Gentil, G. (1983). *Cultural development: Experience and policies* (second edition). Paris: UNESCO.

Kallen, H. (1915). Democracy versus the melting-pot. *The Nation*, February 25.

Kundera, M. (2004). *The unbearable lightness of being*. New York, NY: Harper.

Nandy, A. (2010). *The intimate enemy: Loss and recovery of self under colonialism*. Oxford, UK: Oxford University Press.

Roadside Theater. (2014). *About: Story circles*. Retrieved June 2014 from http://roadside.org/asset/about-story-circles

Sen, A. (2000). Culture and development. World Bank Tokyo meeting keynote address. Delivered in Tokyo. Retrieved June 2014 http://info.worldbank.org/etools/docs/voddocs/354/688/sen_tokyo.pdf

Tebtebba. (2012). *Indigenous people release Rio+20 declaration*. Retrieved August 2014 from http://www.tebtebba.org/index.php/content/220-indigenous-peoples-release-rio-20-declaration

UNESCO. (2012). *Culture: A driver and an enabler of sustainable development*. A Thematic Think Piece of the UN System Task Team on the Post-2015 UN Development Agenda. Retrieved from https://en.unesco.org/post2015/sites/post2015/files/Think%20Piece%20Culture.pdf

UNESCO. (2013). *The Hangzhou declaration*. Retrieved from http://www.unesco.org/new/fileadmin/MULTIMEDIA/HQ/CLT/pdf/final_hangzhou_declaration_english.pdf

UNESCO. (n.d.) Culture for Sustainable Development theme page. Retrieved August 2014 from http://en.unesco.org/themes/culture-sustainable-development

UNESCO. (n.d.) Culture for Sustainable Development web portal. Retrieved August 2014 from http://www.unesco.org/new/en/culture/themes/culture-and-development/the-future-we-want-the-role-of-culture/culture-enables-and-drives-development

United Nations. *Universal Declaration of Human Rights*. (1948). Retrieved June 2014 from http://www.un.org/en/documents/udhr

# 2

# RIVERS AND BRIDGES

## Theater in Regional Planning

*Jon Catherwood-Ginn and Robert H. Leonard*

The Building Home project—a partnership between performing artists and regional planners—employed performance and storytelling methods to facilitate broadly inclusive community dialogue in a three-year comprehensive regional planning project called the Livability Initiative in the New River Valley (NRV) of Virginia. This chapter explores Building Home and its arts-based strategies, describes the challenges that attended it, and argues for the value of such efforts in advancing participatory democracy and strengthening civic practice.[1] A small group of faculty and students from the Department of Theatre and Cinema at Virginia Tech, along with several community artists, actors, and musicians, partnered with the NRV Planning District Commission (PDC) to establish the project. The Commission sought this partnership to engage specific populations in the Valley that it had not successfully been able to include in previous planning processes. Building Home's principals employed storytelling and theater-making techniques to stimulate and facilitate public conversation about residents' experience of life in the NRV of Virginia—as they were experiencing it and as they imagined it could evolve.

In 2010, the PDC, an independent agency supported by local, state, and federal governments, received a three-year grant from the Sustainable Communities Regional Planning Grant Program of the Partnership for Sustainable Communities, which included the United States Departments of Housing and Urban Development (HUD) and Transportation (DOT), and the Environmental Protection Agency (EPA). The Obama Administration initiated this multi-agency approach, arguing that the complexities of life—where people live, how they get to work, how much energy they use, and so on—necessitate a shared effort among several federal agencies. President Obama articulated the logic behind this collaboration:

By working together, [HUD, DOT, and EPA] can make sure that when it comes to development—housing, transportation, energy efficiency—these things aren't mutually exclusive; they go hand in hand. And that means making sure that affordable housing exists in close proximity to jobs and transportation. That means encouraging shorter travel times and lower travel costs. It means safer, greener, more livable communities.

(Obama, 2009)

The Sustainable Communities Regional Planning Grant Program identified numerous elements as essential to community sustainability (e.g., housing, transportation). The call for proposals also referenced the value of building partnerships with arts and culture entities as applicants pursued the grant program's goals (U.S. Department of Housing and Urban Development, n.d.). Including art and culture as keys in sustainability efforts raises real challenges even as it offers an avenue by which to secure authentic inclusivity in a community. As the executive director of the Tuscon Pima Arts Council, Roberto Bedoya, has observed,

[D]iscussions and practices associated with Creative Placemaking [...] are tethered to a meaning of "place" manifest in the built environment. ... And this meaning, which operates inside the policy frame of urban planning and economic development, is ok but that is not the complete picture. Its insufficiency lies in a lack of understanding that before you have places of belonging, you must feel you belong. Before there is the vibrant street one needs an understanding of the social dynamics on that street – the politics of belonging and dis-belonging at work in placemaking in civil society. [...] Placemaking in city/neighborhood spaces enact identity and activities that allow personal memories, cultural histories, imagination and feelings to enliven the sense of "belonging" through human and spatial relationships. But a political understanding of who is in and who is out is also central to civic vitality.

(Bedoya, 2012)

Bedoya's question of "Who is in and who is out" inspired Building Home's leaders to employ strategies rooted in accessibility and inclusivity. As they planned their effort, the authors contacted Michael Rohd, artistic director of Sojourn Theatre, a theater ensemble with extensive experience in the creation and production of new works highly responsive to communities. Rohd is at the forefront of performance-based Civic Practice, which he defines as "activit[ies] where an artist employs the assets of his/her craft in response to the needs of non-arts partners as determined through ongoing relationship-based dialogue" (Rohd, 2012, para. 4). When we described the opportunity to collaborate with the PDC, Rohd offered an important insight: What if you conceived of the arts' role as not only a *topic* of planning but a *tool* for planning? Rather than just planning *for* the arts, why not plan *with* them?

The PDC's executive director welcomed this proposal enthusiastically. During initial meetings with Building Home project leaders, he noted his organization's past difficulty in engaging under-represented communities in planning processes. While typical public involvement methods such as mailed postcards and large meetings would yield some input, their efficacy was often limited by numerous factors including, for example, citizens' transportation challenges, historical lack of agency, and child care needs. He expressed eagerness to experiment with new, thoughtfully constructed engagement approaches. He hoped to demystify for the general public how public input influences regional planning processes and outcomes; ameliorate—if not dispel—some residents' suspicion and disdain of government; and include a significantly more diverse array of citizen perspectives, opinions, and recommendations in the overall project.

During its two years, Building Home organized and facilitated discussions in small gatherings throughout the 1,457-square-mile, four-county, and one-city NRV region. In addition to several incorporated municipalities, this area includes many informal communities and population centers, each culturally distinct. Some are small geographic entities—Wake Forest, New Ellett, Yellow Springs—while others reflect established groups based on particular needs or interests, for example, the Head Start Advisory Council, the Agency on Aging Friendship Café, and the Wake Forest Community Action Club.

Shortly after the Commission received its Sustainable Communities grant, opposition to the effort those funds were to support emerged among a small but vocal cohort of citizens, many of whom identified themselves as members of the Tea Party political movement. This group of conservative activists sought to discredit the Livability Initiative by linking the planning project—through its foundational use of the word *sustainability*—to a United Nation's effort dubbed Agenda 21, which they presented as highly controversial (United Nations, 1992). Though baseless, members of this group believed that this nonbinding United Nations action plan allows the international body to take property from citizens. Nonetheless, these sorts of arguments have been employed around the country to attack local planning efforts. As Llewellyn Hinkes-Jones of *The Atlantic* has observed,

> Several groups have been successful in stopping large-scale public works projects with accusations that have little basis in reality. By acting at a very local level with enough volume, these groups and individuals have been able to overwhelm, or at least derail, council members unprepared to deal with a fusillade of nonsense about international governance and legal minutiae.

(Hinkes-Jones, 2012)

For those working to incorporate the arts into the NRV regional planning process, this opposition and its manifestation in contentious citizen meetings highlighted the limitations of existing mechanisms for democratic deliberation. Both authors had attended many public gatherings in the years leading up to this project, but neither had ever before witnessed citizens calling local elected officials and county administrators "Communists" and "Nazis," as occurred at Livability Initiative public meetings. Such invective from fellow residents, likening the Initiative's community planning efforts to the forced relocation of Jews to internment areas by the Nazis, was shocking. This threat to the project compelled us to question, and quickly: How might we use theater as an alternative medium for public dialogue, so the NRV's citizens could engage in a healthier, more productive form of civic engagement?

## Theater Strategies for Inclusive, Respectful, and Effective Public Dialogue

The Building Home team learned, invented, and utilized numerous strategies to encourage respectful and informed community dialogue. These approaches went beyond conventional dramaturgy—designing how storytelling unfolds— to planning how receiving a story happens.

The team had to become as adept and disciplined in discerning ways to encourage audience engagement and participation as they were in crafting

**FIGURE 2.1** A moment of audience interaction during a performance of Building Home's *behind a stranger's face* in Theatre 101, Virginia Tech, Blacksburg, Virginia. Image courtesy of Bryanna Demerly

story and performance. To address this challenge, Building Home artists found themselves devising strategies for combining their imaginations with those of planners and their audiences. These efforts incorporated the team's experience, research, and training and lessons the group could glean from the work of generations of artists/activists in this country and around the world.

## Story Circles

Donna Porterfield, managing director of Roadside Theater in Whitesburg, KY, taught the Building Home team a particular approach to facilitating story circles.[2] The roots of this practice arose from many places and individuals—most immediately in the work of theater artist/community organizer John O'Neal, who developed a story-circle practice in the 1960s with the Student Non-Violent Coordinating Committee and his allied Free Southern Theatre, and refined his efforts through experience with his theater company, Junebug Productions. This strategy is underpinned by the simple yet critical principle that storytellers are the authorities, the experts, concerning their life narratives. By centering information gathering on each individual, Building Home's principals recognized each participant as the authority of her or his own experiences, values, and unique perspective on the region.

In the contemporary environment of polarized positioning in the nation's politics, Building Home's principals found that it was important to use Roadside's carefully wrought guidelines for the circles to create a space in which participants felt safe to speak candidly without fear of judgment or repercussion. The formal process of acknowledging each participant's authority and agreeing to a protocol and set of rules establishes an environment for the teller to speak from her heart. The Roadside guidelines include

- reaching agreement together about the group's purpose in gathering;
- recognizing that "what's said in the circle, stays in the circle";
- agreeing that everyone may share, but no one is obliged to speak; and
- holding off responding to individual teller's stories until all have shared.

(Roadside Theater, 1999)

To identify a relevant theme for each gathering's story circle, Building Home team members presented a question to each group: What would we need to include to create a complete picture of your community? The facilitators took notes on flip charts during the ensuing conversation, and participants reviewed those logs as a group, adding and editing as necessary to ensure accuracy and completeness. From there, participants worked collectively to articulate a central theme for their story circle. Here are some examples of topics that emerged in the project's story circles:

- memories of economic upticks or downturns,
- the decay of a road and/or bridge, and
- memories of an encounter with substance abuse.

One circle's members chose to tell stories concerning their observation that "People aren't getting the help they deserve; short-term help has happened, but there is not enough long-term help." Their narratives described local, state, and federal programs that participants perceived as serving or failing to address their personal or family needs. Participants shared narratives recounting personal challenges of poverty, physical and sexual abuse, chronic unemployment, and inadequate education. They described their sense of being forgotten as people while becoming instead a program's "clients." Such stories could be raw; they exposed families in extremity, such as the loss of trust between parent and child. Other narratives revealed a high level of despair and disillusionment. Nonetheless, these stories were also often full of hope—expressions of faith in a way of life and a deep love for community.

In Building Home's practice, after everyone had shared a story in a circle, the group identified images and themes that its members perceived as common across the narratives. Storytelling consistently deepened participants' understanding of their circle's identified theme. In the case of the group that explored questions about "getting help," their narratives confirmed that government had provided assistance but also revealed that such support focused principally on short-term stopgaps, whereas the problems recipients commonly faced were longer term in character. Following this logic, the group had an "aha moment" when its members realized that what they were actually looking for were enduring solutions to the difficulties they were confronting, not charitable assistance. They were able to identify that they felt trapped as "clients," whose agency as individuals was de facto being denied. This community-based shift of perspectives—to a sense that what residents needed was less "short-term help" and more "long-term solutions"—contributed an important insight to the planning process.

The Project's story circles revealed a complex array of community concerns, values, and dreams. Participants in Building Home sessions typically reacted to this intricacy with astonishment followed by enthusiasm and positive energy—responses much sought after by theater makers, to say nothing of those who seek to engage the public in government decision making.

One story group identified their shared concern to be "a personal encounter with substance abuse in our community." Several circle members wept as they spoke and heard stories about teenage drug abuse, prostitution, alcoholism, damaged relationships, intergenerational addiction, and mental illness (specifically, how substance abuse and mental illness are so often misdiagnosed and ineffectively treated). Participants exhibited enormous respect and sensitivity to those who shared their stories.

In nearly all of the story circles, the process of sharing narratives highlighted specific circumstances in which communities had reached an impasse. Inevitably, individual stories revealed differences of perspective, opinion, and experience. These unresolved concerns became the focus for deeper deliberation by means of theatrical techniques developed by Augusto Boal. As the following two sections illustrate, Building Home employed Boal's strategies on the basis of their proven efficacy in engendering dialogue and catalyzing grassroots action in communities facing diverse and persistent challenges.

### *Image Theater*

Building Home gatherings would typically follow story circles with engagement opportunities provided by two theater techniques: Image Theater and Forum Theater—strategies developed by Augusto Boal and his Theatre of the Oppressed (TO). Boal developed TO in the 1960s while working with citizens living in the poorest areas of Brazil. He realized that theater could be a powerful medium for the expression of community concerns and could encourage deliberation to address those issues. Boal has described how TO offered the relative safety of role playing to allow participants to "test-drive" potential actions (Boal, 2002). Doris Sommer, director of the Cultural Agents Initiative at Harvard University, has examined the dynamic at play in Boal's work: "what looks like destiny turns out to be a problem with different possible outcomes. [Boal] guides frustration and despair into creative intervention and then into legislative and civic intervention" (Gewertz, 2003, para. 8).

Image Theater invites participants to construct physical evocations of common issues and concerns, to mold or "sculpt" their own bodies and/ or those of co-participants into a gesture, shape, or image expressive of that subject. Participants expand their understanding of the many facets of a concern by re-shaping/re-sculpting the bodies of those in the group. This process creates what Boal has called a "dynamized" dialogue concerning an issue (Boal, 2002). This practice of "speaking through" common vocabularies of gesture and body language opens up new avenues for communication. Within an environment made safe for honest expression and shared discovery without judgment, participants explore ways to address community problems that typically linger below the surface of social consciousness.

In one Building Home gathering, for example, the group shaped a sculpture that depicted one person slipping a hand, undetected, into another person's pocket. As the participants adjusted, refined, and responded to that image, a conversation emerged that clarified and deepened the original observation that long-held, small family farms were now severely threatened in the NRV. Thereafter, the group unpacked the impact of local county policies that supported construction of housing developments in previously rural areas. Participants believed the resulting increase in tax rates that had accompanied such initiatives constituted an unreasonable and destructive burden on farming families. Seen from this perspective, these developments were picking small farmers' pockets, so to speak.

Another group felt that its community was so far down the list of local government priorities that the single road in and out of its small valley location had been allowed to fall into dire condition. Their lone bridge was so overdue for repair that residents feared being stranded, literally beyond the reach of emergency rescue, police, or fire departments. A series of Image Theater sculptures, going from the "real" to the "ideal" image without "magic" (a Boal term for an ending that, while desired, lacks grounding in the known realities of life), yielded a possible means to address the matter (Boal, 2002). A representative from the community appealed directly to the governor. During the scene, the person playing the state's chief executive effectively silenced the community representative. The plight of the emissary mirrored the past experience of community members so well that attendees laughed in gales of recognition. As the group applauded, those gathered also offered comfort and encouragement to their representative, eventually urging her to try again. Participants offered strategies and retorts to the executive's initial rejection. In her next attempt, the group member successfully focused her conversation with the governor on the reality of seventy-five families facing a life-and-death situation unless their bridge and road were soon repaired. The executive stopped talking and listened. In reviewing the exercise, members recognized that "everyone in the room was a back-up" (personal communication, October 22, 2011).

Three months later, in a second gathering with the same community, the Building Home team learned that residents had achieved a measure of success in their effort to obtain needed repairs for their road. The original play *behind a stranger's face*—based on stories shared by citizens in the region and performed around the NRV by the Building Home actors in 2012— recounted the story:

| | |
|---|---|
| JON: | We went back. Visited nearly 3 months later, to the day. The community's leaders—mothers and grandmothers, fathers and grandfathers—said that, since my last visit, they'd met with the Virginia Department of Transportation. Twice. The people of [the community] did the work. Work that began before we arrived and continued after we left. We carry the image and the story. |
| SADAH: | We painted the picture of what things would look like if that bridge caved in. |
| ANDREW: | VDOT responded, |
| SHAWANDA: | and quickly. |
| EDDIE: | They patched the pavement and laid new asphalt. They put in a request to Richmond for a brand new bridge. |
| ANNA: | It wasn't perfect, but certainly "better than nothing." |
| SADAH: | They were talking about building an alternative access road, too: |

LATANYA:     another way in and out.
SHAWANDA:  A petition circled the room. The string of signatures gradually
             grew.

(Catherwood-Ginn, 2012)

### Forum Theater

Boal's second technique, Forum Theatre, provided additional space for community creativity and conversation. Building Home's use of Forum Theater in community gatherings grew organically from impromptu scenes generated by story circles and Image Theater that had presented unresolved issues. Forum Theater provides a safe, open, inclusive space for residents to explore ideas for addressing community ills. Such scenes invite residents to offer alternative strategies—through improvisational theater—to address perceived problems. Participants attempt to solve staged conflicts by providing suggestions for the actors to employ or by intervening themselves as performers (Boal called them "SpectActors"). Observing how the different scenarios unfold, citizens then discuss the strengths and weaknesses of each. The experience of viewing multiple alternatives opens the planning process to well-considered, community-generated ideas for solutions. Meshed with other forms of knowledge, these ideas can set the stage for action, arising from a broad base of engagement.

In one Forum Theater scenario, an African American woman confronted a purportedly racist statement from an otherwise well-meaning white male employer. Several other African American participants offered different solutions to the impasse. In the course of the exercise, it became clear that the alternatives offered were based on distinct understandings of the situation. One person suggested that the black woman needed to stop the conversation and leave, because she was in an impossible and dangerous situation that did not hold any promise of a positive outcome for her; "it's not safe for us to try to solve the white man's problem." Another individual suggested that the black woman compassionately confront her employer arguing that if such instances are not used as teachable moments, such behavior will continue forever. The many strains of this conversation played out through enactment of proposed strategies to address the situation. Passions ran high, but respect for one another and for the process kept participants in the conversation and allowed them to develop a deeper comprehension of the problem. Although the group did not settle on a single "best" strategy, the concern's intricacy and a number of possible avenues of response were fully acknowledged and shared openly. That in itself was a significant advance in the understanding of the moment.

### Facilitation: The Joker

In the context of such complexity, the skills and responsibilities required of a gathering's facilitator—in Boal's terms, The Joker—are considerable (Boal,

2002). This role requires more than leading the various theater exercises and ensuring that every participant has opportunities to speak. The Joker must be aware of the changing agendas of participants as a gathering proceeds and the perspectives of the project's organizing team. The facilitator must strike an effective balance among these agendas and move forward on one (or a compatible set of several) in ways that encourage and energize the group's ownership of the event. This is a hard-earned skill and a sizable responsibility requiring a highly attuned perception to individual and group dynamics, a facility with improvisation as group needs change, and a willingness to acknowledge one's ignorance and employ one's expertise. It is best expressed transparently, acknowledging the origins of agendas openly and often while also seeking to articulate strategies for the group to consider. The Building Home team came to understand the function of the facilitator/Joker as a kind of wild card, an invested game changer, and an insurer of group safety from threat of judgment or intellectual bullying.

## Mapping the Region: Identifying Partners and Building Trust

A key question framed the initial discussions between Building Home and PDC staffers: With whom in the region should project members connect? PDC staff members identified four primary demographic groups that had historically been under-represented in their data-gathering efforts: low-income residents, seniors, African Americans, and youths in the region. With this as a jumping-off point, Building Home leaders developed the following guiding questions in their early engagement efforts:

- Where do individuals within these communities typically gather?
- What are some of the government agencies, nonprofits, and organizations that work with these groups? What is the nature of these citizens' relationship with these organizations?
- What contacts does the team currently have with members of these specific populations? What is the character of these individuals' relationships with their neighbors and peers in their communities? Would the team consider those people "leaders" (official or otherwise) or "followers" in their communities?
- To what extent are these groups organized and civically engaged? What obstacles do they face with regard to internal organization and participation in local government and/or planning processes?
- What were these communities' past experiences with local government and/ or planners? If those associations were positive, how might the Building Home team build on those experiences? If negative, how might Building Home encourage participants to share those encounters? From there, how might the team encourage trust, optimism, and a commitment to participate in this planning effort?

Building Home's participation in the Livability Initiative immediately aligned the team with a number of other PDC consortium partners including nonprofit organizations, public agencies, small businesses, and municipal governments. Members of this group proved helpful in connecting Building Home's principals with many recognized leaders in the population groups with whom they aimed to interact.

Building Home concurrently conducted independent research into the region's various communities and organizations. Partner institutions' numerous connections in the NRV were very beneficial but, even with their help, the team had to devise ways to reach out to many individuals not previously engaged. The capacity of Livability Initiative staff to help to locate previously under-represented residents was limited by PDC staffers' relative homogeneity (i.e., predominantly white, middle-class, middle-aged, and living in the wealthier communities of the Valley). This fact required the project to connect with populations the Commission had not yet reached. Building Home addressed this challenge partially by facilitating story-gathering stations at street festivals and community events. The qualitative data gathered through these "man/woman-on-the-street" interviews with random passers-by provided the team with perspectives quite distinct from the planning commission's typical input.

Unexpectedly, though Building Home's ultimate goal was to engage populations who generally had been outside the PDC's reach previously, securing trust among internal consortium partners proved to be one of the most challenging aspects of the project. After hearing about Building Home, many potential collaborators expressed curiosity and enthusiasm. Just as often, however, the project team encountered criticism and skepticism. As an example, the group met with the staff members of one town who work closely with residents of low-income housing and serve, in a manner of speaking, as gatekeepers. This first gathering with this consortium partner was a "trial balloon," a test of whether Building Home would be given any credence by community officials and, in turn, access to people who had not otherwise engaged in the regional planning process. These staff members expressed resistance to the idea of theater (or any form of art making) as a way to open conversation. As Building Home leaders stalwartly moved through their workshop plan, that opposition increased. The team enjoyed some success when these individuals shared emotional stories related to their work. Images—such as one of developers forcing people off their land—stimulated passionate responses. Nonetheless, the experience also sparked caustic resentment among some staff. These individuals were concerned about having been asked to reveal long-held emotions in a public environment. The Building Home team left the event deeply discouraged, dreading their return later to review the effort with participants.

To their great surprise, however, the group received positive reviews of the experience four weeks later during the follow-up session from the very participants who had previously seemed most resistant to it. In the interim, these individuals said they had come to realize that their experience in the discussions had been profound. They realized and acknowledged that the story circle had opened a space for the expression of unfiltered opinions while also revealing values and important realities. The staff praised the experience because, after hearing such different and personal perspectives, they could now better perceive the complexities of the life situations of the individuals they daily sought to assist. This shift suggested the project's potential for facilitating essential conversations. This Building Home event illustrated an insight from Brent Blair, director of the master of arts degree program in applied theater arts at the University of Southern California that public art making provides "a container for complexity" that is rare and vital for healthy civic discourse (B. Blair, personal communication, August 6, 2012). This first Building Home gathering yielded the realization that the significance of an event does not necessarily manifest in expected ways.

## From Scouting Trips to Preliminary Meetings to Community Gatherings

The team dubbed initial meetings with citizens in their communities as "scouting trips." Project leaders found these gatherings a valuable first step in understanding community dynamics including existing conflicts and divisions, prevailing neighborhood narratives, local histories, and unstated questions. Building Home team members used these get-togethers to gain tentative insights into community contexts before organizing larger group meetings.

The team conducted "preliminary meetings" after scouting trips to discuss the specific purposes and logistics of prospective community gatherings with partners. Questions during these sessions included What are the most pressing

---

### BOX 2.1  MAPPING THE REGION

While the Building Home co-directors sought actively to build trust with consortium partners, they also researched existing community groups and service organizations as sites for potential gatherings. One of the authors contacted public administrators, small business owners, ministers, artists, and activists, paying particular attention to the names of individuals that seemed to echo from county to county across the NRV, people sociologist Malcolm Gladwell has termed "Connectors" (Gladwell, 2000). Catherwood-Ginn described the project for each of those he contacted and also sought additional referrals to people in the effort's targeted populations. Most of this work took place during the summer and fall of 2011 and included attending church services, participating in community-wide New River clean-up efforts, setting up booths at street fairs, and "caning" chairs at a folk-life festival.

concerns your community is facing? How would you like to explore them through theater? What locations would work for such an event? What are essential considerations as we design a tailored meeting for your community? In addition, the group sought to explore the community's gathering spaces, take photographs, and brainstorm possible meeting layouts to minimize physical impediments to participants' engagement in subsequent activities.

The Building Home team always asked its preliminary meeting hosts whether they would be willing to help to organize later gatherings for the project. Some declined, particularly when they described their communities as divided. This moment was generally crucial in the project's evolution in a given location. In such situations, Building Home leaders could "nudge" a potential host in hopes that doing so would foster an opportunity to build that individual's capacity for organizing. This phase of the project, essentially community organizing, strengthened the team's persistence, sharpened its sensitivity to community contacts' dispositions and readiness for action, and kick-started efforts to be creative in finding ways to motivate possible partners. Some of these connections led to ongoing partnerships and substantial civic engagement. Others stalled, even after notable early successes. The varying results encouraged the group to identify opportunities for engagement more quickly, continually assess the status of particular relationships, and reallocate personal energy and project resources as necessary on the basis of analyses of whether and how specific ties were helping to address the project's goal of engaging under-represented communities.

While the team initially considered scouting trips and preliminary meetings as means to an end—the "end" being community gatherings, which were assumed to be the most fruitful phase of the effort—the group was surprised and delighted to discover that these activities instead constituted some of the most illuminating steps in the project. Regardless of their variable outcomes (vis-à-vis organizing subsequent gatherings), such meetings were invaluable. They provided exposure to the unique attributes of communities throughout the NRV, inspiration from official and unofficial leaders in the region, stories and views, contact particulars for concerned citizens, and continuously evolving conceptions of the project's potential. These meetings also honed the team's ability to facilitate dialogue, particularly conversation concerning sensitive issues.

With its organizational base at Virginia Tech, the Building Home project benefitted from many residents' positive perceptions of the university. The team also dealt with some people's distrust of Virginia Tech and frustrations with the institution's existing relationships with their community, a circumstance several residents likened to paddling down a river with an elephant in your canoe. Building Home members were always honest about their relationship to the university. Members of the team recognized their role as representatives of Virginia Tech who could begin to deepen the institution's engagement with its neighbors.

When they began identifying action steps, Building Home's leaders imagined their primary task was to design and facilitate theater-assisted discussion groups. The team quickly realized, however, that the work was also about community organizing, and the gatherings were only one part of preexisting and often hidden conversations among certain groups. The group's facilitators had to discover how to contribute to an ongoing dialogue by learning about the communities in which they intended to work. That is, the team had first to enter those existing conversations as listeners. The key to positive change resided in the various groups' conversations and community assets.

For example, Building Home's leaders identified a low-income housing community as a possible gathering site. After several false starts, one of the project's organizers met an interested individual who lived in that neighborhood. In his own way, this new acquaintance was a local leader in that he was a steward of the property and concerned himself with the well-being of his neighbors. He explained that the site had serious sewage seepage problems, but residents who had complained to its management concerning the issue had historically risked eviction. Many tenants were, therefore, fearful of meeting to talk about that concern or anything else. However, this initial, one-to-one conversation established a relationship that eventually led to a Building Home meeting that included other neighborhood residents.

Considered as a matter of community organizing, these steps were part of trust building. Viewed through the lens of theater, these efforts permitted learning and offered residents opportunities to share stories or individual and group narratives: the givens of who, what, where, why, and how of their relationships and understanding of place. We quickly learned that this process of building relationships one person at a time gave us a depth of understanding we could not gain otherwise, even as those efforts built a base of individuals invested in the project.

## Theory Meets Practice: Community Gatherings and NRV Today

After scouting trips and, as necessary, preliminary meetings, Building Home community gatherings assumed two basic forms: group sessions and what we termed "story corners." The former included story circles and TO exercises. Though group sessions required longer-term relationship building and session design with stakeholders, story corners were easy-to-execute "one-offs." Using portable digital audio equipment, a few folding chairs, and a card table, Building Home team members set up story corner stations at community festivals to record stories and local citizen perspectives.

The coupling of group sessions and story corners not only provided team members the opportunity to facilitate whole-group and one-to-one exercises but the two types of engagement also yielded distinct data. Community gathering reports were concise; only essential information was included, such as field notes and observations, citizens' input, recommendations, and next steps. Story corner recordings, meanwhile, were intimate reflections of lived experience in the region. Memories, gossip, polemics, and raucous laughter all appeared in residents' open-ended responses to such questions as the following:

- What do you consider your community? What makes your community unique?
- When did your community come together around a common purpose? When did your community *need* to unify around a common purpose but did not? Why?
- What would you like to see in the future for your community? What about for the greater NRV?

Each gathering was as unique as the village or town or rural area in which it was held. For this reason, facilitators improvised and adapted sessions to the distinct characters of the towns and neighborhoods in which they worked. In lieu of pressing predetermined agendas, Building Home members endeavored to work within and respect the inherent dignity and perspective of each resident they encountered.

To assess citizens' views about the region's livability accurately, the PDC needed to gather numerous, diverse, and detailed perspectives. Considering this, the Building Home team planned and executed forty-nine distinct community gatherings from September 2011 to May 2012. According to PDC staff, Building Home was highly successful in this effort; "[through Building Home, there was] stuff that came to light that would never have happened [otherwise]" (Catherwood-Ginn and Leonard, personal interview, March 28, 2014).

Following the lessons learned during Building Home's first year, the team embarked on another project in service to the Livability Initiative: a series of Forum Theatre scenes focused on five community topics, collectively titled *NRV Today*. At this point in its regional planning process, the PDC had gathered an enormous amount of quantitative data (i.e., housing stock, community health costs, etc.) and qualitative data (i.e., citizens' expressed values, priorities, and preferences). The Livability Initiative staff processed this flood of information from some 1,200 NRV citizens and approximately 160 participants at monthly working group meetings and produced an informative and sharply designed interim report titled *Livability in the New River Valley* that served as the foundation for Building Home's Forum effort (New River Valley Planning District Commission, 2012a).

The report highlighted a series of specific issues: the percentage of children living in poverty in the region currently exceeds the state-wide average; in twenty years' time, the number of seniors residing in the NRV will nearly double and one in three households in the valley spend more than 30% of their household income on housing and are therefore considered "shelter cost burdened" (New River Valley Planning District Commission, 2012a). To address these concerns, the PDC planned a fresh community involvement initiative. This effort included presenting hypothetical projects and policies that could target issues identified in the interim report. It also sought to gather community members' perspective on those proposals—and citizen-generated *new* ideas—through an online survey called *NRV Tomorrow* (New River Valley Planning District Commission, 2013).

If the survey aimed to gain citizens' responses to potential projects and policies in the *future*, Building Home determined that it could best serve this process by dramatizing and recording citizens' perceptions of life in the NRV *here and now*. Public deliberation and creative interrogation in a series of Forum Theatre scenes dramatizing today's NRV challenges could inform participants' *private* responses to the online survey. Building Home could offer a crucial service to this phase of Livability Initiative outreach by translating such complex realities and projects as "Demand Side Management Programs" into flesh-and-blood characters and relatable human stories.[3]

Dovetailing the PDC's work and Building Home's theater making required the deepest collaboration yet between the entities. Team members pored over the Interim Report, Community Priorities survey, and planners' draft documents as background for devising the proposed Forum scenes (New River Valley Planning District Commission, 2012b). Catherwood-Ginn and the PDC's Community Outreach Coordinator shared a belief in the value of Commission staff-Building Home joint sessions In the end, the Virginia Tech team produced four Forum scenes and an improvisatory panel that dramatized aging in place, downtown revitalization, workforce education for those seeking to overcome past substance abuse, development in the rural landscape, and the need for health education in local schools.

As the group developed these scenes, citizens who opposed the Livability Initiative were mobilizing to protest it. A regional nonprofit organization known as The Crooked Road—devoted to connecting visitors to southwest Virginia by encouraging visits to historically and culturally significant country music, bluegrass, and old time music venues—had been pursuing a National Heritage Area designation from the state legislature for The Crooked Road's ten-county area. People and groups that opposed the tourism project, some of them organized by Tea Party activists, fought this effort, alleging that the designation would negatively affect personal property rights (Bunch, 2013). Enduring continued pressure from such groups, the Crooked Road ultimately abandoned its effort to gain National Heritage status. Buoyed by their "victory" in scuttling the nonprofit's efforts, opponents publicly declared their intention to fight the Livability Initiative even more aggressively than they had before (Dickens, 2013). At about that time, the "Additional Comments" section of the PDC's Community Priorities Survey captured a share of vitriolic expressions of the opposition's viewpoint (emphasis in the original):

2   If all of these "goodies" depend on government financing, then I am against them.

31 This survey was obviously carefully worded to elicit responses that indicate a desire for "sustainable development," a worthy goal as long as it is promoted through education and free enterprise. People who have lived in our locality for many years love this area and care for their property so our community will continue to be a desirable place to live and work. We care about our neighbors and help them when there is a need. We don't need a livability initiative to make us care for our environment and our neighbors. If voluntary community groups want to provide additional assistance, they are free to do so.

58 IF YOU DO NOT LIKE WHAT IS IN THE NRV—GET OUT. DON'T TRY TO CHANGE IT TO SUIT EDUCATED FOOLS FROM "HOKIE LAND." WE SERVE A BETTER GOD, OUR LORD AND SAVIOR JESUS CHRIST !!!!!!!!!!!!!!!!!!!!!!!!!!!!!!!!!!!!!!!!!!!!! !!!!!!!!!!!!!!!!!!!!!!!!!!!!!!!!!!!!!!!!!!!!!!!!!!!

(New River Valley Planning District Commission, 2012b)

As the political climate concerning the regional planning process intensified, one of Building Home's leaders met with the PDC staff to discuss the specifics of the initiative's outreach plans. He asked how she was doing in the face of the planning effort's critics, and she said that she was "terrified." "I'm afraid for my physical safety," she said, and observed, "The dynamics at our public meetings have shifted. After them, I no longer walk to my car alone" (C. Davis, personal communication, March 21, 2014). After receiving a particularly hostile e-mail from a Livability Initiative critic, the staff member indicated she did not feel comfortable having the Building Home team, particularly its undergraduate student members, work in situations that might place them in harm's way and insisted that the group scrap its scheduled public engagement events. She expressed concern for the safety of Forum Theatre facilitators at these meetings and indicated that she believed the potential for violence was real and immediate. As an alternative, the PDC's Community Outreach Coordinator proposed that the Building Home team schedule closed-session events for members of community groups who had expressed interest in engaging with the issues at stake. The team ultimately pursued this alternative.

As part of this new course, Building Home presented an *NRV Today* scene during a meeting of the Head Start Policy Council in Radford, Virginia that arose from analyzing obesity rate statistics among youths in Floyd County and conducting interviews with the leader of the local nonprofit, Plenty!, which has committed to "nourishing community and feeding hungry neighbors by growing and sharing food in Floyd County" (Plenty, n.d.). The scene dramatized an encounter between a female physical education teacher—concerned about the growing rate of obesity and sluggishness among her students—and a well-meaning principal who nevertheless was failing to address the problem. The teacher protagonist described the insufficiency of the allotted time in the school day for physical education for realizing positive health outcomes for students. In the dramatization, she entered the principal's office to request more time with students so as to provide more robust and effective fitness programs, particularly for those whose health was at particular risk. While sympathetic to the teacher's concerns, the principal refused the appeal, citing the greater importance of "test prep" to meet the Commonwealth of Virginia's Standards of Learning and, in turn, ensure the continuance of state funding. The scene progressed from this central dilemma as the teacher employed numerous strategies to achieve her goal.

The Building Home group presented this scene in spring 2013 as the local Head Start program was responding to a recent federal government budget sequestration. Staff members and volunteers alike expressed great concern about how they would continue to have a positive impact on children and their families through Head Start with markedly diminished resources. Considering this, the *NRV Today* scene—which foregrounded a common conflict between different conceptions of how to meet children's needs—struck a chord with council members and prompted a passionate group dialogue about the importance of collective civic action to improve Head Start's salience and standing for public funding. In the group discussion following the scene, one council member shared, "This is on my 'pissed off' list, at the very top of it. Obesity is going to hurt taxpayers even more, so then more children's programs will be cut. Raise hell until children become a priority—with health and education. I will die with my last breath for that" (personal communication, May 8, 2013).

One staff member explained that she was scheduled to meet with elected officials in Richmond, the state capital, in the coming weeks to argue for Head Start's value. She extended an invitation to council members to join her in this effort but shared her anxiety concerning whether the meeting would have a noticeable positive impact. Meanwhile, in a remarkable turn, the group chose to apply Forum Theatre to the problem; the Building Home facilitators and council members collaboratively created a new scene that portrayed the upcoming meeting between a Head Start employee and state legislator as a "rehearsal," of sorts, for the real thing.

In the midst of this scene, the protagonist made her case to the state legislator:

> We are talking about making children a political priority, and in the last 15 years we have seen decreases in children's funding, and never more so than the recent sequestration. The government was very willing to rescue the airlines, but what about our kids? If that was your children and there were no slots for you for school readiness, what [would] you […] do?
>
> (personal communication, May 8, 2013)

The group rallied behind this woman and, after the scene, offered constructive feedback on what seemed to be the most effective strategies to engaging with an elected official.

The success of this *NRV Today* session pointed to the impact that this approach might have enjoyed in the Livability Initiative's second year. The Community Outreach Coordinator at the PDC seemed to agree with this belief, later observing, "[it is] a regret of mine that close to the end of the process, I let that fear undermine the work" (C. Davis, personal communication, March 28, 2014).

## Collaboration, Impact, and Enduring Questions

From July 2011 to April 2012, the Building Home team conducted forty-nine distinct community gatherings with the following groups:

- Upward Bound (2): Montgomery County
- Town of Blacksburg, Housing & Neighborhood Services: Montgomery County
- PDC Livability Initiative Summit: Pulaski County
- Pembroke Heritage Festival: Giles County
- Livability Initiative Consortium ("BUILT" game): Pulaski County
- Sustain Floyd & Community Voices: Floyd County
- Agency on Aging, "Friendship Café" (3): Montgomery County
- Wake Forest community (2): Montgomery County
- Retired Senior & Volunteer Program, Advisory Council (2): Floyd County
- Center for the Arts at Virginia Tech, "Open House": Montgomery County
- Cornerstone housing facility for victims of domestic abuse (2): City of Radford
- Land Policy Task Force: Floyd County
- New River Community Action, Local Advisory Board: Giles County
- Agency on Aging, "Friendship Café": Floyd County
- Virginia Tech, School of Education: Montgomery County
- Head Start Policy Council: City of Radford
- Blacksburg Estates mobile home park: Montgomery County
- Retired Senior & Volunteer Program, Advisory Council: Giles County
- New River Community Action, Local Advisory Board: City of Radford

In total, the Building Home team connected more than 1,000 citizens with the PDC's Initiative, nearly one-third of all Valley residents who shared their input through the Livability effort's multiple avenues of public engagement.

Reflecting on their theater-based methodologies, Building Home's members found that story circles uncover information, perspectives, and knowledge that complement conventional planning surveys and public hearings. As the Livability Initiative's Community Outreach Coordinator has observed, such "traditional outreach approaches"—premised on an "if you build it, they will come" ideology—"make people think in narrow, binary ways where the range of acceptable feedback is to be 'for or 'against' an existing proposal, without inviting citizens to have a meaningful role in scoping out the issues, investigating options, or crafting potential solutions" (C. Davis, personal communication, March 28, 2014). Being framed by the assumptions and intentions of the survey makers and conveners of hearings, such forums often privilege those who possess the resources, social capital, and organization to articulate well-argued claims. In contrast, participants in a story circle can expect equal access as participatory democracy is put into practice, one person at a time, in the form of a self-governed exchange of ideas around local, immediate issues of common concern. The inclusivity of this approach provided a significant contribution to the assessment of community needs in this regional planning project. Repeated requests for the Building Home team to return to host communities suggested that participants—holding the substance of the conversation in their hands—embraced the gatherings as a forum for direct participation in the planning and governance of their communities.

One particularly gratifying outcome of Building Home was the PDC's commissioning of Michael Rohd and his Sojourn Theatre compatriots, Shannon Scrofano and Liam Kaas-Lentz, to redesign a civic planning board game they had previously created called *Built*. Originally conceived for a project with the planning office in Portland, OR, the game is composed of numerous land use pieces (library, factory, parking lot, apartment house, open space, etc.) scaled to accommodate up to twenty people at a time, playing on large map-like boards representing the geographic area under consideration. The game's redesign for the Livability Initiative, called *Built NRV*, changed its focus from an urban to a suburban/rural environment, providing the boards and the playing pieces with characteristics specific to the NRV.

Rohd and Kaas-Lentz trained the Building Home team and staff of the Livability Initiative to facilitate the game. Playing the game in fourteen different locations throughout the Valley yielded substantial public input *and* sharpened facilitators' awareness and relationship to time (considering the game's fast-paced nature), understanding of community infrastructure, and impact of planning decisions on citizens' day-to-day lives. Involvement with the game also sharpened the Project leaders' improvisatory skills as participating groups continually redesigned their ideal communities.

Throughout Building Home's effort, its leaders regularly communicated with PDC leaders and staff. The two groups significantly influenced each other's approaches to stimulating and facilitating community dialogue. As one PDC planner observed in a 2014 interview, the dual excitement and terror of this ongoing co-creation often felt like "building the boat after we've already left the dock" (C. Davis, personal communication, April 3, 2014). She further explained,

> I learned to let go of my ideas about how to do things. I didn't know how rigid I was in my thinking. [...] We skew our approaches based on what we're comfortable with. [...] When things feel scary and contentious,

you want to retreat to the [default]. But that's the time you have to be expansive.

(C. Davis, personal communication, March 28, 2014)

For their part, the artists gained crucial information about the region and its citizens (e.g., aging, employment, community health) through commission program staff participation in Building Home rehearsals and meetings. These local government partners illuminated complex planning concepts for the team and illustrated how the Livability Initiative's bottom-up civic process would proceed from information gathering to implementation. The PDC's staff members went so far as to observe and fact-check theater scenes against their own knowledge of the NRV's diverse communities.

Building Home team members found translating community gathering-based information into formal reports for PDC staff a challenging exercise. Over time, the group discovered the important interplay between fact (what participants said, verbatim) and interpretation (how team members' illustrated, highlighted, and ordered personal perspectives based on what was seen and heard). At the end of their first year of work together, PDC personnel shared their perspective on the advantages and disadvantages of that protocol. One drawback Commission staff cited was that the reports did not sufficiently depict the dynamic character of the live events. The project's partners understood the community gathering processes but sensed that they missed a great deal from not being physically present at the meetings. Conversely, PDC staff members expressed excitement that the qualitative data that Building Home collected more richly illustrated citizens' sense of *place* than any other information the Commission had gathered from the Valley's communities. In one staff member's words, Building Home had fostered "deliberate and deep engagement rather than tokenism" (C. Davis, personal communication, March 28, 2014).

Despite these successes, numerous questions remain from this project regarding tensions inherent in the use of the arts in democratic processes. For instance, in democracy as it is typically practiced in the United States, there exists a tendency among most to look at the general flow of thought in a community to determine what is most important to all of its members. While worthwhile, this modus operandi assumes that insight is always couched inside the "bell curve" of prevailing public opinion. The majority does not always speak truth, however—particularly when that supposed truth allows for the continuance of social ills. Rather, as one PDC staffer put it, the majority of citizens often "speak the paradigm" on topics as varied as housing, health care, and the environment "really well and quite vehemently" (C. Davis, personal communication, April 3, 2014).

True insight, however unpopular, can often be found in a minority group's voice. Sophocles's classical tragedy, *Oedipus Rex*, illustrates this point through Tiresias, the blind seer. Despite the veracity of his claim that the play's titular character *is* the cause of the Theban plague, his fellow citizens brush Tiresias aside. Outside the realm of literature, any historian will attest that democratic rule carries with it a continuing risk of majority tyranny. Winnowing the complexity of citizens' opinions to a common denominator often forecloses honest consideration of the wisdom of the voices that lie outside the bell curve. Considering this, how might elected officials, planners, and everyday citizens intentionally gain the advantage of such thinking to develop plans that attend to the needs of the entire community? And how should such strategies apply in instances—such as Tea Party activist efforts throughout the Livability Initiative—when one minority group's claims are fallacious or without foundation? Building Home addressed this reality and its role in the broader democratic decision process and by faithfully recording and lifting up a diverse array of individual voices for deliberation by appropriate decision makers in the regional planning process.

In practical terms, the question of how to incorporate disparate voices into the Livability Initiative planning process arose in how to incorporate qualitative data into actionable plans. When asked about the character of Building Home's recorded data and how it contributed to the PDC's regional plan, the responsible staff member observed

> That's one of my challenge points. It's also a strength point. [...] We had all of this depth of really nuanced, really contextualized qualitative data that I had no meaningful way to integrate into the quantitative without doing my own version of making it fit through that little "slot." I made everything squeeze through the sieve of [one] database: [like a] play-dough machine. And [it was] me deciding, "What's the core point?" What's the heart of the matter in this paragraph for this person? Is this whole paragraph of growing up in [x community] and feeling unsafe and not knowing who could harm you ... does that get boiled down to "better law enforcement?" Or, "better roads?" It's not tidy. [Yet], it feels wrong to exclude that data from the calculation.
>
> (C. Davis, personal communication; March 28, 2014; April 3, 2014)

This dilemma raises a broader question about grassroots planning processes: How does the mechanism of representative democratic government hear the individual, particularly when a person's or group's viewpoint falls outside commonly held beliefs?

As they reflected on their experience in gathering community comments, Building Home artists and PDC planning partners unanimously attested to hearing moments-of-truth: that is, "when someone said something that [could] stand in for many different ways the issue has been [previously] expressed" (C. Davis, personal communication; March 28, 2014; April 3, 2014). Quite often, such "moments" are suffused with pathos, as was the case during a Building Home story-sharing session with one individual. A resident of a transitional housing facility for women described living in poverty and enduring and escaping from domestic abuse. She argued she was not getting the help she needed from government programs. To improve her circumstances meaningfully, she contended that she needed the community to acknowledge forthrightly that it had contributed to her circumstances.

Building Home team members and their Commission partners mutually recognized that part of what makes such a "moment of truth" so powerful is its emotional punch. As sentiment rests in the listener and not the speaker, however, how can government hear the insight in a citizen's heartfelt statement, assess its reliability, and meaningfully respond to it? Cultivating empathy is paradoxically vital and slippery in considering public needs—particularly because those in government rely primarily on quantitative data to make decisions. As Building Home team members discovered, when speaking with those who are typically unheard in public hearings, a lot of "blind seers" emerge: "It's easy to categorize something [someone says] as crazy." The staffer offering that observation followed it by articulating a critical dilemma for those working toward positive social change:

> I don't know what to do when someone speaks a truth that's *so true* ... and to do what [that person] says [to fix the problem] would mean upheaval of civilization and revolution. [When] what it implies is that everybody's complicit... but instead of doing something real, we just keep chipping away at the glacier with a nail file.
> (C. Davis, personal communication; March 28, 2014; April 3, 2014)

## Conclusion

The Livability Initiative's final report, *Livability in the New River Valley: From Vision to Action*, suggested that the effort's "purpose has been to better understand the views and desires of residents and to serve as a catalyst for positive change in the region" (New River Valley Planning District Commission, 2014). In turn, the "goal of [the final] report [was] to serve as a living document that will help to inform action towards creating the New River Valley citizens want to see in the future" (New River Valley Planning District Commission, 2014). To inform and inspire readers to commit to realizing the Livability Initiative's goals, the narrative chronicled the planning effort's attempts to secure public engagement and outlined its overarching vision, the trends it had identified, and the goals and priority strategies for the region that had emerged from it (New River Valley Planning District Commission, 2014). Significantly, arts and culture drive two of the project's eighteen identified strategies for enhancing the region's livability in the future. This recognition of the unique value of arts and culture in sustaining community health suggests that, instead of simply planning *for* the arts, planning *with* the arts can be a meaningful strategy for catalyzing civic engagement among many citizens.

Building this bridge can be quite challenging in any large-scale public effort in light of the fact that individuals may have widely differing views concerning what steps might make their community more livable. Ann Markusen has highlighted this challenge in her explanation of a common criticism of livability:

> One person's quality of life can be inimical to others'. Take the young live music scene in cities: youth magnet, older resident nightmare. Probably no worthy concept, as quality of life is, has been the subject of so many disappointing and conflicting measurement exercises.
>
> (Markusen, 2012)

Despite this dilemma, Building Home demonstrated that the natural quality of storytelling as a form and forum for communication can provide access for members of diverse communities to participate in democratic dialogue and deliberation. Considering the potential for greater participation in public engagement efforts that include art making and the nuance of recorded qualitative data, it is incumbent upon anyone employing the arts in public decision-making processes to develop reliable and comprehensive methods for understanding, selecting, and implementing expressed goals and strategies. The latter two of these three responsibilities are particularly important and fraught: How might citizens best hear and act on the wisdom of a few, or even a single voice of meaningful insight, when compared to the weight and volume of the many?

In the NRV of southwest Virginia today, residents—equipped with a wealth of community knowledge—still face a host of crucial questions regarding how to implement proposed efforts to strengthen the region's sustainability. As the final report of *Livability in the New River Valley* observed,

> The completion of this project should not mark the end of these efforts, but the beginning of a long-term goal to build networks of support that can bring to bear financial, human, and material resources toward achievement of broadly shared goals and priorities.
>
> (New River Valley Planning District Commission, 2014)

The authors hope that the lessons learned from Building Home will continue to widen and strengthen those networks in the auspicious years ahead.

## Notes

1 Portions of this chapter draw on Leonard, R.H. Building Home—Dramaturgy for theater as civic practice. In *Public—A Journal of Imagining America*. 2(1), 2014. Available at http://public.imaginingamerica.org/blog/article/building-home-dramaturgy-for-theater-as-civic-practice

2 To read more concerning Roadside Theater's story circle methodology, visit roadside.org/asset/story-circle-guidelines?unit=117

3 The PDC included demand-side management programs in its list of potential projects in an *NRV Tomorrow* planning draft document. Power company Con Edison describes increasingly popular demand-side management (DSM) programs as such:

> Utility companies have always managed the supply of energy; making sure enough electricity was available to match customer demand at any given time. Increasingly, utilities are also trying to manage the demand side of this equation. "Demand side management" or "DSM" programs help reduce customer demand for electricity. Using less electricity when demand is high (like on a hot summer day) can mean fewer new power plants and a smaller electric distribution system, saving money and improving the environment for everyone.
>
> Each year, Con Edison forecasts the demand for electricity to determine where and when equipment upgrades may be needed to maintain reliable electric service. In certain cases where upgrades are needed, the Targeted DSM Program is offered in neighborhoods to help reduce the demand on the electric system. Through direct customer participation in the program, the demand for electricity is reduced, allowing Con Edison to delay the need for expensive equipment upgrades in targeted neighborhoods.
>
> Customers also see a direct benefit from reducing energy demand by installing or upgrading to high-efficiency equipment through lower energy bills, improved equipment reliability, reduced maintenance issues and costs, and better overall indoor space quality. Energy efficiency is also a smart way to help the environment since using less energy contributes to fewer air pollutants, preserves natural resources, and promotes the use of domestic energy sources.
>
> (Con Edison. Targeted Demand Side Management.
> *Con Edison: Energy Efficiency*. Retrieved on May 4, 2013 from
> www.coned.com/energyefficiency/targetedDSM.asp)

# References

Bedoya, R. (2012). Creative placemaking and the politics of belonging and dis-belonging. Arts in a Changing America blog., September 1. Retrieved February 8, 2013 rom http://www.artsinachangingamerica.org/2012/09/01/creative-placemaking-and-the-politics-of-belonging-and-dis-belonging

Boal, A. (2002). *Games for actors and non-actors* (2nd ed.). London, UK: Routledge.

Bunch, W. (2013). Crooked Road dropping pursuit of National Heritage Area designation. *Times News*, March 14. Retrieved October 9, 2014 from www.timesnews.net/article/9058557/crooked-road-dropping-pursuit-of-national-heritage-area-designation

Catherwood-Ginn, R. J. (2012). *behind a stranger's face* (unpublished play).

Dickens, T. (2013). Crooked Road drops attempt at National Heritage Area designation. *Roanoke Times*, March 14. Retrieved May 4, 2103 from www.roanoke.com/news/1776386-12/crooked-road-drops-attempt-at-national-heritage-area.html

Gewertz, K. (2003). Augusto Boal's 'Theatre of the oppressed.' *Harvard University Gazette*, December 11. Retrieved February 11, 2013 from http://news.harvard.edu/gazette/2003/12.11/15-boal.html

Gladwell, M. (2000). *The tipping point: How little things can make a big difference*. New York: Little Brown & Company.

Hinkes-Jones, L. (2012). The anti-environmentalist roots of the Agenda 21 conspiracy theory. *The Atlantic Cities*, August 29. Retrieved January 28, 2103 from www.theatlanticcities.com/politics/2012/08/anti-environmentalist-roots-agenda-21-conspiracy-theory/3091

Markusen, A. (2012). Fuzzy concepts, proxy data: Why indicators won't track creative placemaking success. *Createquity.* Retrieved May, 8, 2013 from http://createequity.com/2012/11/fuzzy-concepts-proxy-data-why-indicators-wont-track-creative-placemaking-success.html

New River Valley Planning District Commission. (2012a). Livability in the New River Valley. *Livability Initiative.* Retrieved May 4, 2013, from http://nrvlivability.org/news/livability-initiative-interim-report

New River Valley Planning District Commission. (2012b). NRV Livability Initiative Community priorities survey, December 2012–January 2013. *Community priorities survey results now in!* Retrieved May 4, 2013, from http://nrvlivability.org/news/community-priorities-survey-results-now

New River Valley Planning District Commission, (2013). NRV Tomorrow interactive survey launched! *Livability Initiative.* Retrieved May 4, 2013, from http://nrvlivability.org/news/nrv-tomorrow-interactive-survey-launched

New River Valley Planning District Commission. (2014). *Livability in the New River Valley: From vision to action.* Martinsville, VA: Collinsville Printing Co., Inc.

Obama, B. (2009). Remarks by the President at the Urban and Metropolitan Roundtable. Delivered July 13 in Washington, DC. Retrieved January 30, 2013 from http://www.whitehouse.gov/the_press_office/Remarks-by-the-President-at-Urban-and-Metropolitan-Roundtable

Plenty! (n.d.). Website. Retrieved October 26, 2014, from http://www.plentylocal.org/

Roadside Theater. (1999). Story circles. Story circle guidelines. Retrieved January 28, 2013 from http://roadside.org/asset/story-circle-guidelines?unit=117

Rohd, M. (2012). Translations: The distinction between social & civic practice and why I find it useful. *HowlRound: A Journal of the Theatre Commons,* September 1. Retrieved February 3, 2013 from http://journalism.howlround.com/translations-the-distinction-between-social-civic-practice-and-why-i-find-it-useful-by-michael-rohd

United Nations. (1992). Agenda 21, UN Conference on Environment and Development, 1992. In *Sustainable Development Knowledge Platform.* Retrieved October 19, 2014, from http://sustainabledevelopment.un.org/index.php?page=view&nr=23&type=400

U.S. Department of Housing and Urban Development. (n.d.). Sustainable communities regional planning grants. In *HUD.GOV.* Retrieved October 25, 2014, from http://portal.hud.gov/hudportal/HUD?src=/program_offices/economic_resilience/sustainable_communities_regional_planning_grants

# 3

# ONE NEW YORK RISING TOGETHER?

## Arts and Culture in Neighborhood Ecosystems

*Jan Cohen-Cruz*

In January 2014, Bill de Blasio became mayor of New York City (NYC), announcing his intention to shift the narrative from "a tale of two cities"—one rich, one poor—to "one New York rising together" (One New York Rising Together, 2013). Like New York as a whole, the realm of art and culture can also be seen as a tale of two cities. There is a long-entrenched hierarchy of large, established arts institutions receiving the most support and relating more to other arts institutions than to any other configuration of community (Sidford, 2011). And yet there is an even longer tradition of artistic and cultural expression in distinct neighborhoods adding value where people live. De Blasio's platform offers an opening to align neighborhood-based arts and culture with a progressive, citywide vision. In what follows, I focus on Naturally Occurring Cultural Districts (NOCD)-New York, a consortium of arts and culture organizations in NYC's five boroughs that are linked both with other neighborhood organizations across sectors and with one another across the city. Participation in NOCD both affirms artists who choose to engage socially and locally and provides opportunities for them to learn from one another and to organize in seeking to change municipal policy.

### Framework

There is a particular vitality about artistic expression that arises from a close relationship with its culture of origin. Culture is a specific set of beliefs and ways of understanding and being in the world shared by a group of people and rooted in either geography, given the shared historical roots and way of life of a village or city neighborhood; tradition, such as that which grows out of particular collective experience over generations; or spirit, such as a political philosophy that draws together people from diverse places and traditions.[1] Culture encompasses intellectual, emotional, psychological, material, and sensory aspects of a group's shared life. Art is a concentrated form of cultural expression, depending on the skill sets and tools characteristic of the medium employed, created by individuals and small groups. Art making grounded in a specific culture can and often does challenge prevailing understandings or beliefs that together constitute the dominant culture.

The interdependence of local arts and culture and other entities providing social resources have historically contributed to healthy places to live and work, making inviting what might otherwise have been hostile settings in which to get a footing in life. In the early twentieth century, for example, large numbers of immigrants were socialized in settlement houses, in the best cases, without taking away their cultural traditions to "make them" Americans. Settlement houses continue to provide "job training and employment programs, early childhood education, afterschool youth programs, arts education and performances, computer labs, English-as-a-Second-Language and literacy education, citizenship instruction and legal counseling, mental health and home care, housing, senior centers and Meals-on-Wheels" (United Neighborhood Houses, n.d.).

Artistic programs offered at settlement houses have featured a range of genres, each familiar to a particular immigrant population and unfamiliar to others, connecting people across difference. In the early twentieth century, director Jane Addams of Chicago's Hull-House affirmed theater's "ability to bring men [sic] together into a common mood and to unite them through a mutual interest in elemental experiences" which, performance scholar Shannon Jackson has noted, "provided an environmental medium for cross-class and cross-cultural expansion" (S. Jackson, 2000, p. 212). Addams clearly saw theater's ability to contribute socially and aesthetically.

Other immigrant cultural projects during the same period have been critiqued as assimilationist. The popular United States (U.S.) pageantry movement in the first two decades of the twentieth century involved hundreds of immigrants in enormous spectacles that were often presumed to transform them into Americans with a simple change of costume (Nochlin, 1985). Some pageants literally depicted immigrants arriving in Act I, in native garb, and by Act II, wearing familiar American clothes and waving the U.S. flag. Historian David Glassberg has described this movement's emphasis on a new, strictly American identity and argued that civic officials sought, through pageantry, to "define a common town characteristic and sense of cohesion" even as the flow of immigrants diversified cultural "tastes and interests, as well as particular ethnic, occupational, and neighborhood loyalties" (Glassberg, 1990, p. 282). Clearly, ways are needed to advance geographic cohesion without alienating people from their cultural roots.

In contrast to the pageants' frequently nationalistic response to immigration, Hull-House leaders emphasized the internationalism on which they argued

U.S. democracy ought to be built (S. Jackson, 2000, pp. 224–225). Jane Adams theorized a balance between reminiscence, expressed as a pull to the homeland, and anticipation, creating a new "we" in the U.S. (S. Jackson, 2000, p. 227). Such an attraction continues in New York's neighborhoods today, where more than 37% of the residents were born in other countries (*Huffington Post*, 2013). Settlement houses continue to play an important role for new residents to America, honoring the past while also providing spaces for the creation of a new "we." Though not a direct descendent of the settlement house, NOCD-NY can be seen in that tradition as a consortium of arts and cultural organizations that also play a vital social role. Some NOCD members focus on immigrants, and others do not, depending on their neighborhood's demographics.

NOCD-NY came into being between 2010 and 2011 through a series of conversations among artists, activists, creative manufacturers, nonprofit groups, and policy makers on the role of arts and culture in strengthening NYC communities (NOCD-NY, 2010). These leaders sensed an opportunity to move their work into policy by forming a loose-knit consortium. Caron Atlas, an NYC resident and director of the national organization Arts and Democracy,[2] and Tamara Greenfield, executive director of the NYC-based Fourth Arts Block (FAB), took on a co-convening role to increase NOCD's visibility, stimulate a public discourse about the value of neighborhood-based arts, and develop an action plan.

Susan Seifert and Mark Stern, co-researchers of the Social Impact of the Arts Project (SIAP), developed the notion of a "natural cultural district:"

> A "natural" cultural district is a neighborhood that has spawned a concentration of cultural agents—organizations and businesses, artists and activists, residents and visitors. SIAP research has demonstrated that concentrations of cultural assets are a reliable indicator of neighborhood revitalization. Cultural clusters improve prospects that a neighborhood will see its poverty rate decline and its population increase. They reinforce ethnic and economic diversity. They stimulate social network formation both with and across neighborhoods. These social networks are the critical mechanism for translating cultural assets into neighborhood development.
>
> (Stern and Seifert, 2013, p. 1)

NOCD has applied this concept to a *network* of neighborhood-based cultural districts that cross the city, advocating for public policies that support art as part of *communities* citywide. Urban planner Maria Rosario Jackson, speaking at an NOCD research exchange in 2013, highlighted renewed interest in a comprehensive approach within urban planning circles, citing the California Endowment's Building Healthy Communities initiative in partnership with the Alliance for California Traditional Arts as an example. Building Healthy

Communities features artists and arts organizations partnering with housing groups, human services agencies, schools, and other institutions to address a wide range of issues that ultimately affect health outcomes. Jackson observed, "If, historically, strategies to disempower communities take away creative expression, then why isn't arts and cultural activity a part of strategies to help empower communities?" (M. Jackson, 2013, unpublished presentation). Work must be done to build understanding across sectors about how art and culture are inextricable from other community priorities and contribute to solving local concerns.

NOCD embraces just that transdisciplinary challenge, addressing the magnitude and complexity of issues through the integration of the arts and culture with many fields, in the face of which boundaries wear away. Rather than compete for affordable space as a discrete sector, for example, NOCD encourages arts organizations to see that they have as much to lose as every other local institution when a neighborhood gentrifies and thus look for ways to work together. Gentrification is a well-known phenomenon: artists move to a "poor" neighborhood because it is all they can afford, inadvertently pushing out some of the long-time residents and with them, local culture. Then their art prospers, restaurants and cafes follow, more people of means want to move there, and the artists get pushed out. The neighborhood loses its identity at least twice, related first to the loss of its cultural specificity and then to the loss of its artist community as the people and institutions that shaped it relocate. Moreover, some neighborhoods end up with the same chain restaurants, banks, and pharmacies as Anywhere, USA, replacing even the high-end, but at least unique, restaurants and bars that displaced the artists.

Most NOCD member organizations are located in hitherto economically marginalized neighborhoods. Critic Jen Harvie (2009) has suggested that in NYC, "the received vocabulary for identifying different types of theatre is spatial: there is theatre on the main commercial thoroughfare of Broadway, and there is theatre Off-Broadway, Off-Off Broadway, and so on" (p. 25). By extension, the arts in other neighborhoods—constituting most of the city— are often invisible, situated in what theater critic, "Marvin Carlson terms a 'boundary location–inescapably tied to the city but never truly a part of it'" (Harvie, 2009, p. 25). Such neighborhoods are vulnerable through neglect and, over time, gentrification. In the East Village in NYC in the 1980s, for example, numerous community gardens attracted developers who benefited from the low cost of land at that time. In some cases they then built on the very plots that originally attracted them. NOCD members support the people who have long lived or worked in such areas, rallying municipal protection in the face of powerful real estate interests seeking otherwise to dislocate them. I turn now to locally significant cultural organizations in NYC that play as essential a role to their constituents as do internationally acclaimed institutions to theirs.

## Culturally Committed Artists in Neighborhoods

What draws artists to become involved in particular neighborhoods and how is that relationship reciprocal? Some artists evidence long-term, meaningful ties to a particular place because of family, history, politics, or spirit—in a word, culture, as the sum total of a people's way of life. Others find their way to a neighborhood, perhaps drawn to it as a context in which to give form to their values, through free workshops or participation in public events, such as street fairs. The attraction may include, but is not necessarily limited to, affordable rent.

NOCD members share an appreciation of cultural roots and political inquiries that are reinforced in particular geographical locations and reach the people whose culture/history/experience has informed them as well as, rather than exclusively, art audiences. Although NOCD member Charlie Lai has pointed out that NYC cultural districts are not truly "naturally occurring," as all are a mix of artists with and without roots in their respective neighborhoods, these entities are certainly different from cultural districts *designed* to bring in artists and audiences from elsewhere, which coalesce and highlight art that may be wonderful in itself but have no specific place-based significance. The romantic notion of the artist who eats, breathes, and sleeps nothing but art and may as well situate him- or herself anywhere is outdated; a more multi-dimensional vision has taken its place, as evidenced through the following description of six NOCD member organizations.[3]

### El Museo de Barrio, Linking National and Grassroots Art and Culture

El Museo was founded forty-five years ago in uptown Manhattan by artist and educator Raphael Montañez Ortiz and a cadre of parents, educators, artists, and activists who recognized that "mainstream museums largely ignored Latino artists" (El Museo, 2014, About). The organization's vision was a grassroots, community-based museum aspiring to national and international art status as stewards of Latino/Hispanic art. Tensions exist between those who want El Museo to be *either* part of the museum world *or* part of Latino culture and between those who want to foreground Puerto Rican or other Latino art. El Museo's multiple foci and borderland location (both physically and metaphorically) also result in an interesting, diverse audience. Sometimes art lovers come up Museum Mile—the official designation of NYC's Fifth Avenue from 82nd to 105th streets because of the richness and cultural diversity of the nine museums located there—and get their first taste of Latino art at El Museo. Staff members encourage such visitors to experience more Latino culture in the nearby neighborhood. In an interview in 2013, Gonzalo Casals, then acting director of El Museo, described urging visitors "to go into the neighborhood and check out the food, the music, the distinctly

Puerto Rican community garden" (Casals personal interview, March 4, 2013). For people more aligned with Latino culture than art broadly, the Museo may be the first museum they visit. Then, Casals explains gleefully, "We push them down Fifth Avenue to visit the other institutions on Museum Mile" (Casals personal interview, March 4, 2013).

To appreciate fully the value of art and cultural institutions in neighborhoods, one must look not only at objects produced but at less-obvious ways that artistic assets find expression. Casals has identified three cultural assets that apply both to and beyond the artwork to El Museo's neighborhood (and which other NOCD members also contribute in their locales):

1   Creativity: Historically, East Harlem is a community of immigrants, characterized by cultural forms that carry meaning in its residents' lives. Looking at art and culture as a continuum, beginning with those that leave the most room for individual expression and specific sets of skills that are recognized as art, creativity is expressed in culturally-specific kinds of murals, community gardens, crafted objects in *botanicas* (traditional Puerto Rican shops), such as traditional amulets, bilingual bookstores, and "ethnic store fronts" that people of various Latino/ Hispanic heritages create and that make a neighborhood unique.

2   Dialogue: Artistic work is often the result of and the basis for a participatory exchange of ideas, as compared to the scholarly norm of working alone. Dialogue brings in diverse constituents by virtue of the everyday language in which it can take place.

3   Collaboration: The arts and culture require collaboration, frequently calling for different capacities within the same project, grounded in recognition that people with different expertise and types of knowledge working together are needed to address social challenges.

(Casals, personal interview, March 4, 2013)

## The New York Chinatown History Project and Historical Imagination

The New York Chinatown History Project (CHP) is at the intersection of a specific cultural and geographic location bulwarked by art. Founded by community organizer Charlie Lai and historian/activist Jack Tchen, the CHP is "a community documentation project designed to reconstruct the 120 year legacy of what is now the largest Chinese community outside of Asia" (Tchen, 1987, p. 158). The history initiative brings together scholars, photographers, community workers, artists, and other neighborhood residents to counter stereotypes and articulate their own experiences as a basis for what Tchen has called reclaiming community pasts.

The Museum of Chinese in America (MoCA), a CHP initiative, was founded as a platform for the communication of what those of Chinese heritage have contributed to the U.S. and the expression of who Chinese-Americans are. Tchen notes that unlike most historical projects, the CHP has always worked with artists, and for extended periods of time, since MoCA's beginnings in 1979–1980. For CHP, history is not just non-fiction; the founders always cared as much about the living performance of culture as about the details of past occurrences. This reflects their prioritizing of what Tchen calls artists with a historical imagination—who can think in terms of time not so much as fantasy but as creative and survival processes at different times as expressed through their work. Tchen notes that the artists associated with MoCA communicate something about lived life in a way that written documents cannot. The artists do not improve the historical data but rather evoke how history keeps living (Tchen, personal interview, July 25, 2014).

Artist Tomie Arai, for example, has a long relationship with MoCA, which has influenced both the content and form of her work. With scholar Lena Sze, Arai initiated an oral history and visual art project, *Portraits of New York Chinatown*, which addressed MoCA's role within the downtown NYC community. Recurring through the interviews Sze undertook with twenty-seven neighborhood residents and leaders were concerns about gentrification and displacement. Sze has observed that "oral history, and I believe Arai's work that used oral history to visualize stories, is about constructing meaning out of subjective experience, rather than simply extracting factual evidence as a means of uncovering a single historical truth" (Sze, 2014, p. 3). Sze has noted that Arai captures what it means for people to live in a place in the process of gentrifying.

Elaborating on the difference between what a historian and an artist bring to a historical museum, Sze has written

> Immersed in the details of the affordable housing crisis, of luxury redevelopment proceeding at a seemingly un-checked pace, and of stories of evictions and displacements, Arai wades through this sea of experiences and perceptions to assert that memory, or a historical feeling, of place is never finished or complete, but nonetheless an urgent thing in these fast-moving times.
>
> (Sze, 2014, p. 3)

The context of a historical rather than an art museum for such work suggests that affective memory is an important part of understanding our past and provides an overlapping, but not synonymous, audience, thus fruitfully expanding Arai's reach.

## Fourth Arts Block and Maintaining a Community's Residents and Character

Historically, people from many cultural backgrounds have situated arts initiatives in Manhattan's Lower East Side (LES). The economic downturn of the early 1970s brought a new wave of artists, many of whom identified with under-represented cultures whether ethnically specific or based in gender preference or "queerness" in the sense of other than the mainstream cultural norm in some way. At that time, the area was perceived as dangerous, which is often the language used for neighborhoods with lower median incomes, more people of color and other ethnicities, and fewer municipal amenities, which in fact ought to be a critique of the city, not of the people who live there. So NYC offered artists inexpensive live/work space, recognizing that a critical mass of artists frequently changes a neighborhood's image/story and leads to more tax-generating businesses and people moving in.

Tamara Greenfield, co-director of NOCD-NY and director of FAB, founded in 2001 by arts and cultural organizations on East Fourth Street between Second and Third avenues, said the city was not vetting the art before renting out space. Then some twenty-five years after the explosion of the LES as a venue for an array of artistic and cultural expression, FAB's founders, Greenfield has explained, were

> … committed to keeping long-time organizations in the spaces that they had helped homestead. They have always included a ragtag mix of multi-disciplinary artists and a cross-sector alliance with low-income residents, small businesses, and elected officials who saw the value that these small arts spaces created in the community. Many of the arts groups came out of movements for cultural self-determination in the 1960s, 1970s, and 1980s, and include Spanish-language theater companies, African-American dance companies, and a Women & Transgender theater collective. There are interesting and eclectic ties to and across diverse communities, so these relationships can look really different for different groups.
>
> (Greenfield, personal interview, February 4, 2013)

As gentrification of the LES intensified through the 1980s and 1990s, the city began selling space it had accumulated and which had long been occupied by artists. Housing rights activists, such as the Cooper Square Committee, organized residents of all kinds to press to preserve their spaces against gentrification. They simultaneously resisted efforts to create hierarchy among existing artistic groups based on size, culture, or aesthetics. The rich mix of artists and cultural organizations already located in the LES did not subscribe to such hierarchies and were motivated to be at the same political table and work together because there were potential benefits to be gained for all.

Today, FAB consists of more than twenty-five arts groups (e.g., individual companies self-described as artists), ten cultural facilities (largely places where a range of work, some of it culturally-specific, is supported), and seventeen performance and rehearsal venues. Its services to its members include leading the development and conversion of 100,000 square feet of arts and cultural space, marketing and promoting the district, and offering discount ticketing and other community events and programs. The organization's members attract an annual audience of 250,000, while FAB serves 1,500 artists and provides more square feet for active cultural use than any other block in New York. The mix of established and emerging artists, the diversity of publics they address, and the multiplicity of forms they use have made FAB "an incubator for new work and diverse artistic voices" enhanced by its "racial and ethnic diversity, free and low cost programs, and training for emerging artists and youth" (Fourth Arts Block, 2011, para. 3). While FAB is, in effect, a consortium within the NOCD association, it cannot alone do the same level of cultural organizing that NOCD can undertake citywide.

Ryan Gilliam, executive director of Downtown Art, is a founding member of FAB. She was inspired by NOCD to co-conceive, with Greenfield, the idea for Lower East Side History Month, which launched in May 2014 and involved more than forty local cultural, historical, community development, religious, and activist organizations. Gilliam has explained that since participating in NOCD, her perspective on being a community-based artist has grown:

> From a vision of myself as a practicing artist, with twenty years of experience collaborating with local teens and actively engaging with the local artistic and educational community, [I now see myself as] a viable instigator of a community-wide initiative that crosses boundaries, bringing a larger cross-section of the community into collaboration. Now I see the connection between culture and the city, art and history, and I see history as what happened as recently as yesterday.
>
> (Gilliam, personal interview, August 12, 2013)

Many of the plays that Gilliam makes with local teens address historic themes of the LES, such as "The Great Struggle for Cheap Meat" (2013), on the role of women in organizing a strike to bring down the price of meat in the neighborhood more than 100 years ago. Gilliam also programs three floors of a building on East 4th Street that will open in 2015, "for artists and small companies wishing to develop projects in any art form for which community engagement is a central, integral aesthetic concern" (Gilliam, personal interview, August 12, 2013).

According to Greenfield, what began in the LES as resistance to gentrification has developed into a shared appreciation of historical continuity and diversity, not preservation for its own sake, but because the cultures are still living (Greenfield, personal interview, February, 2013). FAB's challenge is allowing for the continuation and evolution of culture that grew out of a particular place and time. The area's arts organizations have had to continue to resist being forced out, especially in such tough economic times as the post-2008 recession, with less public money available for culture and more profit possible for real estate. FAB helps to sustain the self-determination and institution building that the neighborhood's history made possible; membership in the like-minded NOCD citywide coalition is one of the ways it advocates for those values citywide.

## Urban Bush Women and Cultural Roots

Urban Bush Women (UBW) evidences a different configuration of art, culture, and neighborhood, with the first two of these foci more dominant than the third in the company's work. UBW, founded in 1984 by Jawole Willa Jo Zollar (see Chapter 8), "brings the untold and under-told histories and stories of disenfranchised people to light through dance" (Urban Bush Women, 2014b, para. 1). Zollar envisioned a dance troupe, "founded on the energy, vitality and boldness of the African American community [and] ... the vulnerability, sassiness and bodaciousness of the women I experienced growing up in Kansas City" Urban Bush Woman, 2014a, para. 1). Zollar's observation suggests an aesthetic and cultural root in the company's African American inflected dance forms.

Examples of the influence of African culture on UBW art abound. The presence of a company of women of African descent, of different sizes and shapes, with great strength and multiple kinds of beauty, immediately bespeaks the glory of diversity. The aesthetic and craft of the group's work, which is, unlike ballet, not based on out-turned feet and toe shoes, is a reminder of the many sources of art globally. The integration of culturally specific content and form provides a strong foundation for powerful art making. UBW's piece, *Hairstories*, for example, integrates three idioms of African American music in a piece about black women and hair, challenging racism and sexism:

> Demonstrated through often humorous and sometimes tragic childhood stories of getting hair done, the blues impulse offers a cathartic release that allows overwhelming experiences to be bearable. The jazz impulse is evidenced through a Dr. Professor character who questions assumptions of race and gender in language and movement. Jazz also encourages the constant process of redefinition–to self, to community, and to the past. The final impulse, gospel, suggests that redemption, transcendence, and freedom are found communally.
>
> (Howell, 2011, p. 7)

Then-UBW director of education and community engagement Maria Bauman explained in an interview that Zollar's vision has always included robust exchange between artists and communities (Bauman, personal interview,

February 21, 2013). The company's conception of community engagement evolved through early touring experiences. UBW sought to include audiences in which they could also see themselves—women, the working class, and people of color. They were motivated to give something back to people of similar cultural roots and identities from which their own stories and forms often spring. Troupe members invited working-class people they encountered, such as restaurant servers, hotel workers, or taxi drivers, to come to their shows. Sometimes the cultural organization hosting UBW provided complimentary tickets, but too often such gestures were framed as "outreach," with its unspoken inference of reaching "down" to people who do not pay for seats and thus are not the producers' preferred audience. For UBW, however, relationships between artists and communities have to go two ways (Bauman, personal interview, February 21, 2013). As Zollar depends on her cultural roots for source material, she seeks to ensure that people who constitute that culture have an opportunity to experience what UBW makes of it.

Interacting with peer artistic groups, both dance and theater, that embrace similar values has been pivotal for Zollar. Between 1982 and 1999, the national American Festival Project (AFP) brought a number of such entities together (Roadside Theater, 2014). AFP was an

> alliance of artists and artists' companies working in communities with … activists, organizers, artists, and leaders—in a movement that utilizes culture and the arts as both a grounding place and a means for social change. The Project believes in the inherent value of cultural identity, cultural diversity, and cultural exchange.
>
> (In Motion, 2014, para. 1)

Festival companies were committed to returning art to communities that were its source. The influence of like-minded AFP artists grounded in places significant to them culturally, such as Appalachia for Roadside Theater and a Puerto Rican neighborhood in NYC for Pregones, inspired Zollar to situate UBW in a kindred geographic community. As Bauman has observed, "A core UBW value is that place matters. That mission keeps us honest. How can we ask other dancers to do that and not be accountable to our own neighborhood?" (Bauman, personal interview, February 21, 2013).

In keeping with this view, in 2000, UBW settled in Fort Greene, Brooklyn, a bastion for people of color since the nineteenth century. Some of UBW's projects are Brooklyn-based, including Builders, Organizers, and Leaders through Dance, a workshop series that involves dancers and social activists. Although Fort Greene is an important home base, however, most of the company's efforts are national in scope, such as a ten-day annual Summer Leadership Institute in New Orleans, connecting dance professionals and community-based artists from across the U.S. to encourage widespread integration of the arts in social activism and civic engagement. Zollar frequently collaborates with other artists nationally and internationally. At the time of this writing, she and choreographer Liz Lerman were at work on a performance/social research project, *Blood, muscle, bone: The anatomy of wealth and poverty*, that examines,

> … how wealth and poverty impact the body while asking new questions about how these conditions are defined and imagined … public offerings … might include stage performance, prayer breakfasts, lecture tours, workshops, teacher training, panels, and cabarets.
>
> (Urban Bush Women New Works, 2014, para. 2)

The synergy between UBW's local and national projects is striking; workshops that attract participation across class and sector have also served as research sites for Zollar and Lerman to create a new piece and a series of compelling and generative public events.

### Staten Island Arts and Building Community Cohesion across Difference

Staten Island Arts Executive Director Melanie Cohn has found that artists and arts organizations bring vibrancy to the neighborhoods in which they are located through a wide array of activities and programming such as Art by the Ferry; public theater performances by SI Shakespeare on the steps of Borough Hall; Second Saturdays; SIOutLOUD; St. George Day; Deep Tanks Art Festival; Van Duzer Days; and Harborlore:

> Artists create opportunities for the community—individuals, businesses, social service groups—to come together through different cultural experiences and informally build stronger bonds with one another. And they make the neighborhoods livelier. In turn, the neighborhoods give the arts this amazing diversity. We have great community heritages--Sri Lankan, Central American, West African, Italian, to name a few. These rich traditions exist at the core of Staten Island communities. It's inspirational; the artists and cultural groups draw energy from these shared expressions.
>
> (Cohn, personal interview, May 22, 2013)

While affirming local meaning, the larger world is also important to neighborhood artists. Contact with NOCD members, especially in Fort Greene where tourism is more established, has shown Cohn that "the addition of tourists doesn't take away neighborhood concerns. In fact, successful tourism may help increase audience and economic activity, while still bringing some community issues to the forefront" (Cohn, personal interview, May 22, 2013).

Place is important on Staten Island as well. Cohn highlighted the bonds that are created out of familiarity with what is special about a place:

> Staten Island is different from the other boroughs and is full of well-kept secrets. It is special because of the community's long memory, the loyalty Staten Islanders have to one another, the amazing resources like abundant and beautiful green spaces, and its rich and quirky history. It also has some insecurities and feelings of being overlooked or looked down upon that is part of being the smallest borough in the nation's largest city. These issues come up in the art that is made and how culture is experienced here ... and in the fissure between what many people *think* Staten Island is versus what Staten Island really is.
>
> (Cohn, personal interview, May 22, 2013)

## The Queens Museum and Community Embeddedness

The Queens Museum (QM) demonstrates how an arts institution can develop into a cultural organization by becoming an active part of the surrounding community. Already a world-class venue for art objects, in 2006 then-director Tom Finkelpearl hired a community organizer and tasked her with identifying the interests and needs of people living in its neighborhood of Corona. This led to, among other initiatives, the decision to expand the Museum's identity in response to Queens's many under-served and newly arrived immigrants with limited English language proficiency. For example, the QM spearheaded a community coalition to activate and beautify the Corona neighborhood's public spaces to create a multicultural hub for local residents and businesses. Corona Studio, which marks QM's move to longer-term projects, seeks artists who are "ready, willing, and able" to commit the necessary time to use art for social change.

In 2011, for example, Cuban artist Tania Bruguera, inspired by immigrant-led civil unrest in the Paris suburbs, initiated Immigrant Movement International in the Museum's Corona Studio to put "immigrants in a position of power, whereby their political representation could be strengthened through a political party created by immigrants" (Osman and Fuentes, 2013, p. 88). Bruguera has proven herself to be as at home in fine art spaces as in neighborhood workshops and to take each kind of work as seriously. The space acts as a local educational platform and meeting spot and as an international think tank engaging activists, artists, critics, and academics in envisioning a different legal reality and social role for migrants in the twenty-first century "that can be adapted to the specific contexts of other museums" (Queens Museum, 2012, p. 3).

Through a careful selection of local and international artists whose work engages with social issues, QM has developed a reputation as a home for "art as social practice," an international movement, defined by critic Andy Horwitz as

> ... artistic projects in various disciplines that emerge from engaging with social issues in community, that enlist "non-artists" in the creation and development of the project and have as a goal some kind of

awareness-raising or sociological impact. This doesn't preclude aesthetic considerations or the possibility for the realization of a singular artistic vision, but it implies a set of conditions that are outside of more traditional artistic practices.

(Horvitz, 2012, para. 14)

Art as social practice casts a broad net. For many practitioners, fusing the social with the aesthetic responds to a desire to serve justice aims through their work; for others, this form of art making is just about exploring new terrain for artists. The distinction between the two is significant; the former, which characterizes the work of QM, is grounded in commitments that extend beyond the aesthetic even while, importantly, rooted there.

At an NOCD public gathering in May 2013, Prerana Reddy, QM director of public events, described the expanded idea of the museum beyond the building, gallery, and artworks exhibited. She noted that the QM also includes human resources, including arts educators and community organizers who seek to embed the institution in its community. The Museum now seeks artists, designers, activists, and cultural producers with skills to match issues identified by their community partners. QM has evolved beyond the idea that public art consists of things plopped down in a public space.

The Museum's leaders do not seem concerned about whether participants always know that their projects are conceived within the context of art. For instance, Immigrant Movement International's store front in the Museum's Corona Studio houses classes for immigrants, offers rehearsal space for local dance and music companies, and provides workshops to learn English, performance, screen-printing, bike repair, and urban gardening. Ongoing programs are free and led by artists and other skilled community residents interested in lifelong learning, experimental pedagogy, and mutual aid. The project's diverse cadre of instructors challenges notions that only certain people are cultural producers or that an individual's background defines the areas in which one can become expert. Instead of functioning simply as a venue to house art objects, QM is a model for arts institutions as places that generate, present, and share cultural meaning in various forms.

## NOCD as a Network

### The Need for a Neighborhood-Based Arts and Culture Network

Conventionally, artistic institutions that are well resourced, self-standing (in the sense of not interacting with institutions from other sectors), and attract an art audience are seen as necessarily more worthy of support than those with modest means, situated as part of neighborhood ecosystems, and meaningful principally to local people. Indeed, this oft-held view has fueled an economic development movement of sorts. Carole Rosenstein has addressed this concern:

> Over the past decade, many cities have focused substantial economic development and revitalization efforts and resources on enhancing their "creative" character. Economic development scholar Richard Florida has promoted an enormously influential image of successful 21st century cities as places where social tolerance and natural and cultural amenities draw educated workers and new-economy businesses (Florida, 2003, 2007, and 2008). Florida grounded his work in Jane Jacobs' (1961) path-breaking conception of healthy cities as vital places in which diverse populations use streets, parks, neighborhoods, and downtowns for mixed purposes, both during the day and at night.
>
> (Rosenstein, 2009, p. 1)

The policies that public leaders, however, have developed to respond to Florida's call to build "creative cities" that would support the "creative economy" and attract "creative-class" workers are not in line with Jacobs's vision of what makes a city livable. Instead, these efforts have undermined the diversity of urban populations and uses because they have encouraged gentrification and privileged real-estate development over economic and community improvements that benefit a broader urban population (Rosenstein, 2009). Rosenstein has argued that this sort of municipal cultural policy hurts neighborhoods as follows:

1  Concentrating cultural resources into downtown business and cultural districts and ignoring neighborhood-based cultural assets. For example, more public support goes to large museums and less, if any, to local parades and street fairs.
2  Poorly incorporating neighborhood cultural assets and needs into existing cultural policy infrastructure; in other words, viewing informal, local, participatory acts of expression as other than "real" art with concurrent need for support.
3  Poorly integrating city cultural agencies and sector leaders into broader policy conversation and decision-making, such as negotiating the significance of culturally-specific parades with the resulting noise, dirt, and traffic jams; and
4  Not clearly identifying whom from city government has authority vis-à-vis the public cultural sector.

(2009, pp. 2–6)

NOCD as a group spearheaded by Atlas and Greenfield has sought recognition for the value of grassroots/neighborhood arts and cultural institutions by encouraging partnerships among them and publicizing the significance of their relationships with other neighborhood institutions, including business, education, and housing.

## *Gathering Neighborhood-Based Arts and Culture Constituents*

During NOCD's first two years (2010–2012), representatives of its member organizations met monthly. The organization supported neighborhood-based artists by encouraging contact with one another; explored ways to sustain such efforts citywide, which included testifying at NYC Council public hearings on cultural economies; convened a public forum for community artists concerning ways to access space in a real estate–driven city; and shared lessons the New Orleans cultural sector learned after Hurricane Katrina that could be applied to efforts after Hurricane Sandy in New York.

In early 2013, NOCD organized a public forum, which the organization dubbed From the Neighborhood Up, drawing on the assets of its members. The consortium's goal was to bring together like-minded people working in NYC neighborhoods to broaden the NOCD alliance for future work. The event aimed to further a vision of NYC grounded in the cultural vitality and social networks of its communities. This view became the foundation for a shared policy platform to inform the City's mayoral leadership transition in late 2013. Two ideas were seminal. First, it honored the perspective that, as Wendell Berry has written, "What we need is here" (Berry, 2003). That is, every neighborhood has powerful assets to contribute to a resilient and thriving NYC. Second, recognizing the interdependence of cultural organizations throughout the City, the forum brought them together to develop collaborative strategies to respond to New York's opportunities and inequities (From the Neighborhood Up, 2013).

NOCD's leaders identified the arts and culture sector's relationship to four major community concerns in From the Neighborhood Up: health and sustainability; equitable development; innovative uses of urban space; and sustained community resilience and rebuilding after Hurricane Sandy. Organizers hoped to assemble enough people to discuss these focal areas such that a vote on policy priorities at the gathering would be credible and could be shared with elected officials.

Planning demonstrated the political and aesthetic savvy of NOCD members. El Museo de Barrio was selected as the meeting's venue. Not only did that facility offer appropriate-sized spaces for such a gathering, but its location was also strategic: in a neighborhood not renowned as a cultural destination but easily accessible to all five boroughs. NOCD members' experience organizing performances and exhibitions informed their planning of the forum. Speakers and workshop leaders were selected for their dynamic ability to communicate and facilitate, to reflect the diversity of artists and organizers in NYC, and to obtain their participation.

To experience the interdependence of cultural and other neighborhood organizations, attendees began the day with lunch at one of six community-based organizations (CBOs) located near El Museo, immediately putting local concerns on the table and also discussing the place of the arts in their activities.

Community Voices Heard (CVH) was one of the six host CBOs. CVH is a member-led multi-racial organization—composed principally of women of color and low-income families in New York State—that builds power to secure social, economic and racial justice for all (Community Voices Heard, n.d.). The fifteen to twenty attendees at the CVH luncheon discussed the then-current round of participatory budgeting (PB), a citywide initiative through which community members of eight participating NYC council districts decide how $1 million in each will be spent each year. PB, then in its second year, seemed a particularly good subject of conversation given that it cuts across arts, culture, and other local initiatives that contribute to community vitality. Following lunch, From the Neighborhood Up participants convened at El Museo.

Speakers at the museum articulated the value of the arts and culture in neighborhoods. Equitable community development specialist Mitty Owens described being a father of "a little black girl in Brooklyn," who was developing identity and self-esteem (From the Neighborhood Up, 2013). He emphasized the importance of her contact with both large cultural institutions like the Brooklyn Academy of Music and the Brooklyn Museum, and small venues like a local dance studio with Caribbean instructors. He contended it was crucial that his daughter's everyday experience included "ethnically and women-owned businesses, and a multi-cultural human landscape" (ibid.). For Owens, the importance of NOCD is "the long overdue recognition it gives to how our identity in the world is formed; and as a bulwark against gentrification and displacement" (ibid.).

Other speakers offered examples of how culture broadly defined has been a vehicle for their organization to affirm identity, build community, and raise consciousness about local heritage. Panelist Rosalba Rolon, artistic director of Pregones Theatre in the Bronx, recounted that some years ago the theater asked a community-sensitive radio station general manager to broadcast an arts and culture show. The executive declined, responding that the station concentrates on community affairs. The manager did not see the role of artists in their neighborhood as part of community well-being. Nonetheless, Pregones' presence there—not only in creating and presenting extraordinary performances that emphasize diverse Latino experiences but through starting a community garden and helping in the effort to preserve the WPA-era murals at the local post office—has made clear the multiple ways in which artists contribute to community life as culture bearers and art makers, but the radio station encounter demonstrates how little understood this larger role usually is.

In smaller working groups, NOCD members solicited exchange around its current efforts. Carole Bebelle of New Orleans related her experience with cultural organizing after Katrina. NOCD's equitable development group invited coalitions challenging private development in two historically immigrant neighborhoods in NYC. The groups were a means to another Forum goal: inclusion of this larger group of participants in identifying NOCD priorities moving forward. They voted on policy recommendations to pass on to elected officials, which by and large reflected the transdisciplinary context in which they see arts and cultural work. Priorities included more connections between the arts and cultural sector and grassroots service, activist, and neighborhood organizations; holding developers responsible for providing benefits to existing residents in the neighborhoods in which they work; and incorporating legislators, organizers, and artists in a cultural organizing platform.

The process of selecting priorities is an example of the consciousness that NOCD seeks to instill among people of different sectors: It is not all about any of them alone. The event demonstrated a shift in values from the normally competitive world of producing art to a spirit of sharing resources and information. While the voting process was very similar to that of many public meetings, it is not a typical modus operandi among artists. The priorities demonstrate that many people involved in the arts and culture are also informed or at least concerned about economic policies that could support them.

## Sharpening the Discourse

Soon after From the Neighborhood Up took place, NOCD-NY invited six national researchers on culture and community to talk about their work and help organization participants to think about next steps. The multiple sectors these researchers represented were striking (albeit no one trained in the arts). They included psychiatrist Mindy Fullilove, social scientist Maria Rosario Jackson, the social policy team of Susan Seifert and Mark Stern, philanthropy writer Holly Sidford, and anthropologist Alaka Wali. Among the valuable ideas shared, Jackson called on NOCD to identify tools people can use concretely once they recognize the value of arts and culture in communities. One possibility is to co-host public gatherings bringing together people who work across sectors, including arts and culture. Another is to attach a cultural component to grants supporting equitable urban development. Jackson cited the California Endowment's experiment with incentives to enhance local art and culture as part of job development in one "livable cities" funding initiative.

Another idea echoed by a number of the researchers was changing the narrative of neighborhood-based arts and culture. By naming as cultural a broader range of activities that go beyond mainstream museums, performance spaces, and galleries, NOCD might generate greater interest and support for local cultural vitality. The promotion of cultural riches across entire cities, rather than only marketing those in established districts, is one example. As NYC becomes an ever more popular tourist destination—the Museum of Modern Art is now open seven days a week to accommodate the crowds—all the boroughs are exploring how to entice more visitors. Melanie Cohn reported that Staten Island is building a mall and an observation tower to give people something to do once they take the ferry there besides just turn around and go back (Cohn personal interview, May 22, 2013). Think of what else her organization might make available. In addition to tours to well-known places, many go further afield. Forgotten New

York is a program of the Greater Astoria Historical Society that sponsors tours a half dozen times a year to places of interest throughout the five boroughs. There are hip-hop tours of the Bronx and Harlem, neighborhood walks, multi-ethnic food tours, to mention just a few. Though many are private, some are sponsored by local cultural organizations, giving people a chance to support and get to know the neighborhood at the same time. NOCD's members' understanding of the links between art and culture facilitate thinking about the range of events they produce, from fine arts and traditional theater to neighborhood tours and street fairs.

### "One New York, Rising Together"

The election of Bill de Blasio, the most liberal candidate for mayor, in November 2013 provided an opportunity for NOCD representatives to communicate desired cultural policy to NYC's new political leaders. De Blasio established a "talking transition tent" in downtown NYC for two weeks after the election at which individuals and organizations, including NOCD, were invited to present ideas to the new administration.

NOCD framed its session on arts and culture within de Blasio's "One New York, Rising Together" platform, laying out a vision of arts and culture "rooted in the values of creating a city that cares about our neighborhoods, insists on equality, and embraces civic energy" (Atlas and Sananman, 2013, para. 1). In this document, co-authors Caron Atlas and Amy Sananman, executive director of Groundswell,[4] articulated five strategies "to keep culture at the table during transition planning:"

> Integrate arts and culture across policymaking and practice. ... Build arts and culture into civic participation across the city to reach those who have been historically disenfranchised. ... Revitalize New York City from the neighborhood up by supporting community leadership, cultural hubs, and vital social networks. ... Prioritize equitable distribution of opportunities and benefits related to arts and culture ... [and recognize the] wealth of resources and allies among the artists, activists, and cultural organizations working for social change.
>
> (Atlas and Sananman, 2013, para. 3–11)

NOCD member organizations have in effect institutionalized the insight that artists are about not only individual expression but cultural communication, which is nurtured by and at the same time supports neighborhoods where that culture is not marginalized. For example, the Chinatown History Project brings attention to common histories of racism, struggle, cultural richness, and perseverance in a neighborhood that can be represented by others as simply about food. The Museum of the Chinese in America is both an artistic space, whose shows conform to art world aesthetic standards, and a cultural space, furthering appreciation of the contributions of people of Chinese heritage in the U.S. The histories of multiple cultural groups that sought a place for themselves in the U.S. are connected with the LES even though it is decidedly not a neighborhood accessible to people without means coming to America now. The arts organizations represented by FAB, situated as it is in the quintessential gateway for diverse cultural and ethnic groups to the U.S., are aware that their material survival depends on both public and organizational policies that value their diversity, policies that equally affect their neighbors and depend on joint organizing.

Consciousness of the value of the arts and culture integrated with other local sectors has grown among City institutions in recent years. At a series of meetings sponsored by the Brooklyn Community Foundation, for example, participants extolled the role that the arts play in engaging youths, educating immigrants, advocating on behalf of better housing and jobs, and building community cohesiveness (Sidford, personal interview, 2014).[5]

An increasing number of universities, not just in NYC but around the country, include courses that require students in the arts to interact with community-based projects.[6] The arts community has expanded its own recognition that social goals are often a robust component of artistic projects. This shift is evident in the visual arts in the rise of the movement known as *social practice* and in the performing arts through such phenomena as the weakening boundaries among regional theater, ensemble companies, and community-based practices (Miranda, 2014). Indeed, major foundations that fund the arts have collaborated to found ArtPlace America, which "advances the field of creative placemaking, in which art and culture plays an explicit and central role in shaping communities' social, physical, and economic futures" (ArtPlace America, 2014, About).

There is a distance to go, however, and arts and cultural organizing strategies have moved beyond a single approach featuring individual hero artists/companies in favor of diverse tactics. Occupy Wall Street, with its significant arts component, is a new iteration of the "cultural wings of social movements" approach of the 1960s and 1970s, when companies, including the San Francisco Mime Troupe initially around free speech; El Teatro Campesino supporting farm workers; the Free Southern Theatre bringing grassroots populations into dialogue about civil rights; and Bread and Puppet Theater furthering an anti-war message, reached deeply into communities. Occupy, however, in the absence of sustained and widespread political organizing, was not able concretely to further its goal of advancing economic equity. Especially since the 1980s, the struggle for self-representation among people of different racial, cultural, and sexual identities has found expression through art. The play *The Laramie Project* certainly contributed, at the very least, to catalyzing discussions about homophobia all across the U.S. According to the play's dramaturge Steve Wangh, *Laramie* has been performed more times in U.S. high schools and colleges than any other drama.[7] As Michelle Anderson, however, has argued eloquently in *The New Jim Crow* (2010), the work remaining to overcome racism is formidable. We who advocate for the arts in close working relationships with other sectors embrace a boundary-crossing strategy to expand the role art plays in public life, but sometimes the only metric embraced by funders for such efforts is economic development. The arts have contributed to modest advances around social issues, but enormous need remains, and a diversification of approaches is welcome.

The appointment of Queens Museum's former director Tom Finkelpearl as the city's Commissioner of Cultural Affairs bodes well for aligning the cultural sector with the mayor's social agenda, "One New York, Rising Together." NOCD is already a player in that effort, connecting neighborhood-based artists to one another citywide and promoting significant ways that arts and culture entities can partner with other sectors for the betterment of community life. Along with other cities across the country that are recognizing more integrated roles for the arts in social life, perhaps these holistic examples of the arts on the municipal level will bring with them the necessary financial support to realize their promise.

## Notes

1 This description of culture has been informed by Raymond Williams, Wendell Berry, Kathie de Nobriga, and Dudley Cocke.
2 Arts and Democracy "links arts and culture, participatory democracy, and social justice ... [and] works to increase civic engagement among people who have been traditionally disenfranchised and to build closer ties between arts and culture and sustained and strategic activism" (animatingdemocracy.org/organization/arts-democracy-project).
3 For a complete list of NOCD members, see http://nocdny.org/the-group/.
4 Sananman initiated Groundswell in 1996 "to bring together professional artists, grassroots organizations, and communities to create high-quality murals in under-represented neighborhoods and inspire youth to take active ownership of their future by equipping them with the tools necessary for social change" (www.groundswellmural.org).
5 See also Brooklyn Community Foundation at www.brooklyncommunityfoundation.org/brooklyn-insights.
6 See, for example, the Curriculum project report at Imagining America: www.http://imaginingamerica.org/fg-item/the-curriculum-project-report-culture-and-community-development-in-higher-education/.
7 Wangh and I were colleagues at New York University from the mid-1980s through the mid-2000s and often discussed theater in social context. I could not even guess when he shared this particular information.

## References

Anderson, M. (2010). *The New Jim Crow: Mass incarceration in the age of colorblindness*. New York: The New Press.

ArtPlace America. (2014). About ArtPlace. Website. Retrieved August 15, 2014 from http://www.artplaceamerica.org/about

Atlas, C., and Sananman, A. (2013). Internet letter to Mayor-elect Bill de Blasio and transition team, November 22. Retrieved November 22, 2013 from http://artsanddemocracy.org/detail-page/?program=blog&capID=169

Berry, W. (2003). What we need is here. Retrieved May 1, 2013 from http://poemhunter. com/poem/what-we-need-is-here

Community Voices Heard. (n.d.) Mission. Retrieved June 20, 2014 from http://www. cvhaction.org/mission

El Museo de Barrio. (2014). *About El Museo*. Retrieved May 1, 2013 from www.elmuseo. org/about-el-museo

Fourth Arts Block (2011). *About Fourth Arts Block*. Retrieved August 20, 2013 from http://fabnyc.org/about-fab

From the Neighborhood Up. (2013). A citywide forum on culture and community. Video on Vimeo. Retrieved June 12, 2013 from http://vimeo.com/channels/586794

Glassberg, D. (1990). *American historical pageantry*. Chapel Hill, NC: University of North Carolina Press.

Harvie, J. (Ed.) (2009). *Theatre and the city*. London, New York: Palgrave MacMillan.

Horvitz, A. (2012). On social practice and performance, on *Culturebot*, August 28. Retrieved September 15, 2012 from http://www.culturebot.org/2012/08/14008/on-social-practice-and-performance

Howell, R. (2011). Tools of engagement in Urban Bush Women's *Hairstories*. Unpublished thesis, School of Dance, Florida State University. Retrieved January 15, 2012 from http://diginole.lib.fsu.edu/etd/4917

*Huffington Post*. (2013). More foreign-born immigrants live in nyc than there are people in Chicago, December 19. Retrieved February 5, 2014 from www.huffingtonpost. com/2013/12/19/new-york-city-immigrants_n_4475197.html

In Motion. (2014). Nothing can stop us—The American Festival Project. Retrieved February 4, 2014 from www.inmotionmagazine.com/afp2.html

Jackson, M. R. (2013). Speech at NOCD-NY Exchange of Research and Practice, September 12. Presented in New York City.

Jackson, S. (2000). *Lines of Activity: Performance, historiography, and Hull-House domesticity*. Ann Arbor, MI: University of Michigan.

Miranda, C. (2014). How the art of social practice is changing the world, one house at a time. *ARTnews*, April 7. Website. Retrieved May 10, 2014 from http://www.artnews. com/2014/04/07/art-of-social-practice-is-changing-the-world-one-row-house-at-a-time

NOCD-NY (2010). New York City Naturally Occurring Cultural District Roundtable. Retrieved April 13, 2015 from https://artsandcommunitychange.files.wordpress. com/2011/03/nocdreport3.pdf

Nochlin, L. (1985). "Paterson Strike Pageant of 1913." In B. McConachie and D. Friedman (Eds) *Theatre for working class audiences in the US: 1830–1980* (pp. 87–94). Westport, CO: Greenwood Press.

One New York Rising Together. (2013) One New York Rising Together Retrieved September 15, 2014 from www.archivoelectoral. org/archivo/doc/One%20New%20York%20Rising%20Together BillDeBlasioDemocraticPrimariasDemocratasAlcaldeNYEEUU2013.pdf

Osman, A., and Fuentes, D. (2013). An interview with Tania Bruguera. *On artistic and curatorial authorship*. OnCurating.org. 19 (June), 81–88. Retrieved July 1, 2013 from http://www.on-curating.org/index.php/issue-19-reader/tania-bruguera-interviewed. html#.VDHnnRY3jvh

Queens Museum. (2012). Queens Museum expansion enables increased community engagement through public programs. Retrieved February 10, 2013 from http://prod-images.exhibit-e.com/www_fitzandco_com/QueensMuseum_ ProgrammingRelease_03_18_13_FINAL1.doc

Roadside Theater. (2014). Brief descriptions of eleven festivals. Retrieved September 20, 2014 from http://roadside.org/asset/brief-descriptions-eleven-festivals

Rosenstein, C. (2009) Cultural development and city neighborhoods in *Charting Civil Society*, The Urban Institute, No 21: July 1–10. Retrieved September 2014 from www.urban.org/uploadedpdf/411937_culturaldevelopment.pdf

Sidford, H. (2011). *Fusing arts culture and social change: High impact strategies for philanthropy*. In Washington, DC: National Committee for Responsive Philanthropy. Website. Retrieved January 12, 2013 from http://ncrp.org/files/publications/Fusing_Arts_Culture_Social_Change.pdf

Stern, M., and Seifert S. (2013). 'Natural' cultural districts: A three-city study, report summary. University of Pennsylvania Social Impact of the Arts project. Website. Retrieved April 15, 2013 from http://impact.sp2.upenn.edu/siap/docs/natural_cultural_districts/Summary.15apr13.pdf

Sze, L. (2014). Make it memory, make it now: The life and times of change. In The Museum of Chinese in America's *Chinatown beyond the streets*. Retrieved August 30, 2014 from www.mocanyc.org/files/MOCA_Chinatown_beyond_the_streets_essays.pdf

Tchen, J. K. W. (1987). New York Chinatown History Project. In *History Workshop* No. 24 (Autumn). Oxford, UK: Oxford University Press (pp. 158–161).

United Neighborhood Houses (UNHNY) (n.d.). Website. Retrieved August 10, 2014 from www.unhny.org/about/settlementhouse

Urban Bush Women. (2014a), Jawole reflects. Retrieved January 5, 2013 from https://www.urbanbushwomen.org/jawole_reflects.php

Urban Bush Women. (2014b), Mission and core values. Retrieved January 5, 2013 from https://www.urbanbushwomen.org/mission_values.php

Urban Bush Women New Works. (2014), *Blood, muscle, bone, the anatomy of wealth and poverty*. Retrieved August 20, 2014 from https://www.urbanbushwomen.org/developing_works.php

# 4

# SUSTAINING EMERGENT CULTURE IN MONTREAL'S ENTERTAINMENT DISTRICT

*Anjali Mishra*

For more than a century, visitors have come to the crossroads of Saint-Laurent and Sainte-Catherine streets in Montreal to enjoy its entertainment and nightlife. In 2004, fearing the disappearance of this epicenter, twenty-one representatives of arts organizations, neighborhood groups, and local and provincial governments developed a vision of culture-led revitalization for this downtown area known as the "Quartier des spectacles" (QdS). Ten years later, a major urban design project has outfitted six city blocks with four large granite plazas, architectural lighting, and fountains. Further public works are being planned. The Quartier has become one of the city's premier tourist destinations.

Montreal's leaders and residents are proud of the city's status as an arts center (Ville de Montréal, 2005). Richard Florida's firm, Catalytix, has described Montreal as "a dynamic cultural metropolis that holds creation, invention, and emerging talent in high esteem" (Catalytix, 2005, p. 8). Montreal, located within the only francophone province on the continent, is easily accessible via a one-hour flight from Boston or New York. The city's international reputation as home to Cirque du Soleil, Céline Dion, and Arcade Fire is mirrored by the liveliness of its cultural activities, festivals, and nightlife.

Montreal's economy directly benefits from its cultural workers, who generate revenue from sales of their unique and mass-produced goods, including movies, plays, musical performances, books, and video games. Cultural activities, including major festivals, such as Just for Laughs, also stimulate tourism and entertainment expenditures. The cultural sector generates direct and indirect economic returns for the city totaling more than $12 billion each year (CCMM, 2009). Five of the ten postal codes with the highest concentrations of artists in Canada are in Montreal, including the top three (Hill, 2010). With a population of more than 1.6 million, Montreal is home to 56,100 cultural workers, who represent 6.4% of the city's labor force. In 2010, 13,400 of these individuals were artists who generated cultural content directly (ibid).

Though there are differences among "creative economy" theories, as developed by Richard Florida, Charles Landry, and others, they all concur that the presence of cultural activities increases a city's ability to attract knowledge industries and their workers (Landry, 2000; Strom, 2001; Florida 2002; Markusen and Gadwa, 2010). Hillary Frost Kumpf (1998) has further suggested that arts patrons support adjacent businesses and that the presence of arts venues increases property values and therefore tax revenue. Peter Hall has observed that, "culture is now seen as the magic substitute for all the lost factories and warehouses, and as a device that will create a new urban image, making the city more attractive to mobile capital and mobile professional workers" (2000, p. 640).

Creative workers "require a different type of policy making that cultivates the social world in which art and culture thrive" (Currid, 2007b, p. 158). In Currid's view, art and culture are interdisciplinary, heterarchical industries requiring constant cross-pollination among dense networks of highly specialized individuals. Face-to-face contact allows artists and cultural entrepreneurs to prosper, and a significant portion of such interaction occurs in bars and nightclubs. Such settings are often part of the underground scene. Informal locations are particularly important to creative workers as a milieu for experimentation and inspiration. Artists and cultural workers value bars, nightclubs, pop-up venues, and related sites as places where self-censoring is not required and creative risk-taking is welcomed and encouraged (Currid, 2007a).

Writers in international news media have praised Montreal's prolific underground arts scene. For the *New York Times*, it is "the current hotbed of indie music" (Carr, 2005; Lee, 2006). Thomas Cummins-Russell and Norma Rantisi have detailed how, in music particularly, the relative absence of multinational media corporations has enhanced the development of independent cultural businesses or organizations that cater to niche markets (Cummins-Russell and Rantisi, 2012). The recent success of a number of Montreal's English language popular music bands, such as Godspeed You Black Emperor! and Arcade Fire, has highlighted the breadth of Montreal's alternative cultural scene and the city's success as a talent incubator. A coalition of self-identified independent producers and small venues reported in 2010 that their events accounted for more than 6,000 shows annually, with revenues of $15 million (COLLE, 2010). These activities are significant not only for their economic impact but also for their contribution to Montreal's distinctive popular image of gritty edginess and eclecticism.

Because underground cultural venues and events act as social and creative hubs, they make a neighborhood attractive to artists who patronize them (Zukin, 2010), but their presence also influences location decisions of larger creative industries. For example, Ubisoft, the videogame developer responsible for the popular Prince of Persia offering, located its creative studios north of the downtown area in Montreal's Mile-End neighborhood. Although the area is not home to any major arts institutions, it is known for its concentration of independent cultural venues and artists (Carr, 2005). The firm's communications director has explained that the Mile-End's rich artistic fabric "feeds the creativity of Ubisoft's employees" (Clavel, 2007).

Smaller-scale independent activities have come to define Montreal's identity in a way that is attractive and relevant to young people particularly. Nonetheless, in the QdS, as has occurred in many other tourist areas in cities around the world, increasing real-estate costs are making the area less affordable for eclectic and emergent cultural activities, threatening the availability of spaces for independent artists.

Building on the premise that artistic creation—more specifically, in the present analysis, a thriving underground arts scene—is essential to the strength of Montreal's cultural vibrancy, how are emergent arts entities able to evolve within the QdS, and which government strategies might help to ensure that the area will retain a vibrant underground scene? This chapter first provides an overview of the neighborhood's history and the Quartier des spectacles project. I then identify key features of alternative cultural activities that set them apart from the mainstream:

- they are interactive and evolving;
- their focus is a local community;
- precarious financial situations make survival a constant challenge; and
- many organizations have trouble complying with permitting and other legal requirements.

The chapter then presents the current situation confronting emergent artists and organizations in the QdS. Their challenges are detailed, particularly those tied to the availability of appropriate, affordable, and inclusive space. I conclude by identifying areas of concern the city of Montreal should address in the neighborhood to contribute to its broader goal of enabling continuing alternative creative expression there.

To establish a reliable portrait of the emergent arts in Montreal, and more specifically in the QdS in that city, I conducted twenty semi-structured in-person interviews with festival organizers, musicians and visual artists, cultural organizations, and venue owners active in Montreal's emergent cultural scene. The chapter does not distinguish between alternative, independent, underground, or emergent cultural activities, all of which cater to intersecting niche markets within Montreal's cultural milieu. Rather, this case study seeks to identify common characteristics and shared concerns to develop insights of potential relevance for planners, officials, and cultural leaders interested in better understanding and nurturing these forms of art making and culture in other cities. The discussion of the results from these interviews is also informed by the author's professional experience and continued participation in a number of independent cultural organizations in Montreal.

## Quartier des spectacles: Montreal's Entertainment District

### More than 100 Years of History

Many cities have developed arts and entertainment districts to attract creative workers or revitalize downtowns and former industrial areas. Montreal has had an entertainment district for more than 100 years: the Quartier des spectacles. In the late 1800s, the area became a hub for establishments of which the Catholic Church did not approve, including taverns, theaters, political meeting halls and, later, the first cinemas, located along St-Laurent Boulevard, just outside the old city walls. As Montreal grew around it, the area became a poor working-class neighborhood, complete with grocery stores, tenements, synagogues, and industrial buildings. Taking advantage of prohibition in the United States during the 1920s to appeal to an international clientele, theaters that could not afford upgraded equipment for sound or color picture performances turned instead to burlesque shows and alcohol sales. By the 1930s and for the next several decades, the neighborhood became a weekend party destination for visitors from neighboring cities in the northeast United States, cementing its reputation as a red-light district (Weintraub, 1996).

By the 1950s, the community's mix of poverty, organized crime, and prostitution made it the perfect target for urban renewal schemes. National policy makers aimed to better the living conditions of the poor, provincial politicians wanted to edify the masses through education and the high arts, and the mayor wanted a monumental downtown. Most of the neighborhood was demolished to make way for a public housing project in 1959, the Place des Arts, Montreal's regional performing arts center, in 1963, and the Université du Québec à Montréal (UQAM), one of the city's four universities, in 1969 (Lortie, 2004).

In the 1970s and 1980s, private developers overlooked this part of the city, concentrating rather on the new business district to the west. Artists moved into many of the older manufacturing buildings and renovated abandoned theaters in the QdS. Festivals used vacant lots for free outdoor shows, complemented by indoor performances. Several bars, nightclubs, burlesque theaters, and strip clubs remained—upholding the area's red-light district status and tamping developer interest until the late 1990s.

The city's long-term expansion now places the QdS in the eastern part of the downtown core north of Old Montreal, adjacent to the city's international financial and central business districts, the Plateau (a dense historic residential neighborhood), and the Gay Village. This one-square-kilometer area between Bleury, Berri, René-Lévesque, and Sherbrooke Streets contains 45,000 office workers, 6,000 residents, and 47,000 students (Ville de Montréal, 2014).

"Quartier des spectacles" is French for "neighborhood of performances," a description that remains apt for the area. Tucked among shops and apartment buildings are more than eighty cultural spaces, including thirty performance

**FIGURE 4.1**  Map of Montreal, showing the Quartier des spectacles in relation to surrounding districts (map courtesy of the author)

venues with a total of 28,000 seats (Ville de Montréal, 2014), a concentration seldom equaled in North America. The neighborhood also hosts more than forty annual festivals. The two largest of such events each attract 2 million visitors to their free outdoor shows, in addition to the attendees for simultaneous ticketed events at a dozen area theaters. Cultural activities in the community employ 7,000 cultural workers, including 1,000 positions in education and training (Ville de Montréal, 2014).

## From a Vision to Urban Renewal

In 2001, performance venue owners and artists faced eviction due to planned development projects in the QdS. In that year, theater proprietors, festival organizers, artists' collectives, neighborhood residents and business associations, property-owners, and representatives from all levels of government acted on an idea offered by the Quebec recording industry association to form the Quartier des spectacles Partnership (QDSP), and develop a comprehensive vision for the QdS.

The Partnership summarized its vision for the district in 2004 as a place to "live, create, and entertain downtown" (QDSP, 2004). The QDSP recommended development of a "balanced neighborhood where a diversity of residents and urban functions coexist," keeping a "refreshing marginality" (ibid). The area would act as a "hub for artistic creation, innovation, production, and broadcasting, to become an international cultural destination" in which the street would serve as a way-finding path, connecting activities within the neighborhood and from it to surrounding areas (ibid). In this vision, public spaces would become sites for artistic expression, with permanent infrastructure improvements and facilities for cultural activities. The area's distinctive identity would be reflected in a new vibrancy, made possible by these changes (QDSP, 2004).

In 2007, the city responded to appeals from area festival organizers to prevent construction on vacant lots used as outdoor venue spaces. Montreal's leaders announced a $140 million project to transform those properties in the western part of the QdS near the Place des Arts into a ring of outdoor parks. The city had two objectives as it undertook this effort: to establish permanent space for festivals and to create an international tourist destination that would be attractive year-round (Ville de Montréal, 2007).

The first of these new spaces was finished in 2009 and, as they have been completed, the city government has transferred their management to QDSP. In addition, Montreal has provided funds to subsidize events held in these locations. These public areas are patrolled, manicured, and curated. QDSP leaders have measured their initiative's success by the increase in the number of outdoor events and festivals in the neighborhood, from 281 to 592 between 2010 and 2012. The Quartier's managers also tout the area's increased commercial activity. According to the Partnership's marketing materials, the new projects have increased pedestrian traffic and, therefore, the area's customer base. This changed reality has attracted more than a dozen new gourmet restaurants in the past four years, and other upscale eateries and boutiques are on the way (Fortin, personal communications, 2011). Commodifying culture as the area's anchor has turned the western part of the QdS into a safe upscale international tourist destination.

Between 2004 and 2014, public and private actors invested more than $1 billion in completed or ongoing construction projects in the QdS. That total includes residential development, new cultural facilities for the Montreal Symphony Orchestra, a last-minute ticket booth and a flagship building for the city's cultural information office. In 2011, the city began planning for the eastern section of the QdS, the "Quartier Latin." Promising far fewer investments in new public spaces, Montreal's leaders opted instead for policies that favored the development of a "destination for culture and knowledge." The plan drew on the presence of UQAM, several historic cultural venues, an active nightlife, and an existing mix of commercial and residential activities to maintain the area's appeal to creative firms and workers (Ville de Montréal, 2012).

Demonstrating the feasibility of this plan, WB Games, a division of Warner Bros. Entertainment Inc., recently opened offices in the eastern section of the QdS. Since the plan's adoption in 2012, Montreal has supported a number of pilot projects for creative live-work spaces and temporary public art installations (Ville de Montréal, 2014).

## How Is Emergent Culture Different?

Alternative, independent, or emergent cultural activities are in many ways similar to mainstream or established events except that they occur on a smaller scale. Festival du Nouveau Cinema, one of Montreal's independent film events, for example, is more than twenty-five years old, making it one of the city's longest-lived celebrations of its kind. Pop Montreal, an alternative music festival, showcases more than 600 musical artists during five days, occupying myriad smaller venues around the city. *The Guardian* lists the Casa del Popolo, a concert venue deeply tied to emergent culture with a capacity of about 100, as the best bar in Montreal (Baker, 2007). All of these organizations contribute to Montreal's vibrant underground cultural scene.

In some cases, an artist's audience may be limited because it has not yet reached its potential. In other instances, artists and organizations evolve outside of—or even in opposition to—the mainstream, implying that they cannot or will not be commercialized. Underground arts assume many different shapes and contain many subcultures, each with its own characteristics and requirements. This persistently emergent scene involves players at every level of the production scale: creators who generate content; program organizers; indoor and outdoor venues, such as galleries, theaters, public parks or performance halls; and specialized supply and support service firms.

Small alternative cultural businesses and nongovernmental organizations are typically more flexible than larger and more institutionalized entities. Every arts center, artist, or festival is different, but those that identify themselves as alternative, independent, or developing also often overtly seek to innovate and explore. These individuals and organizations are often more specialized in that they provide a more specific product and appeal to a narrower audience than their more mainstream counterparts. This, however, in no way should be understood as amateurism. Neither the high- or low-brow nature of the art nor the popular character of an activity nor the size of the audience is correlated with a production's quality (Gans, 1974).

Nonetheless, specialization and small size make survival more precarious for these arts organizations. Artists and venues with limited access to funding opportunities and with smaller audiences usually have lower incomes and less secure revenue sources than larger and more established individuals, groups, and production sites. Underground organizations also often rely on the work of fewer individuals, who commit not only their time and passion but also frequently act as primary financial investors. This increases emergent culture's vulnerability to unexpected events, both personal and professional.

Emerging artists, venues, and organizations share a number of characteristics that are less common in larger cultural institutions. As detailed below, alternative entities evolve rapidly, maintaining close ties (and often blurring the lines) between audience and creator. Underground arts are often content-driven: their worth is evaluated by peer-recognition more than commercialization. This community of associates is also one of the pillars to emergent artists' financial survival in a context of limited resources. Finally, alternative events and venues tread a tenuous line when it comes to the legitimacy and sometimes, even the legality, of their activities.

### Intimate, Interactive, and Evolving

The Internet and social networking have given artists tremendous opportunities for increasing their visibility via new promotional tools. Nonetheless, performance, installation, and exhibits remain imperatives in an artist's career. Jesse Osborne-Lanthier, the manager of a QdS underground work and performance space, commented in an interview that pressure for artists to perform and produce new material has increased with the availability of production software and the easier distribution of content via the Internet. Osborne-Lanthier explained that artists who pursue careers in music must constantly release new work and announce public performances to maintain public attention. As the frequency of performances by each artist increases, so does the demand for performance space (Osborne-Lanthier, personal communication, 2012). Peter Burton, executive director of the Suoni Per Il Popolo Festival in Montreal, has explained that one of the draws of his event and underground programs more broadly is the proximity between artist and audience. Casa del Popolo and Sala Rossa, the venues where most of the Festival's shows are held, are small, creating a more intimate setting, reducing the physical distance between audience and performer, and encouraging more frequent and prolonged social interaction between them (Burton, personal communication, 2012).

Osborne-Lanthier also contended that the lack of separation between performers and audience is one of the reasons he prefers smaller venues. He explained that when forty people are in a living room–sized setting, every person becomes part of the performance. Interaction during the show is inevitable: people's sounds, gestures, and reactions all become part of the program, keeping it unpredictable and unique. Smaller scale events also provide an opportunity to discover new work and discuss future projects between sets. The participative and social nature of underground culture keeps it in constant evolution (Osborne-Lanthier, personal communication, 2012).

### Community Rather than Commercially Oriented

This closeness between audience and artists is also reflected in a venue's status within its community. Burton has described how Casa and Sala act as a hub within a "scene" and how those who perform there tend to live in the surrounding neighborhood. These venues were not established in a void but rather provided a location for a community of artists and performers who needed space to meet and to organize shows. As such, the locations have emerged as a neighborhood resource for the arts scene, which ensures its financial autonomy (Burton, personal communication, 2012).

Shows in galleries and independent arts centers generally allow performers and promoters complete control over their environment. In many cases, spaces bear no corporate logos or advertisements besides product labels, and drink and ticket prices are kept low. Organizers intentionally work to keep the spaces approachable and less consumption-oriented (Burton, personal communication, 2012). To maintain their status as creatively relevant, events must demonstrate they are focused on cultural content rather than commercial opportunity and must be attended by creative workers (Curid, 2007a).

Major cultural institutions frequently reach out to more alternative or underground arts organizations to appeal to new and younger audiences. For the past several years, for example, the Museum of Contemporary Art, located in the Quartier des spectacles, has organized a well-attended series of monthly performance and networking events featuring Montreal artists.

## The Challenge to Survive

Emergent cultural activities cater to an audience of limited means: artists and creative workers, students, and younger individuals. Door or ticket receipts; merchandise sales; food and drink income; and grants, donations, and public funding provide the bulk of revenues for these organizations. For events and venues to function as social and creative hubs, they must keep their costs of attendance low, despite often increasing operating costs. With artists' annual median income in Montreal at $15,000 (Hill, 2010), the organizers' pricing of these events directly affects their accessibility. Ticket prices for most events at underground or informal venues are typically around $10, and only rarely rise to $20.

New projects and collaborations are constantly being formed in a dynamic creative scene. However, the creation cycle seldom coincides with granting agencies' yearly application schedules, due to the time necessary for funding request preparation and review (Burton, personal communication, 2012). The difficulty in accessing grant funds quickly for emerging arts activities that can be implemented immediately limits overall project budgets. Artists respond by curtailing expenses or by staging their efforts in places with very low space and equipment rental costs or venues that do not require more expensive ticket prices to cover overhead costs.

Montreal requires public spaces used for outdoor cultural events to remain accessible to the public free of charge. In the QdS, local officials have made particular efforts to reserve public spaces for cultural activities: Regulations in the neighborhood regarding advertising are even stricter than elsewhere in the city, restricting billboards for example. These regulations make it difficult for events to raise funds through corporate sponsorships that require visibility, leaving food and beverage sales as primary revenue generators (Leftick, personal communication, 2012). To succeed, underground spaces work with an extremely high turnover: Several bands or dancers use a single practice space, artists share tools and studios, and venues are open almost every night of the week. Some locations operate restaurants or bars, although this choice precludes access to public funding. "Rent parties" and other such fundraising events are often complicated to organize legally, and unruly partygoers also increase the risk of possible sale and consumption of illicit substances (Osborne-Lanthier, personal communication, 2012). Large crowds in gallery spaces and workshops not designed for such numbers can also attract negative attention from tenants and landlords, jeopardizing future use of the space.

## Does Underground Have to Mean Illegal?

Many arts groups, particularly inexperienced ones, have only a poor understanding of governmental regulations and processes. Even with such knowledge, however, legitimacy is still a challenge for these organizations. Particularly where food and alcohol sales are used to offset overhead for a performance space, alternative spaces without the proper paperwork run the risk of fines and closure by the police due to noise complaints, security issues, and crowd control concerns (Leftick, personal communication, 2012).

For many performance spaces, administrative complexities can sometimes prevent what appears to be a legal operation from obtaining necessary permits. In Quebec, events, whether indoors or outdoors, require a number of approvals from municipal and provincial authorities. City regulations and zoning requirements specify occupancy levels, exits, and fire safety precautions, among other items. In a dense urban environment, new music venues cannot locate in many locations due to the inevitable proximity of housing, schools, or the minimal distances required between liquor license permit holders. Where liquor is served or sold, permits include a series of limitations regarding live music or dancing, so it is not infrequent that an established live music venue may in fact operate with only a restaurant or café license. This was the case, for example, at the Casa del Popolo and Divan Orange when they were listed on *National Geographic*'s 2007 Geotourism Map as noteworthy entertainment venues (National Geographic, 2007; Burton, personal communication, 2012).

Venue owners and promoters without complete required documentation are, perhaps understandably, not always willing to provide public information regarding their properties. The number of illegitimate underground enterprises and the lack of reliable statistics regarding attendance and revenue at alternative arts events pose a challenge for policy makers. This lack of information also makes it difficult to assess the direct or indirect economic impacts of such arts efforts or to attract government funding that is largely awarded based on perceived tourist (and audience) appeal.

## Emergent Arts in Today's Quartier des spectacles

As described earlier in the chapter, the 2004 vision for the QdS was inclusive, paying particular attention to marginal cultural groups. Government and development organizations have spent millions of dollars to choreograph the area carefully for tourists. The ability of emergent cultural venues and organizations to remain within the neighborhood is one clear indicator of the impact of QdS development projects on the underground arts scene.

Reliable data on emerging cultural activities in the neighborhood do not exist. Most studies tend to categorize efforts by artistic discipline (such as music, dance, theater, or the visual arts) rather than levels of institutionalization, making it hard to identify emergent arts. Moreover, the questionable legal status of some underground cultural activities often makes their creators shy of reporting systems. In addition and in any case, the legitimacy of their activities is frequently contested. Events where formal tickets are not sold (such as programs that operate on the basis of a suggested donation to the artist, passes, or entrance fees) are not captured in provincial cultural attendance statistics; neither are poetry or visual arts performances (Fortier, 2013). In addition, public agencies disagree about whether video gaming, multimedia projects, and electronic music are arts or entertainment, and therefore who should account for them (QDSP, 2007). In a neighborhood trying to overcome a red-light district reputation and past, the area's remaining burlesque shows and best-known venue, the Café Cléopatre, are excluded from official statistics. Many artists and event organizers protested the nightclub's projected demolition for a project to expand a public utility's neighboring administrative offices in 2009 (OCPM, 2009). At the time, the president of Culture Montreal, a city-wide arts organization, commented that she did not believe the Café's activities were legitimate cultural events (Ebbels, 2009). The venue still does not appear on the QDSP's listing of public spaces offering arts (QDSP, 2014).

Artists today frequently complain about being priced out of the QdS, an increasingly evident trend. Space in the neighborhood rented for $6 to $8 per square foot in the late 1990s, but such costs now routinely exceed $20 per square foot (Convercité, 2006). Cultural workers with limited incomes can rarely afford more than $10 per square foot for space in which to create. As a result, many artists have moved outside the QdS, where less costly space can still be found, albeit with increasing difficulty (Aubin, personal communication, 2012). Despite rent increases, the city and QDSP answer that according to most indicators—the concentration of activities, the number of tickets sold, the number of workers employed—have all remained relatively constant in the past decade (Convercité, 2003, 2006; Ville de Montréal, 2014). Critics of the QdS charge that the apparent stability in the area's occupancy and lease statistics hides a shift from emergent to more institutional activities and that it is currently far more difficult for smaller, independent organizations to open in the area (QDSP, 2007; RCAAQ, 2009).

In a few notable cases, however, less established venues have secured stable funding and even ownership of their buildings. Underworld, a skate shop, has grown through several moves in the neighborhood. From cramped shows in a small space, the store has more than doubled in size and has expanded to include a music venue on its second floor. The Society for Arts and Technology (more commonly known as SAT) was evicted in 2001 from a manufacturing building slated to be torn down for a symphony hall project. Subsequently, SAT was able to purchase several buildings a few blocks from its initial location and to become an international hub for media research, with offices, a gallery, and several state-of-the art performance spaces.

Nonetheless, artists and cultural organizations have expressed concern in recent years that the neighborhood might lose its potential as an incubator for arts and culture. This anxiety became central to the city's 2012 planning exercise for the eastern section of the district. Christine Racine, the City of Montreal planner in charge of that process, recalled that resident and stakeholder comments in public meetings revealed an underlying concern for the richness of the area's cultural fabric. Recurrent themes of those who offered comments and suggestions to the planners involved were "authenticity," a desire to protect workspaces for artists and their creative activities, and a need to showcase the neighborhood's multiculturalism better (residents come from more than 100 countries; Racine, personal communication, 2012). As a result, the plan sought to reinforce the area's "avant-garde" identity as a central place for experimentation through innovations in zoning, regulation, and public art. Beyond municipal interventions, the 2012 blueprint for the eastern section of the district encourages creative uses of public space and supports economic activities related to knowledge, innovation, and the arts, particularly the multimedia and videogame industries (Ville de Montréal, 2012). The area plan also addresses challenges arising from the area's flagship institutions: Université du Québec à Montréal and a new $2 billion hospital development (located directly south of the area). Within the city, several successful collaborations exist between media arts, the gaming industry, universities, and major hospitals, illustrating the potential for such connections to stimulate the arts, including emergent artists. For example, SAT is collaborating with CHU Sainte-Justine, a regional children's hospital, to create multimedia tools to encourage patients' mobility, autonomy, and social development (SAT, 2011). The mutually reinforcing links between knowledge and creativity that this development exemplifies provide city leaders a strong incentive to ensure that the QdS remains a talent incubator.

## Addressing the Challenge of the Underground

Many of the qualities that made the Quartier attractive to creative workers in the past are still present today. Located at the intersection of the city's main transit lines and within minutes of major highways, the area is easily accessible to a regional customer base. Though larger popular venues and festivals have sought out this location because of its centrality, more specialized activities in the neighborhood benefit from the visibility and foot traffic the former create. The area's educational institutions, many of which have artistic mandates, provide training and development of specialized talent. The QdS remains a place where artists collaborate and local cultural scenes mix. The advantages of location, proximity, and concentration of talent and training are just as pertinent for emergent cultural organizations as for established ones and contribute to maintaining an underground scene in the area.

Though each festival and organization is different, the interviews I conducted revealed a number of shared challenges, detailed in this section. First, because of their limited financial means, artists and organizations are particularly sensitive to the availability of affordable and appropriate space. Noise is a recurrent issue with neighboring residents. Alternative arts entities are also concerned with the temporary nature of their venues, because of rapidly increasing real-estate costs, the need for often-expensive renovations, or their conversions to other uses. Finally, artists and organizations need to be able to claim the locations in which they evolve as their own.

### Finding and Keeping Space at a Low Cost

Artists and their promoters, both those interviewed for this research and those contacted for other recent studies of urban creative culture (Center for an Urban Future, 2005; Markusen and Gadwa, 2010), have emphasized that one of their greatest challenges is securing space that affordably provides required facilities and equipment, within the budgets dictated by their limited revenues. These costs are generally incurred before an event or organization can hope to collect any revenue from patrons or tenants, requiring the availability of up-front capital.

For example, for its tenth anniversary in 2011, Pop Montreal chose to hold a major public event at one of the QdS's new public plazas. Municipal regulations required that the concert be free. Headlined by Arcade Fire, the event drew nearly 100,000 people and garnered excellent reviews. Though the city and QDSP do not charge concert organizers rent for outdoor public space in the district and provide some equipment and street furniture free of charge (a QDSP funding program offsets the cost of gear for eligible events), festival organizers were still responsible for costs such as sound, stage, and lighting equipment and security. Pop Montreal was able to obtain public and private funding for overhead expenses of almost $800,000. This sum would be untenable for smaller festivals, many of which operate on annual budgets of less than $100,000 (Leftick, personal communication, 2012). Increased security costs and liability concerns due to the risk of damaging landscaping elements in the area's new public plazas have dissuaded a number of smaller arts organizations from using the spaces, making them less accessible for alternative events than originally envisioned by city planners (APLAS, 2010).

Eric Lefebvre, a director at QDSP, has observed that since the renovated public areas were opened in 2009, event operators have learned to subdivide them into smaller more versatile spaces. Those locations are currently booked to capacity, with the largest festivals reserving dates several years in advance (Lefebvre, personal communication, 2014). This leaves few openings for more spontaneous, less institutionalized events and thus represents an important challenge to the vitality of the arts in the Quartier.

When explaining why his organization only rarely hosts events in the QdS, Peter Burton, executive director of the Suoni Per Il Popolo music festival, cited Montreal's shortage of well-managed, licensed, low-cost venues open to hosting a diverse range of events for crowds of 200 to 400 people. In 2013, for example, he reported that only a handful of small live music venues were regularly hosting shows with audiences of fewer than 400 people. Among them, Place des Arts' smallest space charged a minimal booking fee of $1,255. Hourly fees for security and sound technicians quickly raise costs in other institutional arts centers, making them prohibitive for most emerging artists and their presenters. The remaining affordable venues are all heavily used. Burton suggested the lack of affordable small locations represents a bottleneck for efforts to showcase Montreal's younger emerging artists whose producers must either plan their events months in advance or resort to illegal or inappropriate spaces (Burton, personal communication, 2012).

Some established organizations have specifically sought to support alternative artists but, to date, with only moderate success. After twenty years of planning and a number of aborted projects, Le Vivier, a collective of twenty-seven experimental musical organizations and ensembles secured a long-term lease in the Gesú, an existing Jesuit church and arts center in the QdS. The collective plans to renovate underused areas for performances, a media library, and administrative and teaching rooms. The landmark status of the building invites artists to express the duality between the past and present, tradition and innovation. Managers are reassuring their members that co-location with a religious congregation will not limit performance content. The building's location within the QdS' network of established venues also facilitates audience development. Permanent space will no doubt help Le Vivier accomplish its mandate to encourage new music (Gingras, personal communication, 2012; Le Vivier, 2014). While this specific example is promising, it is unusual. Additional alternative venues that cater to newer ventures remain necessary.

### *Culture Is Not a Nuisance, but It Makes for Busy Neighbors*

Many theorists have described the virtues of mixed-use neighborhoods, where stores and public places share the street with residential and office uses. Jane Jacobs, when detailing the elements of sidewalk life that provide "eyes on the street," argued that, "enterprises and public places that are used by evening and night must be among them especially" (Jacobs, 1961, p. 36). However, nightlife also has its pitfalls: It generates noise past closing time in areas immediately adjacent to venues and clubs and along the paths to transit, taxis, or parking. In Montreal, the number of complaints from residents about indoor venues has increased significantly since smoking indoors was forbidden in 2006 (Ville de Montréal, 2010). Fueled by citizen concerns about noise, the city began fining performance spaces for such infractions—a practice that led to the permanent closure of several alternative music venues located close to residential areas in 2009.

To complement its indoor programming, Pop Montreal for several years organized an outdoor concert series in a local park located outside the QdS. In 2010, the city forced the festival to cancel its outdoor events because of complaints from the occupants of an adjacent building that had just been converted to residential condominiums. Event organizers have since scaled back the free performances scheduled for the park significantly (Leftick, personal communication, 2012). Montreal's officials defend many of the larger outdoor festivals when they receive noise complaints, citing their positive economic impact. However, the city limits the number of hours when smaller events are allowed to hold performances with amplified music to "strike a better balance between all of the concerned parties" (Ville de Montréal, 2010).

In early 2010, SAT, which is located in the center of the QdS, was required to cancel shows because of neighbors' noise complaints. This prompted criticism from prominent local artists that while the city had claimed that the Quartier would be a space for free cultural expression, unlike residential areas where noise levels are vigorously regulated, alternative artists were no longer welcome (Fragata, 2010), and the area was becoming a "day-care with graffiti drawn by children to cater to tourists rather than Montrealers" (Ghislain Poirier, interviewed in Nicoud, 2010).

Neighbors and landlords have also complained about workshops and practice spaces—about not only noise but other "nuisances," such as sawdust or paint fumes. Tenants with monthly or one or two year leases—as is the case for most less-well-established firms—typically do not invest in soundproofing, extensive waste disposal, or ventilation systems. This was not an issue when artists set up their workshops in older industrial buildings, for which building code requirements were relatively low.

The city's recent decisions to allow office and residential uses in former industrial areas means that owners of older buildings are now faced with undertaking costly renovations to provide ventilation and disposal facilities to comply with new fire safety regulations in spaces where occupants once used chemicals, including dyes and solvents. Many owners instead opt to modernize their buildings for commercial uses to maximize their opportunity to garner increased rents.

In a study conducted concerning one of the QdS's former garment industry buildings containing a number of independent artists' workshops, for example, several occupants complained the landlord now prohibited the use of certain types of materials, including oil paints. He enacted this policy to keep rents low for as many artists as possible, instead of making costly renovations. Though many individuals were thankful to be able to stay, some required use of those substances and, for those artists, this new regulation was tantamount to an eviction (Convercité, 2006).

## The Threat of Eviction

Few cultural organizations or creative workers in Montreal own the spaces they occupy. Because newer artists and smaller ventures face barriers to credit, limited-length leases are common. The short-term nature of these spaces facilitates lower cost start-up and development of creative businesses, but their scarcity is problematic. The firms/artists experience increased risk of eviction and a more subtle danger of their leases not being renewed. Many artist organizations and venues fear that too many improvements will compound that risk by tempting landlords to refuse renewal of a lease and "flip" the better equipped space, to higher-paying tenants (APLAS, 2010).

Rent is also the indirect product of the cost of living and doing business in the area. Creative workers patronize eateries and local stores, but their budgets are not reflections of an area's overall wealth. As noted above, artists rely on access to cafés, bars, and nightclubs to socialize, network, and develop ideas. In light of increasing real estate prices in the QdS, emergent artists caution that as the businesses catering to the arts are priced out of the area, the creative ecosystem of which they are a part will be threatened (QDSP, 2007).

Currid has argued that cultural workers function best in a dense network and, for that reason, their forced displacement from a neighborhood is disruptive (Currid, 2007b). Not only must those who leave find new contacts, but the loss of workers also weakens the existing network. As individual workers can no longer be as productive, dispersion has an adverse effect on the vitality of the arts and culture sector as a whole.

Artists' studios and venues are not protected from profit-oriented real estate ventures. In some instances in the QdS, promoters have refused to renew short-term leases to clear buildings of their occupants in preparation for construction projects. In other cases of "demolition by negligence," heritage groups suspect that owners allowed buildings in the QdS to deteriorate until they were condemned to ensure land clearance (Heritage Montréal, 2014). Tenants and municipal authorities often have little recourse in these cases, as the city can only require that developers assist in the relocation of tenants with leases in good standing at the time building permits are issued.

Cultural venues in the QdS have sometimes benefitted from governmental assistance in their search for new locations. SAT, described previously, is one of those success stories. In another case, Montreal worked for several years to relocate L'X, a punk venue, when UQAM emptied its existing location for renovations in 2004. Relocation proved difficult because potential neighbors were concerned about the club's clientele. L'X reopened as Katacombes in 2006, only to have its owners learn in 2007 that they would soon be evicted from their new venue to permit another development. With the developer's assurance that they could return to their location upon completion of the new project, they relocated "temporarily" once again in 2009. As this is written in 2014, neither project for which Katacombes was evicted has yet been constructed: UQAM cancelled its renovation project and sold the property, and construction has not yet begun on the second development.

Far more dangerous than punk-rock enthusiasts, one of the greatest threats to areas targeted by renewal schemes are unfinished projects, those that demolish without rebuilding. These efforts displace stores, artists, and residents and remove foot traffic. Osborne-Lanthier, whose arts center was a block away from a number of incomplete development sites, contended in an interview that QdS renewal projects had significantly reduced pedestrian traffic. The city had actively cleared street people to facilitate development projects, destroying the informal self-policing networks among the homeless, beggars, drug pushers, and street workers. As a result, safety concerns had increased throughout the area. Osborne-Lanthier's landlord has become uncertain about the future of his building, which could become part of the next major development, and has therefore declined to invest in its maintenance and upkeep. Indeed, after a series of break-ins, Osborne-Lanthier and his colleagues decided to close the center and leave the area in 2012.

## Diverging Aesthetics: The Messiness of Creativity

Jantien Smit (2011) has documented how "creative" entrepreneurs choose to locate in neighborhoods that both reflect and encourage their creativity. They want to live and work in environments they find stimulating. These individuals seek to be visible via the formal businesses they open and operate, the informal transformations of their homes and gardens, or through public expressions such as public art or spontaneous installations.

As underground culture often displays different aesthetic sensibilities, signs of appropriation of a space are frequently interpreted as indicators of blight or poor maintenance. For example, graffiti murals—even when executed with the permission of property owners—are often dismissed as evidence of criminality. More conservative populations often have prejudices against individuals with tattoos, eccentric hairstyles, and unusual attire. These perceptions create a tense dialectic between those who wish to "improve" an area to bolster their status and those desiring to make an area edgy or unique.

Posters are another example of divergent aesthetics. Though the city considers it illegal (and seeks to ticket) those who put up posters advertising their event on public utility poles, artists involved with the underground scene defend the use of posters on utility poles to advertise events, arguing that their right to freedom of expression implies that they should be allowed to communicate publicly, even if they do not have access to commercial media and advertising (COLLE, 2010). These markers signal the presence of underground artists and advertise that experimentation is welcome. Artists have called on municipal authorities to adopt an attitude of tolerance by allowing visual markers of creative activity within the public sphere (ibid).

The new spaces around Place des Arts were designed to meet strict building codes using standard architectural practices and hence do not include visual cues with which underground arts typically identify. Mandated to manage these spaces, QDSP conducts annual public art competitions that target younger or alternative artists. The programs aim to engage the emergent arts and grant them visibility within the Quartier, but they remain a compromise within a more conservative overall QDSP aesthetic. As such, the sites are not used for artistic expression outside of sanctioned public events. Fear of incivilities that may frighten patrons and tourists has added security to QDSP's work (i.e., preserving conditions that will not unsettle the comfort of visitors). Unfortunately, the signage, cameras, and patrol staff associated with this effort give the Quartier's manicured spaces an institutional appearance and make them sterile, as compared to potential sites of underground culture.

## Recommendations to Enable Emergence

Underground culture relies on many of the qualities of any healthy sustainable neighborhood, including a mix of uses, access to transportation, and suitable spaces for work and expression. Emerging arts differ from established institutional and commercial culture in the number of its individual players, its often unstable and informal character, its participatory ethos, and its uncommon aesthetic. Montreal, and more specifically, the neighborhoods in which new artists, organizations, and events congregate, benefit from these individuals' array of vital and vibrant activities, which reinforce the city's overall cultural creativity. As discussed previously, the creative milieu relies upon opportunities for incubation, experimentation, and socialization provided by underground settings (Currid, 2007b). This is particularly true in Montreal, where creative workers in fields outside the arts often participate in the underground scene (Catalytix, 2005).

Emergent arts are also an asset to the QdS as a tourist destination. By virtue of its constant reinvention, developing culture is expressed in a vernacular emanating from a local scene. Tourism organizations have reported that people increasingly travel to places where they believe they will enjoy unique experiences. Underground culture naturally provides a distinctive atmosphere, which would be costly to replicate. In the absence of a local social infrastructure to sustain this diversity, it will also be far more vulnerable to the fickleness of media salience. The QdS's history and current strengths (mass transit service, educational facilities, location, diverse mix of land uses and activities) keep it attractive to emergent artists and organizations, many of which still frequent the neighborhood.

Nonetheless, the interviews I conducted for this study revealed that for those organizations that have elected to do so, remaining in the Quartier presents challenges tied to four main issues. First, current trends suggest that affordable performance, exhibition, studio, and event space within the neighborhood is increasingly scarce. The area's recently completed urban design project has only aggravated issues with respect to availability of spaces on needed dates and overhead costs (insurance, permits, equipment rental, etc.). The financial support provided by the QDSP and the city is crucial to these organizations remaining in the area, and organizers hope that Montreal will design any new public spaces to be more accommodating to smaller events.

Funding sources for alternative cultural entities have not increased at the same rate as real estate prices in the area, compromising access to indoor spaces for organizations and artists with short-term leases. This scarcity is aggravated by increasing conversion of former industrial buildings to residential and commercial (office) space, and further compounded by an overall increase in the cost of living.

Second, appropriate space is increasingly difficult to find and secure within the QdS. New real estate projects often target the venues and buildings in which emergent organizations and artisans work. The proximity of these new occupants imposes costly renovations on artists and their organizations to protect their new neighbors from noise, dust, and other nuisances. Artists suggest that maintaining "light industrial" zoning for the buildings where they work and perform might provide a clear signal to new occupants that they are allowed to continue their residence. The city could also assist by encouraging retail or office uses in spaces that abut workshops and interior or exterior venues, thereby creating a buffer for nearby residents.

Third, the ongoing threat of eviction in Montreal's QdS is pushing many alternative arts organizations to seek space elsewhere. This study's interviewees reported not only that leases are not being renewed to make room for potential redevelopment projects but that their overall safety and the condition of their spaces and buildings have deteriorated because of construction in the area. This situation is all the more problematic because, in many cases, projects have been cancelled or delayed after owners and developers have already emptied existing spaces. Anticipating increased revenue, the city often encourages such initiatives. This makes it an accomplice when cultural groups are pushed out, unless it simultaneously acts to protect them through relocation and stabilization programs. This proactive approach is necessary to ensure continuity in alternative organizations' operations and to complement the more tourist-oriented venues located in the western part of the QdS.

Finally, the eccentricity of the practices and aesthetics of underground culture and their sometimes subversive nature frequently place them at odds with activities that public authorities perceive as more legitimate. However, as described above, underground culture is an essential part of the greater creative ecosystem because it provides uncensored incubation spaces for arts workers while safeguarding the area's distinctive flavor. Furthermore, it is unethical to deny certain cultural groups access to the amenities and advantages a neighborhood has to offer solely on the basis of their beliefs, appearance, or forms of expression. In the city's plan for the eastern section of the QdS, policy makers have favored small-scale projects instead of prescriptive design guidelines (Ville de Montréal, 2012). Paradoxically, strict plans intended to preserve an area's character can in fact freeze it in a dated reality rather than acknowledging the living quality of its heritage—in this case maintaining traditions that enable creativity may be just as important as the architecture prevalent at a given point in history. Montreal's current plan for the neighborhood allows the area's occupants greater freedom to outfit and decorate public space and to hold events showcasing challenging content. Personalization of the public realm as a permanent display of underground arts signals the vitality of a creative milieu in which individuals are not afraid to innovate and experiment.

The city's current planning exercise in the eastern section of the QdS, the Quartier Latin, has given it a unique opportunity to protect the historic presence of emergent cultural activities in this area and, in doing so, strengthen Montreal's attractiveness to creative and innovative talent. However, to contribute fully to Montreal's economy, underground arts should be valued throughout the city and not just in the QdS. Markusen and Gadwa (2010) have argued that initiatives in a single district or part of a city cannot satisfy the needs of a vibrant cultural sector, let alone a constantly evolving underground scene. Maintaining public support for culture throughout the city will ensure that the arts organizations that operate in the Quartier have chosen to be there. This will also keep these entities locally relevant and therefore more likely to remain vital and to flourish.

## References

APLAS (Association des petits lieux d'art et de spectacle). (2010). "Bruit de fond." Retrieved November 20, 2010 from http://www.aplas.ca/tiki-index.php#Bruit_de_fond

Baker, V. (2007). Top 10 bars in Montreal. *The Guardian*, November 23. Retrieved January 15, 2008 from http://www.theguardian.com/travel/2007/nov/23/montreal.bars

Carr, D. (2005). Cold Fusion: Montreal's explosive music scene. *New York Times*, February 6. Retrieved August 5, 2014 from http://www.nytimes.com/2005/02/06/arts/music/06carr.html?_r=0#

Catalytix. (2005). Montréal's capacity for creative connectivity: Outlook & opportunities [unpublished report]. Retrieved April 29, 2005 from http://creativeclass.com/rfcgdb/articles/montreals%20capacity.pdf

CCMM (Chambre de commerce du Montréal métropolitain). (2009). *La culture à Montréal: impacts économiques et financement privé*. Montreal: CCMM.

Center for an Urban Future. (2005). *Creative New York*. New York: City Futures Inc.

Clavel, L. (2007). La Fiesta de la rue Saint-Viateur. *Le Devoir*, June 1. Retrieved August 5, 2014 from http://www.ledevoir.com/culture/actualites-culturelles/145657/la-fiesta-de-la-rue-saint-viateur.

COLLE. (2010). Coalition for free expression [website]. Retrieved July 29, 2010 from http://collemontreal.org

Convercité. (2003). *Étude du Quartier des spectacles*. Montreal: Quartier des Spectacles Partnership.

Convercité. (2006). *Portrait des entreprises culturelles dans le Quartier des spectacles*. Montreal: Quartier des Spectacles Partnership.

Cummins-Russell, T. A. and N. Rantisi. (2012). Network and place in Montreal's independent music industry. *The Canadian Geographer*, 56(1): 80–97.

Currid, E. (2007a). How art and culture happen in New York. *Journal of the American Planning Association*, 73(4): 454–467.

Currid, E. (2007b). *The Warhol economy*. Princeton, NJ: Princeton University Press.

Ebbels, K. (2009). Drawn and quartered. *Maisonneuve*, 33: 47–49.

Florida, R. (2002). *The rise of the creative class and how it's transforming work, leisure, community and everyday life*. New York: Basic Books.

Fortier, C. (2013). La fréquentation des arts de la scène en 2012. *Optique culture, 28* (September). Retrieved February 2, 2014 from http://www.stat.gouv.qc.ca/observatoire

Fragata, Y. (2010). Manifeste pour le bruit: Montréalais, que faites-vous? Blog post, March 26. Retrieved August 5, 2014 from http://www.bandeapart.fm/#/page/blogue-manifeste-pour-le-bruit-montrealais-que-faites-vous

Frost Kumpf, H. A. (1998). *Cultural districts: The arts as a strategy for revitalizing our cities*. Washington, DC: Americans for the Arts.

Gans, H. J. (1974). *Popular culture and high culture: An analysis of taste*. New York: Basic Books.

Hall, P. (2000). Creative cities and economic development. *Urban Studies*, 37(4): 636–649.

Heritage Montreal. (2014). Les résolutions patrimoine et aménagement 2014 [Press release]. Retrieved June 20, 2014 from http://www.heritagemontreal.org/fr/resolutions-2014

Hill, K. (2010). *Mapping artists and cultural workers in Canada's large cities*. Toronto: Hill Strategies.

Jacobs, J. (1961). *The death and life of great american cities*. New York: Vintage Books.

Jantien Smit, A. (2011). The influence of district visual quality on location decisions of creative entrepreneurs. *Journal of the American Planning Association*, 77(2): 167–184.

Landry, C. (2000). *The creative city: A toolkit for urban innovators*. London: Earthscan Publications.

Lee, D. (2006). New music in Montreal. *New York Times*, March 24. Retrieved August 5, 2014 from http://www.nytimes.com/2006/03/24/travel/escapes/24montreal.html

Le Vivier. (2014). Le Vivier s'implante au Gesù [Press release]. Retrieved February 25 2014 from http://www.levivier.ca/fr/select/nouv/index.php?id=1123

Lortie, A. (2004). *Les années 60: Montréal voit grand*. Montreal: Centre canadien d'architecture.

Markusen, A., and A. Gadwa. (2010). Arts and culture in urban or regional planning: A review and research agenda. *Journal of Planning Education and Research*, 2010(29): 379–391.

*National Geographic*. (2007). Montréal: Vive la difference [map]. Geotourism Mapguide.

Nicoud, A. (2010). Lettre au Maire Tremblay: que devient la nuit montréalaise? *La Presse*, April 14. Retrieved April 16, 2014 from http://www.lapresse.ca/arts/201004/14/01-4270245-lettre-au-maire-tremblay-que-devient-la-nuit-montrealaise.php

OCPM (Office de Consultation Publique de Montréal). (2009). *Consultation publique: Le Quadrilatere Saint-Laurent*. Retrieved November 20, 2010 from http://ocpm.qc.ca/consultations-publiques/quadrilatere-saint-laurent

QDSP (Quartier des spectacles Partnership). (2004). *Le Quartier des spectacles: Une destination culturelle*. Montreal: QDSP.

QDSP (Quartier des spectacles Partnership). (2007). *Trois études de cas relatives à l'art et à l'industrie du spectacle à Montréal*. Montreal: QDSP.

QDSP (Quartier des spectacles Partnership). (2014). Quartier des spectales [website]. Retrieved August 5, 2014 from http://www.quartierdesspectacles.com

RCAAQ. (2009). Consultation publique sur le projet 2-22 Sainte-Catherine: Mémoire présenté par le Regroupement des centres d'artistes autogérés du Québec. Retrieved November 20, 2010 from http://ocpm.qc.ca/consultations-publiques/projet-du-2-22-rue-sainte-catherine

SAT (Société des arts technologiques). (2011). Living Lab projects SAT/Sainte-Justine on display [Press release].

Strom, E. (2001). *Strengthening communities through culture*. Washington, DC: Center for Arts and Culture.

Ville de Montréal. (2005). *Montréal Métropole Culturelle*. Montreal: Ville de Montréal.

Ville de Montréal. (2007). *Programme particulier d'urbanisme: Quartier des spectacles*. Montreal: Ville de Montréal.

Ville de Montréal. (2010). *Bilan sur le Bruit*. Montreal: Ville de Montréal.

Ville de Montréal. (2012). *Programme particulier d'urbanisme du Quartier des spectacles*— Pôle du Quartier Latin. Montreal: Ville de Montréal.

Ville de Montréal (2014). Quartier des spectacles de Montréal [website]. Retrieved August 5, 2014 from http://ville.montreal.qc.ca/portal/page?_pageid=7557,81223570&_dad=portal&_schema=PORTAL

Weintraub, W. (1996). *City unique*. Montreal: Robin Brass Books.

Zukin, S. (2010). *Naked city: The death and life of authentic urban places*. New York: Oxford University Press.

# 5

# DIGITAL STORYTELLING IN APPALACHIA

## Gathering and Sharing Community Voices and Values

*Holly Lesko and Thenmozhi Soundararajan*

> We cannot move theory into action unless we can find it in the eccentric and wandering ways of our daily life. ... Stories give theory flesh and breath.
>
> (Pratt, 1995, p. 22)

Stories are not just what we read from books to children or tell for entertainment around the table; they help us define our lives and ground us in place and describe and define our relationships with other people and humanity more broadly. Narratives move, inspire, and connect. They also offer new ways of thinking and being. We offer the following reflection and analysis as a framing of our work with digital storytelling, one form, although a relatively recently developed one, by which individuals have chosen to share their life experiences with others. At the core of our efforts is the aspiration that participatory researchers and activists can create a place with community members in which a wide variety of voices are heard and shared values are identified. We contend that stories shape communities, neighborhoods, and institutions. And while we cannot un-tell the accounts of our histories, we can claim and shift the narrative that guides us for the future. Stories create new myths, evince heritage and cultural identity, and represent one mechanism by which to allow space for otherwise often silenced individual and marginalized voices. The grounding notion of our digital storytelling work is that the incorporation of diverse, and most significantly, disadvantaged and vulnerable voices in public planning and policy processes can expand resident perceptions and understandings of community.

This chapter describes our use of digital storytelling—media production that permits individuals to share elements of their life story in an electronic form. In our case, these stories incorporate full video and sound animation, stills, audio as appropriate—in a project in the New River Valley (NRV) region of Virginia. The effort engaged youths with health concerns affecting their communities. Digital storytelling helped to secure deeper community engagement among participants and across generational divides through the sharing of the youths' video narratives in the community. This case suggests that electronic forms of storytelling can encourage agency and empowerment among those engaged in it while also opening opportunities to catalyze space for community change.

## Background of Narrative Praxis

Each person in the world is living his or her "story": a product of their individual capacities and disposition and the shaping force of a host of political, cultural, familial, corporate, and civic narratives. That ecosystem of story surrounds individuals in local and global contexts alike (McQuillan, 2000). Accounts are powerful because they are a key mechanism by which individuals come to know and define themselves. Through both internal and external narrative, individuals also come to know others and seek meaning and belonging, thus creating unique and also shared visions of the world. Stories are important because they are a primary means by which individuals communicate and share values.

We employ digital storytelling to allow individuals to articulate their stories and concerns in a collaborative process with others while utilizing technology to create an artifact of their narrative to share and for future use. This electronic storytelling process is grounded in a participatory engagement methodology, "an approach ... that deliberately and explicitly emphasizes collaboration [with community residents] at every point in the ethnographic process, without veiling it—from project conceptualization, to fieldwork, and especially, through the writing process" (Lassiter, 2005, p. 16). As we use this media form, every participant, even when developing her or his individual voiceover narration for his or her personal digital story, is part of a collaborative of storytellers who influence, review, and engage in creation of each script. Each finished narrative is thus an articulation of a personal perspective and knowledge but created in and with community—an individual viewpoint developed in the context of a shared experience. As workshop facilitators, we act as collaborative ethnographers as the storytellers develop their videos together. The power of telling and gathering narratives remains firmly with those sharing their accounts, as the focus of the workshop experience is to honor their individual experience.

Sam Cook has defined ethnography as a form of participatory work that represents a, "deliberate effort to be moved by community agendas, reactions, and even resistance. ... Power and its reallocation is the focal concern of collaborative ethnography or anthropology" (Cook, 2009, p. 113). The workshop setting provides opportunities for individuals to explore personal and community challenges and to frame these in their own voices. In this way, digital stories can be used to explore a focal question, policy issue, or current event through the lived experience of each participant. As collaborators, workshop leaders help storytellers capture their narrative. This process provides every participant reflexive opportunities as they develop their evolving work. Individuals also share their stories with other workshop participants, and these exchanges often prove quite powerful.

Anzaldúa has highlighted the power of personal narratives to draw readers (or, in this case, viewers) to consider alternate perspectives, "writing and speaking … are also political acts that spring from the impulse to subvert, resist, educate, and make changes" (Anzaldúa, 2009, p. 187). By capturing stories, especially those of individuals from communities outside the dominant cultural, economic, or political views in a particular arena, digital narratives can counter, challenge, and expand accepted social frames and perspectives. By providing a means by which individuals may own and voice their stories, the digital storytelling workshop can encourage a sense of agency in those sharing their views and experiences.

Our workshops are based on a methodology first developed in the 1990s by Joe Lambert and Dana Atchely at the Center for Digital Storytelling in Berkeley, California (Lambert, 2007). Lambert and Atchely sought to help individuals create three- to five-minute videos that reflected a personal narrative they wished to share. We have sought to take this process further by working with workshop participants to explore how their individual stories reflect broader issues or questions at play in their communities. This step allows the use of electronic narratives for community visioning, organizing, and research. Individuals create digital stories in our workshops but within a context of others working on similar or related questions or themes concerning issues in their community. These peers offer valuable feedback throughout the production process. Those who create accounts in our programs own them thereafter and may use them as they wish. Any later use of digital stories occurs only with the storytellers' permission.

Workshops support the production of a digital story by each participant. Each video is derived from the lives of those involved and may include video recordings, images, photographs, letters, drawings, news clippings, or art that those individuals select or provide. Most digital stories include a voiceover narration (usually by the filmmakers) that anchors the piece by tying its central elements together. We encourage participants to start from their personal place of knowing and experience as they begin to develop narrative arcs for their pieces. This stance provides space for each filmmaker to include the unique details that make their piece a specific and honest portrayal of how they view the concern they have chosen to highlight. We also encourage participants to write about what they know personally about the concern they are highlighting. No one else can tell an individual's story better than that person; workshops provide an opportunity for participants to capture that unique and important account. Digital storytellers can provide narrative in the form of a poem, a rhyme, or a song or via spoken word; all can be powerful and compelling as the evocation of an individuals' experience. We define digital storytelling as a process rather than as a tool. By grounding the use of narrative in a process, those offering the workshop embrace an affective engagement with community members. We aim to prompt participants to realize and express their agency via their individual expertise and voice, not to manipulate them, or to capture a dramatic "sound bite."

Analysts have begun to unpack the impacts of gathering stories from and about community for both research and activism (Graffman and Börejesson, 2001; Lassiter, 2001). We emphasize that efforts to gather and record individual stories must first serve and reflect the personal aspirations of the community members who own them. Digital stories can offer powerful and important content for assessing community needs and shaping common visions and strategies but only if they represent the lived experience and local knowledge of the individuals who create them.

## Central Appalachian Example of Youth Agency through Digital Storytelling

The rich history of story in the Appalachian region has been well documented, but several troubling health concerns are also well established in this part of the country. The NRV is a 1,453-square-mile, four-county area located in Central Appalachia. Valley residents are a traditionally medically under-served population. According to the United States County Health Rankings of 2013, the region ranks well below the median for Virginia on the food environment index due to limited access to healthy foodstuffs. Meanwhile, substance abuse rates in the Valley rank far above state and national averages, as do teenage pregnancy rates (County Health Rankings, 2013).

In 2011, the Robert Wood Johnson Foundation (RWJF) awarded the New River Valley Planning District Commission (NRVPDC) one of thirty Roadmaps to Health grants that supported efforts to create healthier places for individuals and families. The Healthy New River Valley (Healthy NRV) initiative sought to strengthen family and social connectedness while breaking cycles of unhealthy and self-destructive behaviors through assessment of health needs and positive messaging (New River Valley Livability Initiative, 2013). With the support of the grant, the authors were able to work with a group of NRV youths to produce digital stories as a key component of assessment and messaging about health for the Healthy NRV project.

Storytelling workshops served as a vehicle for participating youths to work together and with the authors to assess community health-related needs, identify assets, and locate opportunities for spurring change in area residents' beliefs and behaviors. The young people's digital stories highlighted behavioral and physical health problems and raised issues for community consideration. Drawing on personal experiences and crafted in a collaborative setting (as outlined above), each electronic narrative integrated visual imagery and audio recording into an edited final product. The teenagers' stories explored existing issues in fresh ways and generated community interest as a result.

The project provided in-depth digital storytelling training to nine teenagers or, as they were called formally, youth health ambassadors, during the RWJF project. The youths collected stories from their peers, community leaders, and family members about health concerns and impacts in their communities and developed fifteen videos based on their experiences and the information they gathered. Project leaders produced an additional twenty health issue digital stories with community partners and other adults interested in community change. By engaging both adults and youths in the digital storytelling process, the effort's principals were able to create and honor a richer sense of community perspective and experience. The digital stories addressed a range of health concerns, including how better to support positive diet choices, reduce drug abuse, lower teenage pregnancy rates, and support the needs of a growing aging population. The videos were widely shared locally and regionally in schools and by community organizations and continue to be the topic of public conversations. The health ambassadors presented their work to local governing officials and at the Let's Talk Public Health conferences held at Virginia Tech in August 2012 and 2013. The authors also shared samples of the youths' videos and information about their engagement in the project and with public health concerns at the Imagining America conference in New York City in October 2012, the Appalachian Studies Association conference in January 2013, and at other events throughout the region.

The project's storytelling workshops built fresh community capacity to support grassroots efforts to gather community-based information and turn those data into compelling digital narratives. We had wondered how best to use these stories to help community leaders and members address complex health issues. As it happened, however, a fourteen-year-old health ambassador's presentation of a video addressing teen pregnancy in the region quickly engaged local government officials and encouraged them to suggest they would take steps to address the concern more effectively in their jurisdictions. This sort of reception was typical of the way in which the ambassadors' stories were received at a variety of community presentations across the NRV. As it happened, in short, we need not have been concerned on this count.

By staying connected with the program's youth ambassadors and with the organizations that supported their engagement in the project, we have learned that all of the project's participants have engaged in health-related educational or promotional activities outside the context of the grant. Each has also indicated that his or her involvement in the digital storytelling workshops had enhanced her or his knowledge of and interest in engaging with the community. In particular, the initiative has served as an impetus for ongoing collaboration between its youth participants and a variety of adult community leaders involved with public health concerns in the NRV. Two youth health ambassadors have gone on to lead community health fairs in two counties, and three teenagers have been invited to serve on local nonprofit organization boards and present at those entities' annual meetings and conferences during the past two years.

Indeed, as the project unfolded, we repeatedly discovered ways that the youths' stories helped strengthen connections among residents in the region. The NRV Planning District Commission staff also found ways to link digital workshop participants' stories with graphical representations of statistical data concerning health conditions in the NRV, which both deepened the local population's understanding of health issues and helped engage broader constituencies in regional health improvement efforts. That is, the young people's digital stories offered multiple opportunities for citizen engagement and public deliberation. As noted above, the youth health ambassador's video about teenage pregnancy led to several local government officials committing to address the issue more aggressively. In another example, an ambassador presented an interview-intensive video concerning methamphetamine use in nearby Floyd, VA. The teenager engaged with a school-community audience and asked hard questions. Attendees responded in an open way, and a vigorous discussion ensued. The video depicted a difficult problem and its impacts on individuals and their families and communities. Nonetheless, the digital story left the viewer with hope for the future as it symbolically represented the engagement of the youths of the region. In short, the youth-produced digital stories have helped to broaden the conversation about health impacts on local planning and investment in the NRV. Additionally, the workshop and outreach process has often empowered youths, recasting their roles from that of token or disengaged participants to that of experts.[1]

Connecting health-related data and personal narratives has proven critical to reshaping individual behaviors and informing policy makers about the health needs of the Valley community. The Healthy NRV initiative built important networks and infrastructure for gathering and capturing community stories addressing health and health needs in the region. This enhanced capacity is now informing local policy makers.

## Ways of Knowing and Being Known

We grounded our work for this project in efforts to encourage self-reflection by and self-knowledge among those with whom we collaborated. The digital narratives produced in the workshop process drew on individual stories that reflected their authors' understanding of themselves and the world around them. The youth and community workshops provide opportunities for participants to experience agency and to express their voices while also producing content for dissemination to others.

This said, there is a critical need for scholars, public officials, and community leaders to understand more fully how individual stories are shaped by a range of social resources and circumstances. Stories may empower individuals, but they may also constrain them in important ways. All too often, accounts of members of disadvantaged and vulnerable groups become widely shared by majorities that have little or no basis in the lived experience of those individuals. By creating a space and vehicle for authoring and helping them own narratives in their voices and contexts, digital storytelling workshops can provide opportunities for new voices to enter the community dialogue.

Armed with this self-produced data, individuals can work to share their narrative self-understanding. These attributes of "publicness and transportability" of digital stories allow these short videos to serve as important catalysts of potential social change. The reflection and self-awareness these narratives embody can help to deepen broader popular awareness of civic and social needs and structures while also providing individuals with insights into the values and cultural norms that undergird dominant community understandings of specific public concerns.

Starting inquiry from a place of personal knowing within community is a critical component of digital storytelling. The use of individual narrative in this way provides a vessel for sharing from experience and knowing. Claiming personal voice for both articulating issues and naming assets is important to seeding a multi-faceted conversation concerning community issues. Digitally created stories can serve as artifacts for individuals to share their voice and perspective outside of their community and opportunities to capture other citizens' attention and create space for new ways of thinking and talking about issues, assets, and learning.

The work of electronic narrative is rooted in individual and community collaboration grounded in a belief in the efficacy of shared knowledge creation. Digital storytelling assumes that a wide variety of forms of expertise may exist among all residents of a community. A key goal of this form of art making is to honor the many ways of knowing found in communities among disparate groups of residents. Knowledge is created and recreated between people as they bring their personal experiences and information derived from other sources to bear to address a particular problem (Wells, 1999). The digital storytelling method valorizes all forms of individual knowing including, especially, lived experience.

## Conclusions

The process of digital story creation is as critical as the artifact it creates. Holmes and Marcus have highlighted this dimension of the interconnections among participating community members as creating bonds akin to those produced by involvement in a major theatrical production (Holmes and Marcus, 2008). We have been privileged to witness significant personal and group change in digital storytelling workshops for which we have been responsible. Indeed, our work with this initiative saw this occur for many of the youths with whom we were privileged to interact. We have been encouraged and challenged in our efforts by bell hooks' observation,

All too often we think of community in terms of being with folks like ourselves: the same class, same race, same ethnicity, same social standing and the like … I think we need to be wary: we need to work against the danger of evoking something that we don't challenge ourselves to actually practice.

(hooks, 2003)

We have also drawn on the work of Julian Rappaport:

If we view the power to create, select, and tell stories (that are positively valued) about one's self and one's community as a resource, we quickly see that like most resources it is distributed unevenly, in about the same proportion as other resources, such as money and social prestige.

(Rappaport, 1995, p. 797)

By honoring and valuing individual voices of community, especially those generally under-represented, and creating a context for amplifying and capturing their stories, digital storytelling can enhance not only opportunities for agency of those less frequently heard but also add to the richness and diversity of expression and ideas that communities may consider as they confront and seek change. Kelly has offered an important variant of this point that highlights the importance of including diverse perspectives in community initiatives, "practice … is then woven with the indigenous expression of community approaches where the word 'community' means that citizens are equal and collaborative partners" (Kelly, 1990. P. 450).

Although the stories shared may be centered in a community concern or perhaps a tragic personal event, the purpose of creating opportunities to capture them digitally is always to encourage individual and community possibilities for change. Individuals own their narratives, and the digital storytelling process provides an opportunity to capture and share them more broadly without losing their essence.

The narrative process honors the truth that each story, each person, brings wisdom to the whole. By starting from a place honoring self-knowing, learning and education may occur without fear of self-loss. We are all storytellers and gatherers; the key to building community and to facing and fostering change is to honor personal narratives and to provide context and space for individuals to come to share and know one another. Digital storytelling can be a powerful asset in this vital process.

## Notes

1  The three videos described in the examples can be found on YouTube. The Meth use video, Saving Floyd—Combatting the Meth Madness, is at https://www.youtube.com/watch?v=xw89GogmA3E&list=UUWFV216xuMK2_WYlxTsbKDw

The Appalachia video, LEE final720movie, is at https://www.youtube.com/wa tch?v=gx1G22HIqU0&list=UUsTq229mTGeE5NdIfxBXOcQ The video about greed, Greed in Floyd, is at https://www.youtube.com/watch?v=Yp-cznaW2cI&list=UUWFV216xuMK2_WYlxTsbKDw

# References

Anzaldúa, G. (2009). On the process of writing Borderlands/La Frontera. In A. Keating (Ed.) *The Gloria Anzaldúa reader* (pp. 18–197). Durham, NC: Duke University Press.

Cook, S. R. (2009). The collaborative power struggle. *Collaborative Anthropologies*, 2: 109–114.

County Health Rankings. (2013). County health rankings & roadmaps, Virginia. Retrieved November 21, 2014 from http://www.countyhealthrankings.org/app/virginia/2013/compare?counties=155%2B121%2B750%2B063%2B071

Graffman, K. and Börejesson, C. (2011). "We are looking forward to some cool quotes!" Perspectives in applied ethnography. *Ethnologia Europaea*, 41(1): 97–103.

Holmes, D. R. and Marcus, G. E. (2008). Collaboration today and the re-imagination of the classic scene of fieldwork encounter. *Collaborative Anthropologies*, 1: 81–101.

hooks, b. (2003). *Teaching community: A pedagogy of hope*. New York: Routledge.

Kelly, J. G. (1990). Changing contexts and the field of community psychology. *American Journal of Community Psychology*, 18: 769–792.

Lambert, J. (2007). Digital storytelling. *The Futurist*, 41(2): 25. Retrieved September 5, 2014 from http://ezproxy.lib.vt.edu:8080/login?url=http://search.proquest.com/docview/218580074?accountid=14826

Lassiter, L. E. (2001). From "reading over the shoulders of natives" to "Reading alongside natives," literally: toward a collaborative and reciprocal ethnography. *Journal of Anthropological Research*, 57(2): 137–149.

Lassiter, L. E. (2005). *The Chicago guide to collaborative ethnography*. Chicago: University of Chicago Press.

McQuillan, M. (Ed.) (2000). *The narrative reader*. London and New York: Routledge.

New River Valley Livability Initiative. (2013). "Livability in Action NewsLetter.' Retrieved September 15, 2014 from http://nrvlivability.org/

Pratt, M. B. (1995). *S/HE*. Ithaca, NY: Firebrand Books.

Rappaport, J. (1995). Empowerment meets narrative: Listening to stories and creating settings. *American Journal of Community Psychology*, 23(5): 795–807.

Wells, G. (1999). *Dialogic inquiry: Towards a sociocultural practices and theory of education*. Cambridge, UK: Cambridge University Press.

# 6

# SHAPING THE ARTFUL CITY

## A Case Study of Urban Economic Reinvention

*A. Scott Tate*

## Introduction

Cities and regions regularly incorporate art and culture in strategies for economic development. In part, the phenomenon has been driven by the increased importance of place marketing and branding in our neoliberal era. In a hyper-competitive global economic marketplace, development leaders construct "creative" identities to "sell" to both internal and external audiences (Griffiths, 1998; Hague, Hague, and Breitbach, 2011; Kearns and Philo, 1993). At this level, the work of cultural development is aimed at crafting the idea of a place or altering an established location's identity (Shields, 1991) and shaping a new imagined geography (Massey, 1995) or urban imaginary (Cinar and Bender, 2007). Marketing and branding constitute a portion of such endeavors. Indeed, a significant scholarly literature addresses place marketing and branding. However, a need remains: "to give attention to the complexity involved in place transformation which the branding literature seems to ignore or simplify" (Nyseth and Viken, 2009, p. 4).

This chapter explores a question that emerges from this perceived imperative for more robust analyses of place re-identification processes: What does it mean to craft and promote a city as a place for arts and culture? Communities are shaped by policies, programs, and physical improvements and through less tangible but still powerful means: symbols and stories, branding tactics and marketing campaigns, events and performances, changing aesthetics, and spatial functions.

Drawing on research conducted for a more extensive ethnographic case study (Tate, 2012), this chapter examines one city's efforts to employ arts and culture-focused place reinvention (Nyseth and Viken, 2009). Such a reorientation offers many positive development possibilities, and public decision makers and residents frequently support arts projects. Arts-based urban identities encompass both tangible and intangible elements, and the line between the perceptual and the material is a fuzzy one. Indeed, leaders who pursue arts-centered place marketing are not only touting the existence of cultural assets but may be influencing an array of corresponding policies, practices, and projects that alter the spatial, economic, social, and cultural makeup of their city. Marketing messages are a small part of such initiatives but often may reflect more comprehensive processes of community re-identification. The systemic impacts of broader cultural development efforts are complex, often mixed, and difficult to gauge easily.

Subsequent sections offer an overview of the challenges associated with such place reinvention and a short summary of the study's approach; background and description of the case site, Roanoke, Virginia; a discussion of themes and their implications that emerged from intensive exploration of this city's cultural development experience; and concluding observations aimed at assisting cultural leaders, public officials, development practitioners, and community researchers pursuing such initiatives.

## Problem Overview and Study Approach

Few studies have sought to address the question of arts-focused place re-identification in the particular, utilizing "thick description" (Geertz, 1983) and exploring the wider universe of contested meanings and interests at play in place reinvention processes. Moreover, existing analyses tend to be dominated by research on global cities and larger metropolitan areas. Small and mid-sized cities are far more numerous than megalopolises, yet there is a "woeful neglect of the small city in the literature on urban studies" generally (Bell and Jayne, 2009, p. 2).

This inquiry focused on one place in depth. It describes Roanoke, VA's cultural regeneration project while seeking to elicit the complexity of its urban imaginary as a set of ideas in flux and tension. Though not their sole focus, Roanoke's city officials, planners, arts and cultural entities, and others have been engaged in a concerted effort to utilize arts and culture as a key driver of economic and community development. Community officials cite Roanoke's $2 million annual investment in arts and culture as "significantly higher" than any other comparable municipality in Virginia (Carr, personal communication, 2011). The city has invested significantly in public art, encouraged an explosive growth of festivals and events, and undertaken major capital improvements to downtown cultural anchor institutions. Art as a development strategy is surely one part of Roanoke's efforts to reinvent itself economically.

This study offers one response to the diagnostic challenge that researchers and analysts encounter when struggling to conceptualize and examine urban cultural development initiatives. A number of studies have identified a prevalent "legitimizing," "upbeat," "globalist," narrative of "culture as development"

(Banks and O'Connor, 2009; Jensen, 2007: Miller and Yudice, 2002; Strom, 2003). Strom has observed that "Each city's narrative is unique, but 'culture as development' has become such a prevalent strategy that variations on these stories can be found in cities throughout the United States" (Strom, 2003, p. 261).

Communities that subscribe to this imaginary of art and culture believe a focus on such projects and programs will yield positive economic impacts, including attracting specific labor groups and tourists. Cities also hope these strategies will create jobs (Bianchini et al., 1988; Florida, 2002; Myerscough and Bruce, 1988; Pratt, 1997). There are numerous success stories of places that have experienced downtown revitalization, increased visitation, and other positive economic impacts related to cultural development initiatives.

Nonetheless, careful analyses indicate that causal relationships between investment in cultural industries and facilities and associated economic impacts are tenuous and uncertain (Evans and Foord, 2003; Markusen and Gadwa, 2010; Noll and Zimbalist, 1997); may increase social and economic inequalities (Florida, 2005a, 2005b; Mercer, 2005; Stern and Seifert, 2008); and disproportionately concentrate benefits on downtown cores and arts districts while drawing resources away from non-core neighborhoods (Mercer, 2005; Stern and Seifert, 2008; Rosenstein, 2009). Despite this evidence, city officials, developers, and tourism professionals continue to seek to advance an arts-focused imaginary for their communities through policy decisions, planning strategies, development projects, and various forms of boosterism, including marketing and branding efforts.

The rhetoric of "culture as development" tends to overstate the positive impacts and to understate the more negative or mixed implications of such strategies and their specific elements. The skewed character of the arts-based development narrative contributes to failures of cultural policy design and implementation.

This chapter draws on an ethnographic case study. Case analyses investigate a selected phenomenon in depth and incorporate a number of different data collection approaches (Hamel, Dufour, and Fortin, 1993; Yin, 2009, p. 18). The descriptor "ethnographic" suggests a study that employs some form of participant observation as one of its data collection methods and that seeks to understand one or more phenomena through the everyday experiences of people (Crang and Cook, 2007, p. 1).

I selected Roanoke, VA as a site likely to inform understanding of urban imaginaries because the city is actively engaged in efforts to become a place "synonymous with arts and culture" (Carr, personal communication, 2011). The case seemed likely both to have intrinsic significance and to offer theoretical insights as a more or less typical example of the processes through which the intersections of art, economy, and place are negotiated by arts activists, political officials, and cultural leaders in a small city (Stake, 1995, p. 3; Yin, 2009, p. 48). This was also an opportunistic sampling. My research began as a citywide arts and cultural planning process was getting underway. My interviews occurred while process-related experiences were fresh in participants' minds. My study data consisted primarily of key informant interviews supplemented by participant observation and unobtrusive data drawn from public and private archival materials. Throughout, I sought to identify themes related to place re-identification activities and concerns, including respondent processes of meaning construction and negotiation around an arts-focused urban imaginary.

## Case Background and Description

Roanoke, VA today is a medium-sized city with a core population of 98,465 (U.S. Census, 2013) and an area population of more than 250,000. Ringed by the Blue Ridge Mountains, the community is situated in a valley in western Virginia. Present-day Roanoke emerged from a colonial era settlement known as Big Lick. Many early pioneers arrived from the north through the larger Shenandoah Valley via what became known as the Great Wagon Road. The immigrants were often newly arrived Scots-Irish, English, German, and Dutch individuals and families who, "travelled on foot or on horseback, carrying their household goods on pack horses" (Warren, 1940, p. 7). A small community gradually developed.

In 1880, Big Lick consisted of a collection of churches, general stores, blacksmith shops, saloons, and tobacco warehouses with 669 residents (Dotson, 2007, p. 4). Most of the valley was open farmland and wetlands and crossed by a single railroad line. About this time, however, Philadelphia-based financial companies and investors were intensifying their engagement with railroad construction, land speculation, and mineral extraction throughout the southern Appalachians.

Attracted to the area by its proximity to southwest Virginia's coalfields, its abundant land, and by local incentive dollars, representatives of the newly formed Norfolk and Western Railroad (N&W) arrived in Big Lick in early 1881. The N&W began surveying sites around the marshes and in the pastures and fields east of the village for a junction, along with a company-owned hotel, depot, machine shops, railroad office building, and housing for workmen and officials (Dotson, 2007, p. 8).

The transformation from the small town of Big Lick to the city of Roanoke was swift and stunning. From 1882 to 1890, Roanoke's population grew by 2,000 percent, and "no city in the South grew faster" (Dotson, 2007, p. 1). Regional boosters christened the burgeoning town as the "Magic City of the New South" (Dotson, 2007, p. 1). A travel writer of the period described his first impressions of the city from an incoming train:

> Roanoke blazes up ahead like an illumination; red-mouthed furnace chimneys lift like giant torches above the plain; the roar of machinery, the

> whistle of engines, the ceaseless hum of labor and life in the very heart of a quiet, mountain-locked valley.
>
> (Ingersol, in Dotson, 2007, p. 15)

Dotson (2007) has described Roanoke's rapid rise in the 1880s and 1890s and argued that the city evidenced characteristics that some urban historians have associated with "boomtown syndrome." These included public revenue shortfalls, lack of adequate public services, sanitation difficulties, infrastructure challenges, social tensions, housing inadequacies, an unattractive cityscape, and increasing rates of alcoholism, rowdiness, crime, disease and vice (Dotson, 2007, p. 29).

A national economic downturn in 1893 briefly halted Roanoke's growth, although the city's population reached 50,000 by 1920. Expansion slowed significantly thereafter. Prohibition and economic depression took their toll on Roanoke's economy as thriving local businesses, such as the Virginia Brewing Company, collapsed; dozens of African American– and white-owned saloons closed, and the N&W slowed its construction and machine works operations. Many who originally came to Roanoke for its "magic" migrated to northern cities during the 1920s and 1930s (Dotson, 2007).

City economic boosters sought to rekindle faster-paced economic growth by rebranding the community as the "Star City of the South" in the 1940s. In 1949, the city's chamber of commerce erected what remains the largest manufactured star in the United States (Colbert, 2010, p. 170) as the centerpiece of a marketing initiative. It is still perched atop Mill Mountain, one of the few peaks located inside a city's limits in the U.S. The star's 2,000 feet of neon tubing emit 17,500 watts of light, visible up to sixty miles away (Colbert, 2010, p. 171).

Despite the best efforts of city boosters to shape an economically prosperous "Star City" in the 1940s and 1950s, Roanoke's economy was challenged during that period as the N&W ceased passenger rail service and closed its locomotive manufacturing operations in the 1950s, throwing thousands out of work. Company-built houses also gradually deteriorated during this period, contributing to the decline of several of the city's lower- and middle-income neighborhoods (Dotson, 2007).

While black and white schoolchildren began attending integrated schools in Roanoke in the 1950s, segregationist practices and policies continued to have pronounced adverse impacts on the predominately African American sections of the city. Urban renewal in Roanoke, most active from the 1950s through the 1970s, for example, destroyed historically vibrant black neighborhoods in the city's northeast quadrant. Former *Roanoke Times* reporter Mary Bishop (1995) and Columbia University scholar Mindy Thompson Fullilove (2004) have captured Roanoke's story of urban redevelopment and racial segregation with thoughtfulness and sensitivity.

The negative impacts of urban renewal on traditionally strong African American neighborhoods reduced downtown housing and suburban commercial developments and contributed to the demise of a once-thriving city center. Central Roanoke in the decade preceding 1986 had been so altered by the rise of suburban shopping centers as to give the downtown "an eerie deserted feeling after dark ... with no crowds downtown at Christmas" (Beagle, 1986, p. 12).

Though not on the same scale as its Magic City days, downtown Roanoke is in the midst of a transformation that long-term city dwellers perceive as remarkable. The number of downtown residents rose from a scant fifty in 2000 to 610 by April of 2010, a rise of more than 1,600 percent (Boone, 2011). Since that time, that number has continued to rise with the creation and lease or sale of more than 500 additional downtown apartments.

The change in the past ten years has been significant, and every one of my interviewees confirmed or commented on this trend in some way. J. Nelson, a leader of a Roanoke arts organization, said the city today is "a whole different place now ... as far as the past 12–13 years" (personal interview, 2011). A. Dennison, a local artist, described Roanoke during the last several years as "going through a transformation" (personal interview, 2011).

The identity of twenty-first century Roanoke includes a resurgent downtown, thriving health care and professional economic sectors, and abundant outdoor recreation opportunities. Nonetheless, despite the many positive trends, Roanoke today remains a "wounded city" (Schneider and Susser, 2003) with lingering sores that include inequality, cultural loss, and a distrust of local government by low-income and African American citizens (Shareef, in Fullilove, 2004, p. 99). In addition to neighborhood and race-based divides, heavy concentrations of poverty continue to exist in Roanoke. The 2013 poverty rate in the city was 21.1 percent, nearly twice the state average of 11.1 percent (U.S. Census, 2013).

Nonetheless, Roanoke boasts rising numbers of technology-based, health care, and creative sector businesses. Arts and culture have been prominent features of the city's current resurgence. All of my interview respondents suggested the community had become a place known for its arts and culture. As W. Thompson observed,

> In moving back to Roanoke eight years ago, I saw a huge change [sic] ... a paradigm shift of some sort where [the city's] focus was not only going to be on health care, but it was also going to be on arts and culture. And I think that has been evident ... It's just been boom, boom, boom, boom, one thing after another. The Marginal Arts Festival this year was incredible. ... You know at one time it used to be, and maybe still is to a certain degree, that Asheville was the place to go for arts and culture. But I'm beginning to see that people are not talking about that being the place to go. More and more I hear people say that the arts and culture are in Roanoke. And it's doing nothing but growing by leaps and bounds every year.
>
> (personal interview, 2011)

As the director of the Roanoke Valley Convention and Visitors Bureau stated in a newspaper interview in 2011, "We are known for our railroad heritage, but now with galleries sprouting everywhere, we're really developing a reputation as a hub for the arts in Virginia" (Bair and Wright, 2011). In addition, many of my interview respondents echoed the thought that, in Roanoke, "arts and culture is creating this amazing sense of community" (J. Nelson, personal interview, 2011).

The city has a number of arts and cultural organizations. Roanoke's Center in the Square houses several of these entities and recently underwent a $27 million dollar renovation. The new Center in the Square is home to the Mill Mountain Theatre, the Harrison Museum of African-American Culture, Opera Roanoke, the Roanoke Ballet Theater, the Science Museum of Western Virginia, and the Western Virginia History Museum. The Center's facilities include a rooftop deck, a planetarium, four aquariums, and a butterfly habitat. The following sections briefly trace the origins and key features of three key exemplars of Roanoke's ongoing arts-based economic reinvention: the Taubman Museum of Art, the Roanoke Arts and Cultural Plan, and the Roanoke Marginal Arts Festival.

### The Taubman Museum of Art

The Taubman Museum of Art is the most visible example of Roanoke's identification with arts and culture. The Taubman is a strikingly prominent addition to the city's downtown architecture, a $66 million building designed by Los Angeles architect Randall Stout in a contemporary style akin to the work

**FIGURE 6.1**   The Roanoke, Virginia, city skyline, featuring the Taubman Museum in the foreground

of his well-known mentor Frank Gehry, designer of the Guggenheim in Bilbao, Spain. Knox and Mayer have cited the Taubman as "a good example of a cultural facility designed not only to provide exhibit space for an art collection but also to signal the town's aspiration to be 'on the map'" (2009, p. 158).

The Taubman arose from a predecessor's growing pains. The Art Museum of Western Virginia rented space in the Center in the Square. On January 31, 1999, the Museum's board announced that its existing facilities were no longer adequate, due to new collections and visitation numbers. In June 2000, Roanoke's mayor announced plans for a new building, containing new space for the art museum and an IMAX theatre. The city council pledged $4 million to the project (Kittredge, 2008).

The proposed new facility received several bequests of significant, especially American, paintings. The Museum board hired Georganna Bingham, an arts leader with established fundraising success, as executive director and chose Stout as architect for the project. Stout grew up in east Tennessee but had designed buildings around the world as a senior associate in Frank Gehry's firm before opening his own practice in 1996.

In an area with a high number of residents whose attitudes have been described as "very, very conservative" (Nelson, personal interview, 2011) and "resistant to change" (C. Phillips, personal interview, 2011), Stout's innovative design for the new museum had its detractors, many of whom continue to criticize the facility's architecture. The facility's board announced the architect's plan for the building in 2005, and it sparked a "lively debate" (Kittredge, 2008). Stout described the design as a metaphor for the region's natural landscape. Others have compared the structure to a spaceship or, more disparagingly, as "the wreck of the Flying Nun" (Kittredge, 2008). For her part, the museum's first executive director said, "It's a piece of art. People respond very differently to art" (Bingham, in Kittredge, 2008).

The city eventually dropped the IMAX theatre from plans for the structure due to its estimated cost. Groundbreaking occurred in 2005 and, in 2006, the museum announced higher than anticipated construction costs due to materials and labor price increases. In 2008, the facility was named the Taubman Museum of Art to honor its most generous donors, Nicholas and Jenny Taubman. Nicholas Taubman had been CEO of Roanoke-based Advance Auto Parts and served as U.S. Ambassador to Romania during the George W. Bush presidency. The Taubmans pledged an initial $15 million to the project and have remained the museum's largest donors (Kittredge, 2008).

The new facility opened with a gala attended by 1,200 people, each paying $250 to join honorary event hosts that included then–Virginia Governor Tim Kaine and Roanoke native and former professional football player Tiki Barber. On Saturday, November 8, 2008, the day after the ball, the museum opened to the general public, and admission was free.

Roanoke officials and arts supporters collaborated to make the opening weekend a citywide celebration, complete with jugglers and jazz bands, puppets and street performers, ballet performances, and blues guitarists (Kittredge, 2008). That weekend brought 14,000 visitors to the museum. While Stout's building continued to generate interest and discussion, the Taubman's visitation numbers declined after the strong opening, and it failed, in its first year, to meet its estimated annual attendance of 170,000 people.

Partly as a result of its lower-than-expected number of visitors and despite its visibility and recognition, the museum soon experienced fiscal difficulties. The first year's operating budget was $3.75 million, while actual expenditures totaled $6.8 million (Allen, 2010). While initial expenditures reflected some start-up costs, outlays were nonetheless much higher than projected. As John Williamson, the organization's first board president, has observed, "Reality began to set in pretty quickly after the opening, and it's been a struggle ever since" (Allen, 2010).

Board members had focused on fundraising and construction in the years leading up to the opening and successfully raised their targeted goal of just under $70 million. The organization had initially hoped to keep construction costs at less than $50 million and establish a $20 million endowment for ongoing operations. Meanwhile, actual construction costs rose to $66 million, allowing latitude for only a $2.7 million endowment. That amount took a further hit with the financial collapse in 2008–2009, which caused the endowment's value to shrink from $2.7 to $2.2 million (Allen, 2010).

The museum's leadership responded to its somewhat disappointing first year by reducing the organization's staff from fifty-two to twenty-three (Allen, 2010). Bingham retired as director in 2009. The Board selected a new director, to whom I refer in this chapter as M. Hart. Hart worked with the board to craft a revised strategic plan, and he described in an interview with me how a part of his work has included "trying to inform patrons about what it takes to have a quality art museum in Roanoke with only a minimal public investment" (personal interview, 2011).

During Hart's tenure, one part of the Taubman's core positioning strategy has been to engage the general public more often and in a greater variety of ways to help Roanokers identify the institution as "their museum" (Allen, 2010). Hart organized and led two town-hall meetings at the Taubman to inform—and solicit feedback from—patrons and the general public on his efforts to address the organization's financial challenges. I attended the second such meeting on Wednesday, May 18, 2011. The setting was striking, as the gathering occurred in the museum's soaring, glass-fronted atrium. Hart reported that the arts facility had

> delivered on all the major promises made at [an earlier] meeting. Reduced admission and membership prices, free admission for Roanoke public school students, more free events, more collaboration with regional artists, more art classes—all of those things have come to pass.
>
> (Allen, 2011b)

J. Nelson, the leader of a major arts and cultural organization in Roanoke, shared how she had been struck by how Hart had addressed a neighborhood meeting by

> talking with them and saying, do you know about the museum, and is it important to you or no, and if it isn't, why isn't it? And ... there was [sic] a plumber or electrician, something like that, and he [stated] there is nothing at the museum for me, I am not interested so [Hart] said, well, I will tell you what, you have never seen our HVAC system, and if you come over there, it is state-of-the-art and it's the coolest part of the museum. I will give you a back scene tour.
>
> (personal interview, 2011)

Hart worked diligently to make the Museum more accessible to the community. As noted, for example, the Taubman has partnered with Roanoke City Schools to offer free attendance to its students. Through strategic corporate sponsorships, the museum also expanded its existing Spectacular Saturdays program from a monthly free attendance day to a weekly feature with no admission fee for all, focused around family and youth-friendly activities. My family and I attended several of these events, remarking each time on the number and diversity of people there. We struck up a conversation with an older gentleman on one Saturday who remarked how lucky we were to have this museum in Roanoke, just like you'd find in a "real" big city. In addition to reaching out to the general public, Taubman officials have worked since 2010 to build strong relationships with established artists in Roanoke.

In late 2012, Hart stepped down as Taubman executive director shortly after voicing public concerns about the museum's financial health. Benefactors stepped in, led by the Taubman family and a $150,000 contribution from Advance Auto Parts, underwriting year-round free general admission to the general public. The Taubman board of directors named Della Watkins, formerly with the Virginia Museum of Fine Arts in Richmond, the museum's new executive director in January 2013 (Squires, 2013).

### Arts and Culture Plan

The decision to craft an arts and culture plan for Roanoke has its own origin story. Virginia adheres to the Dillon Rule, meaning cities and municipalities enjoy only those express powers authorized by state statute. In 2006, the Commonwealth's legislature passed a law authorizing a select number of jurisdictions to create designated districts and to impose differential taxing of arts-related enterprises in those areas. Soon thereafter, officials and arts leaders from cities not granted this authority began lobbying the Commonwealth's General Assembly to expand the law to include them.

In late 2009, as discussions concerning arts districts continued around the state, Roanoke's planning office brought together interested stakeholders, including staff members from the Arts Council and the Taubman and a number of other cultural organizations, to discuss forming a proposed "Arts District." In public forums, city officials described the meeting as a watershed moment. Participants debated the location and implications of such a district, who would be included, who might be left out. Then Hart, then executive director of the Taubman Museum of Art, asked, "How does such a district fit into the city's arts and cultural plan?" (C. Phillips, personal interview, 2011). Hart described the rationale for this question to me in an interview as an attempt to encourage city officials and arts leaders to think strategically (personal interview, 2011). City officials, in interviews and public meetings, indicated they had been surprised by the query. Roanoke's planning staff responded by proposing a city-wide arts and cultural planning process, as explained on the community's Website,

> ... we started to realize that the [arts district] program should be one of many tools to encourage development of arts and culture in Roanoke. Such tools should be part of an overall strategy—a strategy that was conspicuously absent. That's when we embarked on a process to develop a plan. While City staff working with the Roanoke Arts Commission (RAC) is leading the process, we want the plan to support and guide anyone involved in the development of Roanoke's arts and cultural scene.
>
> (City of Roanoke, 2011a)

The idea was discussed internally at the city's RAC meetings and then brought to the Roanoke City Council, which charged the Commission and the Planning Department with carrying out a planning process that would result in a city-wide arts and cultural strategy. Roanoke's planning staff began laying the groundwork for preparation of an official arts and cultural blueprint in spring of 2010.

A city ordinance had earlier established the Roanoke Arts Commission in 1983 to "advise and assist City Council on matters relating to the advancement of the arts and humanities within the city" (City of Roanoke, 2011a). The Commission's fifteen volunteer members have long included a mix of arts advocates, nonprofit leaders, business professionals, and private citizens. The RAC is all-volunteer but is supported by a paid, full-time Arts and Culture Coordinator, a position established in 2006 and housed in the city's economic development office. The Arts and Culture Coordinator supports the Commission, oversees the city's Public Art Program, and serves as an arts and culture planner and development official.

City Council had precedent for tasking the RAC with developing the Arts and Culture Plan. The Commission had been centrally involved in the creation of the City's first Public Art Plan in 2003. Roanoke's City Council established the city's public art program in 2002 and simultaneously charged the RAC with developing a detailed plan for public art. Council approved hiring a consultant to assist with that process in 2004. The Commission worked with that contractor to conduct a series of four public workshops, community surveys, and key stakeholder interviews to inform the plan's development (City of Roanoke, 2011a). That effort was eventually entitled "Art for Everyone: Roanoke Public Art Plan" (City of Roanoke, 2011c).

The City Council formally adopted the new strategy in 2006, and it became part of Roanoke's comprehensive plan. The city also hired an Arts and Culture Coordinator at that time and assigned her the primary duty of implementing the plan in coordination with the RAC. A new Public Art Policy formalized the responsibility in winter 2006. It conferred joint authority on the Commission and city staff (in the form of the Arts and Culture Coordinator) to develop comprehensive guidelines for implementation of the new initiative.

Under the policy's provisions, the RAC and the Coordinator recommend appropriate sites and advise on policy and procedural matters pertaining to public art throughout the city. The community commissioned its first public work of art in October 2008, a thirty-foot tall stainless steel sculpture, *In My Hands*, by Baltimore artist Rodney Carroll. The piece is on display in front of the Roanoke Performing Arts Center. Later that month, the RAC launched a temporary exhibit dubbed "AIR: Art in Roanoke," which placed eight pieces in sites around the city for a period of eighteen months. The Commission has since overseen the installation of several other permanent works and a second temporary exhibit, AIR II. The group has also worked to develop walking tours of the city's collection of approximately 100 public art works (City of Roanoke, 2011b).

The public art project has helped to form Roanoke's arts and culture identity, as this arts organization leader observed,

> Of course the public art, I mean I have to keep saying the Public Art Project is amazing, to have that in our greenways, to have that in our public spaces, where everywhere you are going, I think there is even more and more for them, a drive to do that, so that when you are in public places that you will see art, it will be part of your experience of those places.
>
> (J. Nelson, personal interview, 2011)

The RAC coordinated the initial planning process, supported by the Arts and Culture Coordinator, planning department officials, and additional community arts and cultural leaders. The Commission conducted focus groups with arts and culture stakeholders in May 2010 to refine an approach to craft the arts plan. The RAC developed a vision statement to guide the process during summer 2010 and formally adopted advocacy, celebration, collaboration, education, innovation, and inclusion as working values on October 12, 2010 (RAC, 2011).

Overall, the city held eleven public meetings to gather input for the initiative, including three events held during October 2010. More than 1, 200 respondents completed an on-line survey and commented on Roanoke's arts and cultural offerings and opportunities. In addition, the RAC and the city's arts and culture coordinator worked with other team members to examine more than twenty-five arts and cultural plans from other communities in the U.S. The Commission also utilized a consultant organization, Partners in Performance! The firm, which specializes in strategic planning for collaborative arts- and culture-based efforts, provided analytical data and offered feedback on the plan and the RAC's decision process (City of Roanoke, 2011b, p. 5).

The Commission was initially unprepared to lead development of the arts and cultural plan. Prior to this assignment, board meetings had usually been "fun," consisting of discussions of upcoming events and activities of the different arts and culture organizations or of possible artists and works for the public art program (J. Martin, personal interview, 2011). As work on the city plan progressed, however, RAC members disagreed concerning the effort's goals. A central question became, "Who are we trying to serve?" (J. Nelson, personal interview, 2011). The arts and cultural plan included a considerably broader range of concerns than Commission members and city officials had originally anticipated. Some RAC representatives expressed apprehension about such a broad-based approach and opposed shifting the framework's focus from supporting individual artists and arts-based organizations.

Moreover, serving as a Commissioner proved doubly challenging when individuals also represented institutions. The role of institutional representative, such as a museum executive director, for example, necessitated active engagement in the planning process on behalf of organizational interests, while the RAC role required collaborative development of a plan for the city's overall benefit. As a result of these tensions, the group's meetings shortly were "no longer fun" (J. Martin, personal interview, 2011). The process was, "… a hard one, because we all are going to have our territory and we all want to protect that territory" (J. Nelson, personal interview, 2011).

In an interview with me, the city's Arts and Cultural Coordinator observed that several RAC members, many of whom were executive directors of local arts and cultural organizations, voiced their discomfort as possible plan elements unfolded (M. Reed, personal interview, 2011). For example, some Commission participants argued that engaging neighborhoods and extending arts and cultural activities throughout the city would draw emphasis away from the plan's animating purpose that for some, at least, was to solidify support for a downtown arts and cultural district.

Meanwhile, arts and cultural organizations in Roanoke were experiencing increased financial constraints. As the number of arts organizations and venues in the city has grown, the area's overall population and wealth have remained relatively static. The 2008 recession-created financial challenges in the U.S. and continuing globalization of the world's economy also increased the relative conditions of competition and scarcity confronting the city's arts entities. As a result, arts and cultural organizations in Roanoke have struggled to maintain financial support from private donors and from local, state, and federal governments.

An interviewee who has led one of the city's larger arts organizations discussed some of the fiscal difficulties confronting the arts sector in Roanoke:

> Right now the money is such a big thing in trying to figure out … how do we identify what are the most important pieces that have to be part of an arts community to support it, and which things maybe need to—I am sorry, I just need to be very careful how I put all this, but which things may need to be pulled together and infused into another component to make that stronger? There has to be that question of, do we need two or three or four theatre groups? Or do we need people to come together and become one strong, really well done quality, and not to say that the different ones aren't, but in a community like this, where the funding is already so sparse, to spread it out so much, is that really what's best for our community? And I think that always for us has to be that bottom line question. Are we doing what's best for our community at large? In supporting the arts community, it's not about the Arts Council, it's not about the Taubman Museum, it's not about the Symphony, it's not about even one of our little burgeoning arts organizations, it's about this community … Are we helping our community, or are we hurting by asking it to try to support so many things and it's not really able to support them in a way to where they can continue to produce high quality art and bring that back out to our community? So are we actually doing a disservice to the community if we are doing mediocre [things]?
>
> (J. Nelson, personal interview, 2011)

Roanoke City Council unanimously adopted the Arts and Cultural Plan in August 2011. The final framework provided an overview of the process that created it, and its executive summary listed three cross-cutting thematic findings of synergy, collaboration, and creative solutions (City of Roanoke, 2011b p. 5). Interestingly, the plan's recommendations are conservative, as stated in its summary, "In this time of limited resources, this plan does not propose new or additional City funding to support arts and culture in the Roanoke area" (City of Roanoke, 2011b, p. 5). The arts reporter for the regional newspaper, *The Roanoke Times*, concluded in his wrap-up of the year (2011) in arts and culture, "What effect the plan will have in the long term, however, remains a bit of an enigma" (Allen, 2012, p. E-6).

The final plan included specific recommendations under the rubric of three broad goals of economy, livability, and lifelong learning. Below are excerpts from the plan, which provided a defining sentence for each of its three aspirations:

- Develop our economy—A Vibrant Region-Healthy Economy
- Strategically advance arts and culture as a significant contributor to the growth of the region and an essential element in the Roanoke brand by supporting our strongest assets while fostering

a sustainable, collaborative public/private network that retains the flexibility required for innovation among artists, entrepreneurs, and arts organizations.

- Increase livability—Livable Communities and Engaged Neighborhoods
- Integrate arts and cultural activities in neighborhood-level planning so that our cultural heritage and contemporary assets are included in events, physical design and revitalization strategies of neighborhoods in a fashion that highlights local talent city wide.
- Foster an environment of lifelong learning, participation and education.
- Increase access for all residents to the vast resources of schools, colleges, universities, institutions, organizations and publicly available arts and cultural assets.

(City of Roanoke, 2011b, p. 7)

For each of these aims, the plan described some general policy approaches and strategic initiatives, then offered a matrix of specific actions with a suggested time frame and a listing of the entities tasked with implementation. For example, the first action item under "develop our economy" was to "structure city grants, capital and line item funding to implement plan recommendations for collaboration, neighborhood outreach and pursuit of diverse audiences" (City of Roanoke, 2011b, p. 13). The report identified the RAC as the primary entity responsible for this activity and listed a number of possible partners.

It is too early to know the impact of the plan's proposed activities. A committee composed of several arts commission members, city officials, and other key stakeholders meets monthly to coordinate the plan's execution (Allen, 2012, p. 3). Judgments concerning the framework's significance vary, but the formal incorporation of arts and culture aspirations into the city's comprehensive plan represented a significant step for the community,

> I don't know honestly that the plan has created a whole lot of new things as much as it has put it in a package so that people can see it. And that it is part of now what is the governmental plan, so that there can be backing for it and support for it on that level, which is really important.
>
> (J. Nelson, personal interview, 2011)

Dan Casey, a columnist who writes about city concerns, argued in a *Roanoke Times* commentary in 2011 that the city's overall policy stance toward art and culture had shifted positively in recent years. Specifically, he recalled how, in 2009, a local sculptor was prohibited from installing an artistic bike rack on a city sidewalk but that in 2011, Roanoke had changed streetscape ordinances to encourage public art in the form of benches, bike racks, and bus stops. As Casey stated,

Two years ago, the city was prohibiting [functional public art]. Now, its fine print allows them. Its officials are celebrating them. And in some cases taxpayers are footing the bills. Folks seem excited. You can call this whatever you want. Looks like progress to me.

(Casey, 2011, p. 9)

Many of the individual artists I interviewed, however, voiced mixed feelings about the city's stance. Artists and gallery operators L. Runnel, F. Neely, and E. Calhoun said the city of Roanoke had not been a major impediment to their businesses, but neither had it provided them financial or technical support (personal interviews, 2011). Each suggested the city should provide funding in small amounts to assist individual artists with arts-based projects and neighborhood festivals. The limited community funding available is awarded instead to arts institutions, although a recent shift toward awarding neighborhood organization grants represented a move in what these individuals considered a positive direction. My interviewees also suggested the city could make it much easier for artists to display work in downtown empty storefronts, which artists do in other cities, and that changes were needed in current regulations that prohibit or curtail busking and street performers.

The RAC plan seems to have spurred a significant dialogue about arts and culture in the city. As one arts organization leader said, "So I think those are conversations that are happening and I think that they are constructive and healthy conversations. But I think that we are in the midst of that." (J. Nelson, personal interview, 2011).

## Marginal Arts Festival

The Roanoke Marginal Arts Festival (MAF) is a "six-day festival of art beyond the predictable that nurtures local identity and promotes contemporary art from the local to the international" (Marginalarts.com, 2011). The MAF completed its seventh iteration in 2014. My first direct experience with the MAF in 2011 was memorable. My son and I had scurried to a standing spot along the parade route in downtown Roanoke. My son heard the parade first: "Drums!" Then, he pointed, "Look, puppets!" My eyes followed his finger and, indeed, there were marionettes, towering, ten-foot-high puppets slowly weaving. We also spotted a squadron of butterfly-winged dancers, a rat float, and space creatures. Meanwhile, a phalanx of figures adorned with the names of financial institutions would periodically stumble and fall to the ground, a moving "financial collapse." The crowds were sparse but excited and mobile. Spectators would watch the procession weave past and then scamper to another spot along its circuitous journey winding through the major streets, parking lots, and even an alley or two toward its final destination near the city's epicenter, beside the Taubman Museum and adjacent to the Wells Fargo building, the iconic City Market Building and the double set of railroad tracks that divide the city center from the northern neighborhoods and the English Tudor-Style Hotel Roanoke.

An Absurdist Street Carnivale immediately followed the parade and included an array of activities. Onlookers and procession participants joined together in tossing rubber chickens and merrily stomping, jumping, and dancing on giant sheets of bubble wrap. Performance artists orchestratedly smashed a piano. As we drove home, my son clutched two souvenir piano fragments of varnished black wood and proclaimed, "That was cool!"

As the organizers had proclaimed,

> This is the sort of festival Monty Python would put on! If you like the absurd, audacious, ludicrous, laconic, sublime or the serene, you'll find all of those things at MAF 2011. We welcome funny walks, ex-parrots, deadpan wit and rubber chickens of all sorts. Like the Pythons, Fluxists, and Dadaists, this festival draws upon historical arts movements as well as contemporary ideas in art to offer a fun, engaged and educational experience for all ages.
>
> (MAF, 2011, p. 1)

Arts festivals have a long history, and MAF organizers viewed their event as continuing "3,000-plus years of human festival tradition" (Marginalarts.com, 2011). The faculty and students of Community High School, a small private arts-focused secondary school in Roanoke initiated the city's first annual marginal arts festival in 2007. Arts movements in many cities aimed at recognizing and celebrating "fringe," "underground," or "alternative" artists and arts activities inspired the MAF's organizers.

Fringe arts festivals have emerged and expanded rapidly since the middle of the twentieth century. The first such event was created in Scotland as a response to exclusion, to the "marginal" placement of less recognized arts forms at the Edinburgh International Festival. That event began in 1947 as one strategy to emphasize the role of arts and culture in post–World War II Europe's redevelopment. As such, festival organizers emphasized the selection and inclusion of works of "agreed excellence" by artists whose merit was "beyond doubt" (Bruce, 1995, p. 147, quoted in Lane, 2003, p. 7). The fringe festival movement arose as a reaction to the exclusion of local Scottish artists and playwrights from the major international festival occurring in their own country (see Bruce, 1995; Lane, 2003). These individuals refused to accept this snub and constructed makeshift performance spaces around the festival's edges, at its "fringe." The Edinburgh Fringe Festival was born, eventually exceeding the size of the original event and morphing into a major worldwide attraction held for three weeks each August and now known as the "largest arts festival in the world" (Edfringe.com, 2011). A central Festival ethos, written into its charter, is that its organizers are "proud to include in our programme anyone with a story to tell and a venue willing to host them" (Edfringe.com, 2011).

Like their counterparts elsewhere, Roanoke MAF organizers have grappled with what it means to be fringe, with the role of art, and with the idea of the city itself. The Festival has been cited by such far-flung sources as the New York City–based *Brooklyn Rail* for being, "more anarchic and socially present than many of its [fringe festival] peers" (Fry, 2009, p. 1).

The Roanoke MAF's origins were rather unglamorous. Community High School was "looking for a fundraiser and we decided on Fat Tuesday" (N. Loman, personal interview, 2011). More specifically, the private school was interested in a non-traditional fund-raiser, and its educational focus, along with a majority of its faculty and administration, was arts-based. Fat Tuesday in Roanoke was a quiet time. The School held a fund-raiser on that day in 2006 that was sparsely attended, as the "only people coming were parents and friends of the school. It was a Tuesday night, in dead of winter, and we needed a way to include more people" (N. Loman, personal interview, 2011).

Loman, a faculty member at Community High School, took on the task of developing the event. He researched the time before Lent and the history of festivals during that period. His studies led him to a focus on art:

> ... there were a lot of tie-ins for how contemporary art really functioned ... it does sort of act as an alternative for many people to the cathedral in the church ... it does have a satirical commentary built into it on social issues ... it's not always the kind of art I like, but a lot of contemporary art has taken on this social and spiritual leadership role. I was just interested in advancing the idea of a contemporarized Fat Tuesday or Carnivale.
>
> (N. Loman, personal interview, 2011)

In addition to focusing on art, Loman crafted the event with the larger arts and culture milieu of the city of Roanoke in mind. As he recalled, "my idea was to start with this intention to include the type of things that were missing from the local arts scene" (personal interview, 2011). An interesting facet of the MAF that began with its first year was an emphasis on events organized and led by curators. The organizers' responsibilities ranged from selecting a venue, coordinating with that site, preparing a space, recruiting and coordinating with artists, and staffing the event. Some curators ended up painting walls, hanging canvasses, and completing tasks to which they had previously been unaccustomed. For many MAF stewards, "logistics were *hard*" (A. Stuart, personal interview, 2011, her emphasis).

Loman explained that Festival curators were expected to produce experiences that served as a critique and aspired to fill gaps in the local arts scene rather than simply to reproduce activities already available. Loman's vision of curation was a do-it-yourself one. Curators, moreover, did not need to be artists but rather people who had a vision, an idea, and who could assemble and organize a group to produce an event around that concept.

L. Runnel, F. Neely, and E. Calhoun curated a major exhibit for the 2011 MAF. The three met as students at Hollins University, a private liberal arts institution for women located on the outskirts of Roanoke. At the university, they had lived in the arts house, a themed residence on campus. Upon graduating, they shared an interest in staying in Roanoke, partly due to connections formed in the city's arts community while students. E. Calhoun commented that in her hometown of Charlottesville, VA, artists did not typically work with one another, but in Roanoke everyone is "so excited to collaborate" (personal interview, 2011). F. Neely added that, "Roanoke is surprisingly big but you still have an opportunity to contribute and connect … it is rapidly growing, in really good ways" (personal interview, 2011).

Neely began working with the MAF during her junior year at Hollins. The trio's decision to form their own gallery was born partly of necessity. Roanoke appealed to them, they felt a part of the city's arts community, and they needed their own studio. Existing spaces were too expensive or too large. There were literally no low-rent studios available. So, they found an old building for rent that enabled them to have small individual studios that opened into a larger gallery space. The three christened their new location the "Unicorn Stables Project." When I visited their location, I followed a labyrinthine hallway that twisted up and into a large open area, expansive but welcoming, with couch and chairs and glowing light sticks.

All three women emphasized how the MAF and the individual relationships they had developed with artists had provided each with opportunities for growth, partnership, and marketing. The trio curated an exhibit, and the Unicorn Stables Project became a featured venue for the 2011 Festival. That fact attracted a *Roanoke Times* journalist who wrote a lengthy profile of the three, their gallery, and their MAF exhibition with the headline, "Secret Histories of a Space Age" (Allen, 2011a). The three credited the Festival with helping their studio attract media and public attention by "elevating their profile" (L. Runnel, personal interview, 2011).

The MAF effort was in the same spirit as their ongoing shows, in which their openings are "like performance art," in which everyone is encouraged to don costumes (F. Neely, personal interview, 2011). The trio has organized group theme shows with up to twenty visual, multimedia, and experimental artists. The events are mini-celebrations through which the local alternative arts network "celebrates community and each other" because "there is something magical about bringing people into a single space and seeing how they react" (F. Neely, personal interview, 2011).

Neely argued, "In Roanoke, it is very easy to contribute to culture … everyone here is making something happen" (personal interview, 2011). Runnel added that "five years ago, when I first came to Roanoke, there was not much to do downtown, not much zeitgeist," but now it seems like "new things are happening every day" (personal interview, 2011). There is a kind of "fearlessness to make things happen" (Runnel, personal interview, 2011).

MAF organizers have also gradually moved toward a more comprehensive understanding of both community and marginality so as to include neighborhoods and class, race, ethnicity, gender, and sexual orientation concerns. As the Festival's 2011 program guide suggested, "This year's festival, perhaps more so than ever, is taking the 'community' part of Community High to heart" (MAF, 2011). The Vexilloid Project that year, for example, represented an intentional, if not entirely successful, effort to engage neighborhood residents in the Festival.

A. Dennison was born and raised in Roanoke but spent much of his adult life in California before returning to the region a few years ago. Shortly after he moved back, Dennison met some of the artists, including Loman, who were active in alternative arts in Roanoke. Loman asked him to participate in the first Marginal Arts Festival, and he "has been involved ever since" (A. Dennison, personal interview, 2011). Dennison emphasized in his interview that the MAF has come a long way from its beginnings, which were "fairly small." In 2011, he took on organizing the Festival parade and leading the Vexilloid Project. He found curating the event more complex than he had expected because the project involved working with city administrators to secure permits and the police department to identify routes and traffic control support (A. Dennison, personal interview, 2011).

Vexilloid describes vexillary, or flag-like, objects used by organizations or countries as a form of representation. The Vexilloid Project sought to engage residents in telling stories of their neighborhood and working with local artists to design a place-specific vexillary for them (N. Loman, personal communication, 2011). Dennison and Loman worked together closely to lead the Project. Dennison described the work to me as "very challenging." In his view, the effort was important, a way to demonstrate that "art is not just an elitist thing that nobody understands" but also a way to express, discuss, and support community identity (A. Dennison, personal interview, 2011).

The response from neighborhood groups was "initially enthusiastic," but then it became difficult to keep people involved (A. Dennison, personal interview, 2011). Dennison and Loman attended meetings of six neighborhood groups around the city before deciding to focus on the Southeast Action Forum in southeast Roanoke. Overall community engagement with the project was low, however. This was particularly striking in light of the initial vision for the initiative:

> We also want to identify the creative individuals of the neighborhood: the artists and writers, poets, musicians, and crafts people of course, but also the unusual or overlooked eccentrics, the seamstresses, dancers, decorators, enthusiasts, activists and cartoonists. We want to talk to the historians, archivists and honored personalities, as well as troublesome renters, 'tweens and teens, immigrants, and the homeless. We want as many different perspectives on the notion of "neighborhood identity" that

we can get. We want to record the conversations and collect them into a document for public record. The Vexillum will be designed by neighbors, and assisted when necessary from outside, using the documents gathered as a source.

(N. Loman, personal communication, 2011)

Festival organizers hoped to employ the Vexilloid effort deliberately to engage people from city neighborhoods, particularly predominantly African American or more culturally and socially diverse areas. In speaking with the artist-leaders of this effort, I sensed both their pleasure at the Festival's growth and its vibrancy and their disappointment with the Vexilloid Project and the MAF's ongoing struggle to include or engage more people from marginalized groups and neighborhoods in the city more successfully. Dennison argues the Festival has engaged artists and others who felt disconnected, since "four years ago, I was marginalized, now, I don't feel that way" (A. Dennison, personal interview, 2011). He would like to use the arts to help other now marginalized groups have the same experience.

## Discussion

In some ways, Roanoke is a cautionary tale. The city aimed high with the construction of the Taubman Museum of Art and hoped for a Bilbao-like result (Frumkin and Kolendo, 2014). The term *Bilbao effect* refers to the positive urban development impacts of spectacular buildings such as the Guggenheim Museum in Bilbao, Spain. Many development practitioners and scholars have credited the museum's opening in 1997 with "transforming a gritty port city in northern Spain into a tourist magnet" (Lee, 2007). As Lee has suggested in his *New York Times* feature on the museum, "The iridescent structure wasn't just a new building; it was a cultural extravaganza" (2007).

However, the Guggenheim was not solely responsible for Bilbao's transformation. The city crafted a plan and implemented actions that included cleaning up its waterways, investing in its transportation infrastructure, and completing other downtown commercial and residential development projects (Plaza, 2007). Still,

Even for those who couldn't spell "Bilbao," let alone pronounce it (bill-BAH-o), the city became synonymous with the ensuing worldwide rush by urbanists to erect trophy buildings, in the hopes of turning second-tier cities into tourist magnets. The so-called Bilbao Effect was studied in universities throughout the world as a textbook example of how to repackage cities with "wow-factor" architecture. And as cities from Denver to Dubai followed in Bilbao's footsteps, Mr. Gehry and his fellow "starchitects" were elevated to the role of urban messiahs.

(Lee, 2007)

Roanoke was clearly following an established international trend, and the Taubman enjoyed a successful grand opening before financial and operating difficulties ensued. Bilbao, like Roanoke, has industrial roots with a population of approximately 350,000 people. Roanoke's metropolitan region has slightly more than 250,000 people. In its first year, however, the Guggenheim Museum welcomed nearly 100,000 visitors a month, and the large numbers continued, reaching roughly 1 million visitors per year during its first decade (Lee, 2007). The Taubman's visitation numbers failed to meet first year projections and continue to be a concern as of this writing. On March 19, 2014, *The New York Times* included a special feature in its Arts section on museums. The Taubman was featured as a museum "plagued by financial problems" (Wallis, 2014) and referred to as one of the "living-dead institutions, zombies whose preoccupation is daily survival" (Ellis, in Wallis, 2014).

Roanoke's culture story, however, is not so simply dismissed as a negative exemplar. Indeed, arts-influenced development efforts have played a central role in the city's continued downtown revitalization, neighborhood renewal, and earning of external accolades. Despite its struggles, even the Taubman has been a central piece in a remarkable city-wide economic re-identification. Downtown Roanoke continues to undergo development projects led by both public and private investment. The Taubman Musuem of Art's iconic facility is a key economic anchor, attention attractor, and architectural highlight. The museum has shifted focus toward greater public accessibility, enhanced inter-institutional collaboration, and efforts to strengthen the larger arts ecosystem in the region. The Taubman's influential role in forming the city's arts and cultural plan is one example.

Roanoke's experience with its arts and cultural plan is significant for, "Despite the fact that the creative city rubric has the potential to tie urban planning, economic development and arts and cultural policy efforts together, this has for the most part not happened in most American cities" (Markusen, 2006, p. 2). Roanoke's arts and cultural plan at least temporarily engaged these formerly siloed sectors in a joint effort. As Markusen has also observed,

> Few cities large or small have the expertise to bridge current balkanized bureaucratic structures, and few know how to work with multiple constituencies for cultural policy to develop an agenda that works. Some slap down "cultural districts" on maps without thinking about their viability or impact on neighbors or competitors. Some commission cultural plans from outsiders that have no after-life, since they are not generated through the efforts of local coalitions.
>
> (Markusen, 2006, p. 19)

Roanoke, rather than duplicating its effort with the Public Arts Plan that overwhelmingly relied on outside consultants, shouldered the task of crafting the Arts and Cultural Plan itself, with its own resources. The process was uneven and messy, generating tensions and creating still largely uncertain outcomes. Nonetheless, the initiative helped city officials develop a broader perspective on arts and culture and led to the final plan's focus on livability and engagement across the entire community.

Efforts to create the arts and cultural plan generated discussions that broadened city officials' focus beyond art's economic value as a development tool and toward its ability to further other shared community goals. This raises the question of whether Roanoke might now be moving toward a more holistic approach to arts- and culture-based development. In 2014, the city was named one of the "most livable" cities in America, by the U.S. Conference of Mayors (City of Roanoke, 2014). The recognition cited a program that emerged directly from the arts and cultural plan and its emphasis on cross-departmental and inter-organizational collaboration to extend performing and visual arts directly to Roanoke's neighborhoods. That initiative, Parks & Arts, identifies park spaces in or adjacent to under-resourced residential areas and partners with community organizations to develop events that include artists, dancers, musicians, and related activities. For residents who had not visited the Taubman or attended a performance of the Roanoke Symphony, Parks & Arts has helped bring these institutions into different parts of the city and provided a new experience.

The RAC and relevant city officials and the leaders of some of Roanoke's major arts institutions seem now to be placing greater importance on community and on working with artists engaged in alternative, or community-based, arts. The arts and cultural planning process is not solely responsible for this shift, nor is the Taubman. Rather, the change is occurring for several reasons, including financial concerns that incentivize collaboration and greater public engagement in an environment of resource constraints; the emerging prominence of Roanoke's alternative arts scene, thanks in part to the MAF; and heightened public awareness attained through conversations generated by the arts and culture planning process and the RAC.

MAF organizers describe their intent as an effort to expand the domain of arts and culture beyond the institutional and the mainstream. Festival activities have demonstrated this commitment. Yount, a local curator and artist, acknowledged Roanoke's traditional arts institutions were not overtly antagonistic to alternative artists but that institutional barriers did exist. He suggested the staff of larger cultural entities were less familiar with working with unconventional artists:

> My perspective is [Roanoke City and the formal arts institutions] haven't impeded anything. I think the institutions in general aren't used to working with people who do things the way we do things, so they don't know what their role should be and they might suspect that we are more trouble than we are worth and [the organizations are] not familiar with trying to facilitate DIY [Do-It-Yourself] grassroots experimental, collaborative activities. You know [the institutions] are set up to do different things.
>
> (Yount, personal interview, 2011)

The MAF's founders have sought to broaden the scope of the city's arts and cultural scene by encouraging greater recognition of alternative artists and arts forms. The Festival today counts institutions such as the Taubman, the Arts Council, and the RAC as principal supporters and partners. Indeed, many of my interviewees commented on the presence and significance of Roanoke's "alternative" or "edgy" arts community. Reed, the City's Arts and Culture Coordinator, also expressed this awareness in an interview with a *Roanoke Times* journalist:

> ... and are there some ways that we can financially support individual artists? There's a great group of artists ... doing this project called PROject proJECT. They're doing light shows downtown, and so we've been working with them on how to make that happen. So one of our big goals is to support these, for lack of a better term, guerilla art movements, things that artists are getting together and doing. Support them because that's what makes the city different and exciting.
>
> (Skeen, 2011)

## Conclusions

The case of cultural development and arts-based reinvention in Roanoke offers several possible lessons for development practitioners and urban researchers. The first observation concerns Roanoke's incorporation of multiple strategies: not only a cultural facility but a city-wide planning process, a public arts program, and an alternative arts festival, just to list those cited in this chapter. In selecting approaches, localities such as Roanoke might also look to balance attention to hard infrastructure with a focus on efforts to strengthen social capital, enhance collaboration, and build networks. Many of my interviewees commented on Roanoke's "arts scene." The Taubman has drawn extensive attention and scrutiny on its own terms, but it has also contributed to a larger arts ecosystem. City leaders supported multiple efforts and did not use the Taubman's financial struggles as a rationale for rejecting arts-based approaches. If anything, the community's public officials have consistently forwarded and welcomed cultural development efforts. Currently, the city is exploring options for establishing a more permanent public-private endowment model to support a range of arts institutions in Roanoke.

A second consideration suggested by Roanoke's experience for urban economic reinvention might be described as a "big tent" approach. Gradually, the city and its cultural institutions broadened their notions of arts and culture and of community. As the Marginal Arts Festival example illustrated, it may be useful to question what is missing from a region's cultural development portfolio. Not so long ago, fringe arts were virtually invisible in Roanoke whereas in 2014, alternative artists are a well-established and visible presence. In general, the city's arts efforts became more community-focused, engagement became paramount, and previously marginal arts activities became more recognized as the projects matured and generated momentum. Indeed, the horizon of possible approaches to arts- and culture-based development is quite broad (Currid, 2009; Knox and Mayer, 2009). Roanoke's arts- and culture-planning process highlighted the need to extend arts activities into neighborhoods and to nurture a wider variety of cultural activities.

Last, the importance of leadership and organization building is central. Efforts that thrive, or that survive in hard times, as the Taubman and the MAF have done, require champions. Beyond spark-plug figures such as Loman and Hart, attention to organization building and collaborative leadership seems paramount, certainly so in the case of Roanoke. The city's arts ecosystem includes several smaller cultural organizations, many of which are struggling. Leaders who are skilled at organizational development and who can diagnose problems and implement radical solutions when necessary are crucial. This does not mean that the onus is entirely on a cadre of cultural elites. Rather, the work of organization building requires a web of supporters, networks, funding streams, and policies. How does the cultural ecosystem help sustain organizations and mediate resource competition as needed? As seen in the arts and cultural planning process in Roanoke, conflict and collaboration are both present and necessary in multi-organizational efforts.

Roanoke's experience with arts-based economic "reinvention" suggests that such initiatives are marked by strong variety and complexity. The term *reinvention* tends to summon images of quick fixes and rapid transformations. Instead, economic change through the arts is more commonly uneven, longer term, and messy. The stories of the Taubman Museum of Art, the Marginal Arts Festival, and the Roanoke Arts and Cultural Plan each share these elements of mixed impacts, uneven progress, staged evolution, and contentious moments. In many ways, the evolution of each effort is distinct, and any lessons are necessarily limited.

Collectively, the three examples from Roanoke's larger project of cultural development constitute an argument for greater specificity, nuance, and a longer-term view in the broader discourse concerning arts-based approaches. News media, development professionals, and community researchers sometimes too readily designate projects and places as positive or negative development exemplars. Roanoke's tale contains lessons from both ends of that spectrum and ultimately provides a more mixed case. The Taubman may be an example of much that can go wrong with arts-based development, such as an over-emphasis on facility development and "star-chitecture" at the expense of organization building and arts ecosystem. Nevertheless, on closer examination, the museum also offers insight into ways to strengthen arts-based development, such as by enhancing connections among members of the arts community, conducting more substantive engagement activities, and better employing organizational development initiatives. Ultimately, a more tangled narrative results that is more difficult to decipher, harder to condense into a headline, but perhaps even more important to share.

Shaping the artful city is a process and a commitment to learning by doing. Research and experience in Roanoke suggest that this journey is more complex and fraught than commonly recognized, but also that the trip may still be well worth making.

## References

Allen, M. (2010). Taubman Museum of Art reveals lofty new goals for fundraising. *The Roanoke Times*, November 12. Retrieved November 15, 2010 from http://www.roanoke.com/news/roanoke/wb/267170.

Allen, M. (2011a). Sci-fi art. *The Roanoke Times*, February 26. Retrieved February 27, 11 from http://www.roanoke.com/extra/wb/278302

Allen, M. (2011b). Taubman in better shape, but still has work to do. *The Roanoke Times*, May 29. Retrieved May 30, 2011 from http://www.roanoke.com/extra/arts//wb/287998

Allen, M. (2012). Taubman Museum's portrait is etched in red ink. *The Roanoke Times*, January 8. Retrieved January 12, 2012 from http://www.roanoke.com/news/roanoke/wb/303245

Bair, D. and Wright, P. (2011). Quick trips: Art is the new star in Roanoke, Virginia. *The Miami Herald*, May 29. Retrieved October 11, 2011 from http://www.visitroanokeva.com/articles/index.cfm?action=view&articleID=30&menuID=291

Banks, M. and O'Connor, J. (2009). After the creative industries. *International Journal of Cultural Policy*, 15(4): 365–373.

Beagle, B. (1986). Times past. *The Roanoke Times*. Special Centennial Edition. Roanoke, VA.

Bell, D. and Jayne, M. (2009). Small cities: Towards a research agenda. *International Journal of Urban and Regional Research*, 33(3): 683–699.

Bianchini, F., Fisher, M., Montgomery, J., and Worpole, K. (1988). *City centres, city cultures*. Manchester, UK: Comedia and Centre for Local Economic Strategies.

Bishop, M. (1995). *Street by street, block by block*. Unpublished Report, Virginia Room, Roanoke Main Library.

Boone, J. (2011). For business and young professionals, a new way of life in downtown Roanoke. *The Roanoke Times*, February 13. Retrieved July 22, 2011 from http://www.roanoke.com/276715

Bruce, G. (1995). *Festival in the north: The story of the Edinburgh Festival*. London, UK: Hale.

Casey, D. (2011). Bold bike racks in Roanoke area show functionality, too. *The Roanoke Times*, July 14. Retrieved July 22, 2011 from http://www.roanoke.com/columnists/casey/wb/292842

Cinar, A. and Bender, T. (Eds.) (2007). *Urban imaginaries: Locating the modern city*. Minneapolis, MN: University of Minnesota Press.

City of Roanoke. (2011a). City of Roanoke Website. Retrieved July 22, 2011 from http://www.roanokeva.gov

City of Roanoke. (2011b). *Arts and cultural plan*. Retrieved July 22, 2011 from http://www.roanokeva.gov/artsplan

City of Roanoke. (2011c). *Public art plan*. Retrieved October 11, 2011 from http://www.roanokeva.gov/85256A8D0062AF37/CurrentBaseLink/N26WGNMV999LBASEN

City of Roanoke. (2014). City of Roanoke Website. Retrieved August 5, 2014 from http://www.roanokeva.gov/85256A8D0062AF37/vwContentByKey/N25Z7NUX818LBASEN

Colbert, J. (2010). *Virginia off the beaten path: A guide to unique places*. 10th ed. Guilford, CT: Morris Books.

Crang, M. and Cook, I. (2007). *Doing ethnographies*. Durham, UK: Sage.

Currid, E. (2009). Bohemia as subculture; "Bohemia" as industry: Art, culture, and economic development. *Journal of Planning Literature*, 23(4), 368–382.

Dotson, R. (2007). *Roanoke, Virginia, 1882–1912: Magic city of the New South*. Knoxville, TN: The University of Tennessee Press.

Edfringe.com. (2011). *About us*. Retrieved October 18, 2011 from http://www.edfringe.com/about-us

Evans, G. and Foord, J. (2003). Shaping cultural landscapes: Local regeneration effects. In M. Miles and T. Hall (Eds) *Urban futures: Critical commentaries on shaping the city* (pp. 167–181). London, UK: Routledge.

Florida, R. (2002). *The rise of the creative class: And how it's transforming work, leisure, community and everyday life*. New York, NY: Perseus Books.

Florida, R. (2005a). *Cities and the creative class*. New York, NY: Routledge.

Florida, R. (2005b). *The flight of the creative class: The new global competition for talent*. New York, NY: HarperCollins.

Frumkin, P. and Kolendo, A. (2014). *Building for the arts: The strategic design of cultural facilities*. Chicago, IL: The University of Chicago Press.

Fry, W. (2009). Annual hoo-rah Marginal Arts Festival parade. *Brooklyn Rail*. Retrieved August 23, 2011 from http://www.brooklynrail.org/2009/04/artseen/1st-annual-hoo-rah-marginal-arts-festival-parade

Fullilove, M. (2004). *Root shock: How tearing up city neighborhoods hurts America, and what we can do about it*. New York, NY: One World.

Geertz, C. (1983). *Local knowledge*. New York, NY: Basic.

Griffiths, R. (1998). Making sameness: place marketing and the new urban entrepreneurialism. In N. Oatley (Ed.) *Cities, economic competition and urban policy* (pp. 41–57). London, UK: Paul Chapman.

Hague, C., Hague, E., and Breitbach, C. (2011). *Regional and local economic development*. New York, NY: Palgrave MacMillan.

Hamel, J., Dufour, S., and Fortin, D. (1993). *Case study method*. Thousand Oaks, CA: Sage.

Jensen, O. B. (2007). Culture stories: Understanding cultural urban branding. *Planning Theory*, 6(3), 211–236.

Kearns, G. and Philo, C. (Eds). (1993). *Selling places: The city as cultural capital, past and present*. Oxford: Pergamon Press.

Kittredge, K. (2008). A guide to the Taubman Museum of Art. *The Roanoke Times*, October 1. Retrieved from http://rtstories.com/artmuseum/frontpage

Knox, P. and Mayer, H. (2009). *Small town sustainability: Economic, social, and environmental innovation*. Boston, MA: Birkhauser Verlag AG.

Lane, A. (2003). *The edges of fringe: Development and structure of the American Fringe Festival*. (Doctoral dissertation). Retrieved from ProQuest

Lee, D. (2007). Bilbao, 10 years later. *The New York Times*, September 3. Retrieved from http://travel.nytimes.com/2007/09/23/travel/23bilbao.html

Marginalarts.com. (2011). *Marginal Arts Festival*. Retrieved from http://www.marginalarts.com

MAF (Marginal Arts Festival). (2011). *Marginal Arts Festival program guide*. Roanoke, VA.

Markusen, A. (2006). Urban development and the politics of a creative class: Evidence from a study of artists. *Environment and Planning*, A 38: 1921–1940.

Markusen, A. and Gadwa, A. (2010). Arts and culture in urban or regional planning: A review and research agenda. *Journal of Planning Education and Research*, 29(3): 379–391.

Massey, D. (1995). Imagining the world. In J. Allen and D. Massey (Eds.) *Geographical worlds* (pp 5–53). Oxford: Oxford University Press.

Mercer, C. (2005). From indicators to governance to the mainstream: Tools for cultural policy and citizenship. In C. Andrew, M. Gattinger, M. S. Jeannotte, and W. Straw (Eds.) *Accounting for culture: Thinking through cultural citizenship*, (pp. 9–20). Ottawa, Canada: University of Ottawa Press.

Miller, T. and Yudice, G. (2002). *Cultural policy*. London, UK: Sage.

Myerscough, J., and Bruce, A. (1988). *The economic importance of the arts in Britain*. London, UK: Policy Studies Institute.

Noll, R.G. and Zimbalist, A. (1997). *Sports, jobs, and taxes: The economic impacts of sports teams and stadiums*. Washington, DC: Brookings Institution Press.

Nyseth, T., and Viken, A. (Eds.). (2009). *Place reinvention: Northern perspectives*. Burlington, VT: Ashgate Publishing.

Plaza, B. (2007). The Bilbao effect. *Museum News*, 86(5): 13–20. Retrieved September 16, 2011 from http://mpra.ub.uni-muenchen.de/12681/1/MPRA_paper_12681.pdf

Pratt, A. C. (1997). Production values: From cultural industries to the governance of culture. *Environment and Planning A*, 29(11): 1911–1917.

RAC (Roanoke Arts Commission). (2011). *Roanoke Arts Commission web-site*. Retrieved July 22, 2011 from http://www.roanokeva.gov/85256A8D0062AF37/CurrentBaseLink/N26WGLTM150LBASEN

Rosenstein, C. (2009). *Cultural development and city neighborhoods*. Charting Civil Society, 21. Washington, DC: Urban Institute.

Schneider, J. and Susser, I. (Eds.) (2003). *Wounded cities: Destruction and reconstruction in a globalized world*. New York, NY: Berg Publishers.

Shields, R. (1991). *Places on the margin: Alternative geographies of modernity*. New York: Routledge.

Shields, R. (1999). *Lefebvre, love and struggle: Spatial dialectics*. New York, NY: Routledge.

Skeen, M. (2011). Arts, culture can draw businesses to area. *The Roanoke Times*, July 24. Retrieved August 9, 2011 from http://www.roanoke.com/business/wb/293791

Squires, P. (2013). Taubman Museum of Art names Della Watkins executive director. *Virginia Business*, January 7. Retrieved January 22, 2013 from http://www.virginiabusiness.com/regions/article/taubman-museum-of-art-names-della-watkins-executive-director

Stake, R. (1995). *The art of case study research*. Thousand Oaks, CA: Sage.

Stern, M. and Seifert, S. (2008). *From creative economy to creative society*. Philadelphia, PA: University of Pennsylvania, Social Impact of the Arts Project

Strom, E. (2003) Cultural policy as development policy: Evidence from the United States. *International Journal of Cultural Policy*, 9(3): 247–263.

Tate, S. (2012). Civic tinkering in the small city: Intersections and imaginaries of art, place, and marginality. Unpublished doctoral dissertation Blacksburg, VA: Virginia Tech. Retrieved from : http://scholar.lib.vt.edu/theses/available/etd-04132012-140503/unrestricted/Tate_AnthonyS_D_2012.pdf

U.S. Census. (2013). *Roanoke, Virginia census data*. Retrieved February 8, 2013 from http://quickfacts.census.gov/qfd/states/51/51770.html

Wallis, D. (2014). Start-up success isn't enough to found a museum. *The New York Times*, March 19. Retrieved March 20, 2013 from http://www.nytimes.com/2014/03/20/arts/artsspecial/start-up-success-isnt-enough-to-found-a-museum.html?_r=0

Warren, I. M. (1940). *Story of Roanoke*. Roanoke, VA: Works Progress Administration.

Yin, R. K. (2009). *Case study research: Design and methods*. 4th ed. Washington DC: Sage.

# 7

# COMMUNITY CULTURAL DEVELOPMENT AS A SITE OF JOY, STRUGGLE, AND TRANSFORMATION

*Dudley Cocke*

## Introduction

This chapter reports the search by a rural, professional theater company, never numbering more than a dozen members, for a cultural development paradigm that utilizes the inherent intellectual, emotional, spiritual, and material traditions and features of a community to encourage individual agency in support of community well-being. Based on its theatrical experiments, Roadside Theater eventually would claim that by sharing (performing) and examining one's personal story in public settings marked by manifold perspectives, not only can one learn to speak for oneself from the depth of one's own experience but one can learn to act in concert with others to achieve what is fair and just for the whole in which one resides. This assertion would be decades in gestation as the theater company's artists and producers learned from hundreds of communities in its home region of Appalachia and across the United States.

If community cultural development (CCD) means developing the intellectual, emotional, spiritual, and material traditions and features of a community, CCD has been the core of Roadside Theater's efforts since its inception forty years ago. Beginning its work in its own backyard, Roadside eventually—for ideological, aesthetic, and economic reasons—turned its attention to helping communities beyond its Appalachian homeland develop their inherent artistic assets as a means of celebrating local life, of wrestling with community problems, and of catalyzing potential personal and collective transformation.

## Beginning

Roadside Theater's journey of discovery began with several questions nagging the theater's founding members:

- Could a small group of community-trained musicians, storytellers, and writers create a professional theater in a place—the coalfields of central Appalachia—with no history of the same?
- Could the content and form of such a theater be fabricated from local sources found within an area of approximately twenty counties in parts of five adjoining states—eastern Kentucky, southwestern Virginia, southern West Virginia, western North Carolina, and upper eastern Tennessee?
- And could the ensuing regional dramas appeal to people anywhere?

With these questions in mind, a group of young Appalachian musicians and storytellers started rehearsing traditional Jack and Mutsmeg (the female version of Jack) tales and performing them in schools and local community centers in central Appalachia. During a three-year (1916–1918) visit to the United States, English ethnomusicologist Cecil Sharp had observed that these centuries-old archetypal stories and ballads were more intact in Appalachian communities than they were in the British Isles, where they originated (Yates, 1999).[1] In their spirited retellings, the Roadside actors spontaneously traded characters, batting the old stories' lines back and forth, and generally "cutting a big shine." Upon ending a tale like *Jack and the Heifer Hide*, with its rousing shared finale, "And the last time I went down to see Jack, he was a-doin' well," the performers would

**FIGURE 7.1**   Roadside Theater artists perform a traditional Jack tale (photo courtesy of Roadside Theater)

break into song accompanied by fiddle, banjo, and sometimes the twang of a jaw harp: "I wish I was a hole in the ground / I wish I was a hole in the ground / If I was a hole in the ground / I'd be a mountain upside down / I wish I was a hole in the ground."

The group that undertook this work took the name Roadside Theater and began offering performances wherever the ensemble's actors hung their coats. Area schools usually could afford between $50 and $75 for an assembly performance, and $3 was the standard adult admission to an evening Roadside show in a community center or church hall. Appalachian people of all ages loved what the company was doing—there just was not enough local money to support it.

Since the arrival of large-scale coal mining in the 1890s, central Appalachia has been a rich land with poor people. Singer-songwriter John Prine succinctly suggested why in a famous song, "Paradise": "Mister Peabody's coal train done hauled it away" (Prine, 1971). From this perspective, the region has been a mineral colony, at first of national and thereafter of global, energy corporations that have taken its natural wealth and left little behind. Fortunately for the band of young Roadside storytellers and musicians, a local job-training program for youths, the Appalachian Film Workshop, had transitioned in 1972 into a nonprofit corporation, Appalshop, which was busy documenting Appalachian life through the voices of the region's people. Appalshop intentionally had established itself in Whitesburg, Kentucky, the hometown of lawyer and author Harry Caudill and of Tom and Pat Gish, publishers of *The Mountain Eagle* newspaper. Caudill and the Gishes' were outspoken critics of poverty and its causes. "It Screams" was on the masthead of *The Mountain Eagle*, and after the newspaper offices were torched in 1974 by an arsonist hired by a Whitesburg policeman, the next edition proclaimed, "It Still Screams." Harry Caudill's (1963) angry book, *Night Comes to the Cumberlands: A Biography of a Depressed Area*, painted a picture of an isolated region colonized after the Civil War by national corporations rapacious in their extraction of the mountains' wealth of coal and timber and without regard for the area's people, many of whom, like Caudill's ancestors, were of Scots-Irish and Cherokee descent. Caudill's insider analysis attracted the attention of the John F. Kennedy Administration staff working on poverty policy and, subsequently, the Lyndon B. Johnson Administration officials who would launch the national War on Poverty in 1964 from the front porch of the Fletcher family home in Martin County, KY.

In 2014, on the fiftieth anniversary of the War on Poverty, Appalshop is an example of a federal job training program that succeeded, but there is a twist concerning why. In 1969, when the Appalachian Film Workshop began its work, the airport closest to the training initiative's location in Whitesburg was three-and-a-half hours away, and there was no bus or train service to the community. This meant the Workshop's absentee supervisors in Washington, DC were unable to guide the development of its program closely, and this relative lack of oversight resulted in the trainees learning by doing: They took the government-issued equipment and started making films. Their subjects were their neighbors and kin—a hog butchering on a frosty morning, a midwife assisting a birth (twins as it turned out, to everyone's surprise), and foot washing at the Old Regular Baptist Church. The power of telling their own culture's stories quickly became apparent to the trainees, who believed that even their amateur results were more revealing and authentic than the War on Poverty renditions permeating the professional mass media. In 1971, when the government ended its support for such job-training centers, the trainees and their local supervisors, Bill and Josephine Richardson, began the process of incorporating as a charitable organization with the educational mission to tell central Appalachia's story through the voices of the people living there. With a similar purpose and a felt need to develop an alternative to working in the mines, young local musicians and storytellers were welcomed into the Appalshop fold of documentary filmmakers. In less than two decades, Appalshop would develop into the region's leading producer of music recordings, plays, and radio and film documentaries.

Because Appalshop's productions were popular, the organization's leadership decided to apply for government supported grants. In Roadside's case, the result was that for two consecutive years, the Kentucky Arts Council rejected the theater's applications for assistance. Judging from the distribution of its tax generated grants and the tone of its staff members in public meetings and private conversations, Appalshop staff concluded that the Council's attitude, if not its policy, was that a professional theater could not possibly exist in such a backward part of the state. That outcome convinced Roadside's principals that the shortest route to the Kentucky state capital, Frankfort, was through New York City.

As it turned out, Roadside's new play, *Red Fox/Second Hangin'* (1976), was a hit in the Big Apple, first downtown at the Theater for the New City (1977) and then uptown at the Manhattan Theatre Club (1978). *Red Fox*, as it came to be known, told the story of the first coal boom on the Cumberland Plateau and the life-and-death debate it stirred among local people. In front of projections of photographs of the period and of the play's real-life characters, three performers (all distant kin of the play's protagonists) offered the story with overlapping lines and unisons:

Gary Dale: You see now about that time, there's an awful lot of rich city folks figured that there was a lot of money to be made in these mountains,

Hoyt: and they just figured,

D. H. and Gary Dale (as rich city folks): they'd be the very ones to make it.

Gary Dale: They knowed for a long time that there was iron ore and timber and coal back in here, but they hadn't been able to figure out how to get it out.

Hoyt: By 1885, they'd about got all the bugs worked outta that little problem,

D. H. and Gary Dale (as rich city folks): and was ready to start amakin' their money.

Hoyt: Everybody was expectin' to make them a king's ransom. It was just like the California gold rush.

D. H.: Now, they's a little town 20 miles from the Mud Hole called Big Stone Gap,

Hoyt: and they's people pourin' into little bitty Big Stone Gap,

D. H. and Hoyt: from all over this world!

D. H. (as a duke): There's even a duke,

Gary Dale (as a duchess): and duchess

D. H. and Gary Dale: from London, England.

Hoyt: Them fellers set about to make little bitty Big Stone Gap

Together: into the Pittsburgh of the South!

D. H.: They's runnin' full page advertisements in the *New York Times*,

Gary Dale (reading from paper): proclaiming as how, "This country has everything to offer to make you a fortune. They have timber, coal, and iron ore, all in one spot. The natives have no idea of the money they're sittin' on, and there are men who know how to talk to these natives,"

D. H. and Hoyt: like Devil John Wright,

Gary Dale: "and not pay anything for it, either."

(Anderson and deNobriga, 1994, pp. 79–80)

The tone of the New York reviews reflected the difference between the play's initial downtown audience and the one uptown. In the West Village, *Red Fox* was hailed by *The Village Voice* as "a series of hard male pranks … akin to *Wisconsin Death Trip*" (Sainer, 1977, p. 89), while *The Christian Science*

**FIGURE 7.2** Roadside Theater performs *Red Fox/Second Hangin'* (photo by Dan Carraco)

*Monitor* proclaimed the uptown performances "remarkable entertainment, the likes of which New York folks don't encounter every day" (Beaufort, 1978, p. 26). After *The New York Times* announced *Red Fox/Second Hangin'* was, "as stirring to the audience for its historical detective work as for the vanishing art of frontier yarn spinning" (Franklin, 1977, p. 17) and *The Louisville Courier Journal* reported the play was "a part of this country's past the entire nation can treasure" (Mootz, 1978, p. 21), Kentucky Arts Council (KAC) staff flew north to see the production—and, in its next granting cycle (1978), the KAC joined the National Endowment for the Arts (NEA) in supporting Roadside's work.

From its inception, the ensemble's members understood that the stories they told and the way they conveyed them were different from mainstream theater. In Manhattan, Roadside was identified with avant-garde companies, such as Mabou Mines and the Wooster Group. At home in the mountains, if anyone troubled to categorize the group, it was as folk theater. In fact, Roadside was probably the only professional theater company to receive support from the NEA's Folk Arts Program.[2] For folklorists, the decisive factor was that Roadside artists had learned their craft not in the academy but instead in and from the Appalachian communities in which they had grown up. Roadside also received numerous grants from the NEA Theatre, Opera Musical Theatre, and Expansion Arts programs.

The New York City experience confirmed that the Whitesburg-based company had developed a unique theatrical aesthetic and fresh content based on what its members had known all their lives: storytelling, ballad singing, oral histories, and church. The theater group had demonstrated that the local and specific, when rendered faithfully and imaginatively in the voices of the culture's young people, could touch audiences anywhere. Roadside had brought to the stage some of the inherent genius of its Appalachian community, and what had been a marginal economic enterprise became a nonprofit organization capable of eventually supporting as many as nine full-time ensemble members and nearly half as many part-timers.

With the *Red Fox* experience under its belt, Roadside set about in 1980 completing a cycle of Appalachian plays that chronicled the period from the first European settlement to the present. When completed, the series became the first collection of indigenous Appalachian dramas.[3] The five productions presented a radically different version of the region's history than that published under the auspices of the coal companies that continued to play overweening roles in the economic life of the region. Performance fees from national tours of the plays became a significant part of Roadside's budget, typically accounting for more than half of the theater's annual income. This revenue helped underwrite the extensive performance work the company continued to do in its home region, whose residents remained economically strapped. By 1989, as it began its fifteenth year, Roadside had crisscrossed the country multiple times, performing, as it did so, in thirty-four states.

## The Fork in the Road

The old adage "watch out for what you wish for" began rattling around in the mind of at least one company member as the ensemble traveled from performance to performance. The "road" is notorious for its homogenizing effect on performers and their art. W. H. Auden captured this effect in his poem, *On the Circuit*: "Though warm my welcome everywhere, / I shift so frequently, so fast, / I cannot now say where I was / The evening before last." (Auden, 1991, p. 729).

While the young company members found ways to entertain themselves as they traveled, the question became the effect of constant touring on the plays *themselves*.

After fourteen years of successfully offering its productions nationally, the ensemble's members made a decision that surprised many of the people who had been following their work: Roadside now would perform only in communities that contractually committed to bringing an inclusive cross-section of their population to the theater's performances and workshops. Within the company, the decision was made quickly after an epiphany its artistic leadership had while on tour in Nevada: The elite audience for professional theater was re-shaping Roadside's plays to fit their own class-determined sensibilities.

This audience magic was made possible by the disconnection between the rural, working class origins of the plays' form and content and the social class of those who attended professional theater. The 2011 study, *Fusing Arts, Culture, and Social Change*, reported,

> … the majority of arts funding supports large organizations with budgets greater than $5 million. Such organizations, which comprise less than 2 percent of the universe of arts and cultural nonprofits, receive more than half of the sector's total revenue. These institutions focus primarily on Western European art forms, and their programs serve audiences that are predominantly white and upper income.
>
> (Sidford, 2011, p. 1)[4]

As Roadside's members became increasingly knowledgeable about the history of United States theatre, they began to identify their efforts with the drama produced during the labor and civil rights movements of the last century. Like the producers and artists allied with those social justice movements, the company's artists were focused on preserving and perpetuating the intellectual, spiritual, emotional, and material traditions and features of economically exploited populations.

This decision—that presenters of Roadside's work commit to bringing together audiences that reflected their entire community—was risky economically because there was no way that its Appalachian audience of modest economic means could begin to make up the income difference if the company's national bookings faltered as a result. The decision also tested Roadside's relationship with its Austin, Texas–based engagement and producing partner, Theresa and Michael Holden, of Holden Arts and Associates, who now would have to ensure that this provision of diversity and inclusion was included in every contract. Because the Holdens were trained as artists themselves and shared Roadside's interest in community engagement and agency, however, they immediately agreed to it.

In contrast to its audiences while on tour, Roadside's home support comprises almost entirely working, middle-class, and economically poor people, in other words, the region's general population. Attendees do not come to Roadside plays simply as spectators but, rather, to bear witness to their cultural identity. This is confirmed by community members' habitual eagerness to contribute stories and music of their own to Roadside productions—and, as the plays are developing, their readiness to attend staged readings of the works in progress to share their insights on what is working and what might next occur to deepen or further enliven the scripts.

In the Appalachian storytelling, music, and church traditions, performers speak directly to the audience without elaborate sets or a "fourth wall." No curtain is drawn. Roadside has long sought to arrange its performance spaces so as to dissolve the physical and psychological distance between performers and their audience. For example, company members view orchestra pits as barriers to participation. They perceive the need for undue electronic amplification similarly. Auditorium lights are never so dark that the audience cannot see itself. As with an oft-told family story, Roadside actors know the entire script by heart, not just their individual parts. If a performer is inspired to riff with audience members in spontaneous call-and-response, the other actors are ready to back her or him up and then land back into the script at just the right moment in the appropriate key. Here is an example of call-and-response from a transcript of a video of a live performance of *Pretty Polly* at Cleveland Technical College, Shelby, North Carolina (1986).

| | |
|---|---|
| Angelyn: | I think I'll tell one *(a story)* about your Uncle John. |
| Tom: | I got two Uncle Johns—one lives on one side of the mountain and the other one lives on the other side. Which Uncle John are you talkin' about? |
| Angelyn: | Honey, he's the one that lives on the outside of the mountain. Well, I figure it's better to tell it in front of you, than to tell it behind your back. John lived in a little cabin there on the mountainside, and he was a bachelor feller. Poor old thing, bless his heart. |
| Tom: | He was a bachelor by choice! |
| Angelyn: | That's right—the ladies' choice. Well John had a little garden |

...

*Audience Member calls out: What did he grow?*

Angelyn:   (taking a step toward the audience member) He had three ol' spindly bean plants and a big 'mater plant ...

*Audience Member: and I bet he had some corn!*

Angelyn:   Well yes, he had a great big field a corn ... Now I always wondered what he done with all that corn.

*Audience Member: He was making corn liquor.*

Angelyn   (to fellow actors on stage): Why looky here boys—they done heared about John all the way down here in North Carolina! ... (to audience member) Now John wadn't no different than most—ever'body likes a little libation now and again ...

*Audience Member: With all that corn, now and again must have been every day!*

Angelyn:   (to audience member) Are you one of them Mullinses from over around Skeet Rock? If ya' are, your Mommy told me to send you home if I run into you anywheres. She said the law was a lookin' for you, so not to take the turnpike.

Tom:    (to Angelyn) Now I don't know about no corn liquor, but I do know that Uncle John raised a few chickens.

Angelyn:   Well yes, Uncle John did raise a few chickens, of which he was particularly fond, especially when proper cooked. It was this fondness that was responsible for the eventual depletion of his entire flock—for depleted it did become—until finally they's only one old rooster left. But mercy sakes alive, what a rooster that thing was—why he was two or three feet tall!

                          (*Pretty Polly*, 1986)[5]

The community ownership of Roadside's work often surprises visitors, whether from the theater community or beyond. One weekend, in 1984, for example, the arts program director of a national foundation came to the company's home theater in Whitesburg to evaluate the ensemble's work. As usual, the 150-seat theater was packed with more than 175 people. At the play's intermission, the foundation director was livid. "The woman to my right and the man to my left are both singing along to your original songs and sometimes completing a character's line. You've set me up, which is decidedly not in your self-interest," she said. "Oh dear," I replied, "Please pick any seat you want for the second act." When the play ended, the foundation officer came to me and apologized, saying the same thing had happened in her new seat and that she was moved beyond words by what she had experienced. I commented to her that the Appalachian culture's tradition of participation is a reason that it has been able to resist the forces of homogenization and commercialization seeking to bottle and sell it—for a people without a fair share of economic independence, cultural autonomy is that much more important.

After performing on tour for hundreds of economically well-off audiences, a tipping point must have been reached, for the actors found themselves cutting short or even deleting text that was not registering with these spectators.

Something had backfired, because Roadside's aesthetic, with its concern for audience members' finding their own story in the play, seeks to encourage actors to undertake such editing. As it was playing out, if enough audience members had preconceived ideas about poor and working-class people that occasioned redactions critical to honoring their history and traditions, the plays could veer dangerously close to becoming a parody of their intentions. After one such performance, a company actor remarked that despite the full exertion of her willpower she could feel herself becoming Ellie May Clampett, the stereotypical young hillbilly woman of television's "Beverly Hillbillies" fame.[6]

Roadside's insistence that communities presenting its plays commit to the concept of inclusion at first attained mixed results. Initially, the ensemble thought expanded audience recruitment efforts would secure its goal. Accordingly, the company developed a promotional "tool kit" that included press releases, flyers, posters, and prerecorded radio spots that reflected the working-class origins of the coming attractions and sent it to each presenter. Roadside also developed a manual describing how best to use the promotional material and a three-month calendar outlined the timing of a model publicity campaign. On a regular schedule, a company member made friendly calls to each presenter to learn how audience recruitment was going and to help address any problems. The extra effort and expense paid off. Roadside now toured to full houses of diverse audiences, and the actors (and consequently the plays) were back in their groove. However, unexpected issues loomed.

In 1988, after months of working on promotion with the local presenter in a mid-sized Alabama town, a large crowd greeted Roadside: "This is twice as many people as show up for our performances!" exclaimed the presenter to Roadside's tour manager. It was standing room only, and it was obvious from the racial diversity and the social signs of speech and dress that the crowd was a cross-section of the city. The actors were excited, and judging from the buzz in the auditorium, so was the audience. The quick and knowing reactions of the working-class audience members helped lead other patrons through the drama. There was a prolonged standing ovation; some stormed the stage to take pictures of their families with the Roadside actors and, most important, to share their own stories. The company left town thinking it surely would be invited back to continue such an inspired exchange.

Four months later, Roadside's tour manager called the presenter and said, "Haven't heard from you. I guess you want us back next season. Good for the box office!" Unexpectedly, the presenter replied he could not commit. The company's booking manager called back nine months later and received the same answer. So, finally, on the third call, the Roadside representative said, "I can tell you're not going to ask us to return. Why?" And the presenter said, "The play was really good. We never had such a big crowd before—or since. But our board of directors just didn't like the way y'all talked." Alabamans did not like the way Appalachians talked? So the Roadside tour manager asked, "What do you mean?" The presenter replied, "One board member said that if we keep having those people in our audience, they might want us to start programming country music, and we can't have that!" "Oh, I see," the tour manager replied, and she thanked the presenter for his time.[7]

What had happened was that some people did not enjoy sharing their evening with certain "other" individuals in the community who might know more than they did about parts of life. For those citizens, the arts are akin to their country club, a chance to get away and be with "their" kind. Paradoxically, tax-exempt status and public support were making their social class-rooted theater experience possible.

From experiences similar to the one in Alabama, Roadside's actors began to realize their challenge on tour was greater than attracting an audience that looked like the entire community, as difficult as that could be, but was instead ensuring that everyone had an opportunity to participate in decisions about their community's public arts and culture programming. It also was becoming clear to the company's members that diverse community audiences, like its own supporters at home, wanted to participate in the artistic experience itself, as opposed simply to consuming it as a spectator. It was with this realization in mind that Roadside's leadership began thinking of story circles as a potent form of public participation.

## Story Circles

Roadside's original ensemble members grew up without television, immersed in a world of local narratives. That oral tradition, often in ballad form, is the most prominent feature of Appalachia's shared Scots-Irish heritage, and it has shaped the content and determined the form of the company's plays. If you have ever enjoyed the experience of sitting with friends and kin singing, spinning tales, and recounting oft-told histories, you can quickly grasp the roots of Roadside's approach to theater making. The play's tellers sometimes carry the narrative, sometimes portray characters, and often call out a phrase in unison with lines suddenly doubling and overlapping within a general motif of call-and-response. In the company's Appalachian performance tradition, and in those with which its members have been invited to participate (the southern African American and Puerto Rican customs, for example), call-and-response includes the audience. The result is the rich choral effect of harmony and counterpoint that is group storytelling, whether on a front porch or in an auditorium.

Not only does oral tradition effectively generate content for building plays but, after performances of the staged show, story circles with audience and cast participating provide a nuanced feedback loop for audience members to integrate a production's experience into their own lives and for the presenting artists to deepen their understanding of their performance. The sharing opportunities story circles represent continue the play's action into a new act, providing a way for participating community members to develop deeper individual and collective meaning of what they have experienced. Story circles also are effective at eliciting valuable feedback and understanding for performers and thereby contributing to enriching the possibilities for presentation of plays in the future.

Based on the experience of many such public circles, Roadside's members concluded that the stories people were able to tell themselves and others, those they could imagine and understand, defined not only what they perceive to have occurred but what they thought could be possible in their individual and collective lives (Cocke et al., 1999, p. 4). In the course of communicating personal stories, difficulties in a community often rise to the surface, including issues from which its members are suffering. For example, in 1995, Roadside staged a play in a rural Montana county in which residents were bitterly divided concerning a proposal to close the jurisdiction's last one-room school and to consolidate its small high schools into one larger entity to serve all of the county's teenagers. Many students and parents supported the change, but several older members of the community were strongly opposed. Participants in story circles held after Roadside's performances turned to this controversy as their topic. At first, younger people shared stories about difficulties getting the classes they needed to get into college. Then the first older person, a woman in her eighties, began her story with, "They just don't have good fights in [our] schools like they did when I was a girl." She went on to describe the Saturday night dances at the one-room schools she had experienced as a teenager and how some of the young men would go outside to take a nip, and a fist fight over a girl would inevitably ensue, be broken up, and the event continued. She also painted a picture of weddings held at the schools during the summer full moon so participants could waltz in the moonlight. After her story, the next teller, a younger man with teenage children, said,

> I couldn't understand why you were so against getting a better education for our children. Now I see that the old schools weren't just places to learn reading and writing, they were the heart of the community. If big consolidated schools can't be that, how can we develop heart another way?[8]

Because narratives are powerful and can easily be used to dominate and exploit rather than to empower and enrich and secure collective development, Roadside's members are very formal about how they employ story circles. In essence, the group sits in a circle, and each person tells a personal story based on a mutually agreed theme. A Roadside facilitator introduces the sharing by suggesting that narratives should have characters, a setting, some aspect of conflict, and a beginning, middle, and end. No one can join a story circle late, and everyone must participate. Calculated by the amount of time allotted for the circle divided by the number of participants, each person is asked to share a narrative of approximately the same length. The experience begins when the first person starts and then moves to the individual to that person's right. Even if someone tells a controversial story, there is no cross-talk in response. Participants must wait to respond through their own narratives. As the telling

**FIGURE 7.3** Roadside Theater conducts a story circle during a residency at the University of Richmond, February 20, 2013 (photo by Zhivko Illeieff)

moves around the circle, one may pass if not ready to share, for the opportunity to speak will come around again.

As practiced by Roadside, the story circle encourages deep listening. Naturally, when the circle's theme is decided, participants immediately begin thinking about what story they are going to tell. However, facilitators suggest that they not share the narrative that first comes to mind but rather offer a story that arises from listening to those shared by others. There is no timekeeper, as each group will create its own rhythm: For example, after listening to the preceding story, the timing of beginning one's own account is the teller's choice. After everyone has told his or her story, the group reflects together, now allowing interpersonal dialogue, about what just happened. Were there common or strikingly divergent themes? Was there now a new narrative in the middle of the circle?

Story circles engender appreciation for the unique intellectual, emotional, and spiritual qualities of each participant and develop oral expression and listening skills. Each individual's story is a present to those in the circle, with the quality of the listening also a gift in return to the storyteller.

Informed in 1990 by some audience members that racism was once more on the rise in their southern communities, Junebug Productions, the New Orleans African-American theater that grew out of the Civil Rights Movement's Free Southern Theater, and Roadside jointly decided to create and tour a musical play about the historical relationship between black and white poor and working-class people in the South. Roadside and Junebug had been collaborating since 1982, when Junebug director, John O'Neal, and Dudley Cocke decided to share their company's respective plays with each other's home audiences—one predominately white Appalachian and the other principally African American. In 1990, the two directors agreed the new play would treat the period from the slave trade and first landing of indentured servants in the United States to the end of the Vietnam War. To build a foundation for the drama, the two ensembles sat together in circles telling one another personal stories about their experience with race, place, and class. These narratives and the group's discussion of their meaning helped company members better hear one another and themselves and, as the participating artists began to understand their differences, the group was better able to assess its shared history and current circumstances. After arriving at a script that those involved thought was a genuine reflection of their experiences and testing and revising it with their home audiences in Louisiana and Kentucky, the two companies set about touring the production, their stock in trade.

Before playing a venue, the ensembles asked potential sponsors of *Junebug/ Jack* whether their community was ready to think about local race and class issues. If the producers felt ready or wanted to take a chance, the combined troupe would bring the play to their town or city. As the group began traveling to communities across the South, the challenge became how to get black and white working-class and poor people to attend. In the main, such folks do not gather together, much less go to the same professional theater productions (Sidford, 2011). However, those who had labored on the work believed that if they did not obtain just such an audience notwithstanding—no matter how popular the drama might be with others (and it was)—they had failed.

After exhausting the array of previously mentioned promotional strategies, including getting the word out to barbershops and bars, where politics are discussed, the *Junebug/Jack* company members in one typically animated post-performance discussion hit on an idea: Every location wishing to present the play would agree to form a racially diverse and religiously ecumenical choir to perform in the show. Reflecting each community's diversity, these choruses could include singers from African American churches, members of predominately white congregations, performers from women's choirs, and perhaps participants from high school glee clubs. Several months before the professional actors arrived, Roadside/Junebug sent each community chorus the show's music and asked it to designate an individual to conduct evening rehearsals, if they had not done so already. A few days before the opening performance, the show's director (the author, as it happened) staged the chorus into the show.

Several things occurred in the course of this production process. First, the play's presenter had to begin thinking about the entire community while identifying individuals who might serve in the chorus. The singers did not volunteer to discuss race and class—They came together because they loved to sing and this professional drama looked like a good opportunity to shine. In the course of rehearsing the music, they naturally hit on a sound that had never been heard in the community, simply because all those different talents had never been joined before. Choruses did not come together consciously to sing beautifully crafted, down-to-earth songs about the cruelty, heartache, and paradoxes of 400 years of race and class struggle, but that is what they wound up doing anyway. Choir membership would typically increase the *Junebug/Jack* cast from a small cadre of six professionals to a group of twenty or more. Junebug and Roadside artists agreed that residents' participation only raised the artistic quality of the production—and noted how much local talent goes unappreciated for lack of a meaningful book and finely crafted musical score.

**FIGURE 7.4** Junebug Productions and Roadside Theater artists performs *Junebug/Jack* (photo by Jeff Whetstone)

A cross-section of the entire community was present when shows opened as a result of the engagement of the chorus and the various communities from which its members came. Friends and family of choir members came to see the play. In addition, because the performances enabled everyone to feel confident about his or her traditions, audience members became eager to witness and to learn more about the *other* ways of life on offer: to experience how the African American people sang, or how the white people sang, or what inflections young people brought to the song.

The community choir that performed *Junebug/Jack* in New Orleans in 1997 to launch a statewide tour was thirty-two-strong. The group proceeded down the church aisle of what was once a bowling alley, the venue of that kickoff performance, singing the traditional gospel tune, "This Little Light of Mine." The play's musical finale encourages everyone in the auditorium to join in, and as audience members get up to sing and dance, any semblance of a division between stage and spectator seating is blurred. The actors and choir lead everyone in the finale's syncopated chorus (Cocke, Newman, and Salmons-Rue, 1993). Here's a sample:

Michael
A lot of black people all over the world
Still fighting a terrible fight
Thinkin' 'bout the past but lookin' to the future
Beginning to see the light
History has proven that it's unacceptable

To keep a people down
Pain and suffering all those years
Shackled and whipped to the ground.
Families disrupted, where is the justice?
Millions gone to slave ship seas.
With faith intact they broke their backs
Three hundred years of labor for free.
Now the only request after giving their best
Was for forty acres and a mule
Asking and waiting and asking again
Still treated like a fool.
It's been a long time since 1865
Some changes are hard to see
But freedom for you and freedom for me
Everybody in equality!
Chorus (*all*)
What did they do with what they took from you,
What did they do with mine?
No use complaining what they took from you
They been stealing from us all a long time.
Ron
For over 100 years people in the mountains
Lived in peace and harmony
Helping one another, living on the land
They knowed what it meant to be free.
Then some men from the banks, church, and government
Men from the industry
Took a look at the mountains, put their heads together,
Said with disbelief:
"There's something wrong with this picture here
And there's gonna be hell to pay.
You need money to spend, credit cards and bills
To live the American Way."
You can't buy my pride
You can't sell my hope
You can't steal my identity
And when the air we breathe is sold a breath at a time
Hillbillies will still be free!
Chorus (*all*).

(Cocke, Newman, and Salmons-Rue, 1993, pp, 67–68)[9]

When the song ended, the church's preacher asked the 500 audience
members to bow their heads as she led a prayer for the actors' safe keeping.
This was timely because earlier that week, Ku Klux Klan leader David Duke

had been stirring things up in the communities Roadside and Junebug were about to visit.

In the days after these performances (and in a process very similar to that the two ensembles had employed in creating the play), audience members were invited to join circles to tell personal stories about the dynamics of race and class in their community. With a newfound permission based on the common experience and trust arising from their engagement with the play, they told one another of encounters and incidents that were typically complex, hard, and emotional—and untold before in "mixed" company. The biggest impact, indeed a kind of social catharsis, created by *Junebug/Jack* during its performances from 1991 to 1997 did not occur during the play but in the community members' telling and sharing of their stories after the formal performances.

## Community Cultural Development

When television starts telling a community's stories for it, when its older and younger members no longer share their lives and mass media replace the front porch, the living room, and the local county store, what happens to a population's sense of themselves and its collective possibilities? This question provided the motivation for Roadside to codify and further develop its community cultural development theory and practice.

Roadside's CCD praxis, like its plays' form and content, grew out of experiences in its home community. After a 1989 performance of *Mountain Tales and Music* at a local high school in Clintwood, Virginia, the school's drama teacher asked the company's artists to help teach her class. That same year, Roadside was working with the town's Senior Citizens Center, so the troupe's members suggested to the students that they begin collecting stories from the older folks at the Center. The high school students were not initially a bit interested in this idea. Nevertheless, Roadside invited the class to a performance at the Senior Center of its play, *South of the Mountain*, which is set in the first half of the twentieth century in the county where the performance was to occur. As the drama unfolded, the older people in attendance increasingly interrupted the actors to tell their own version of the times. This was mildly interesting to the students, whose experience was only with fourth-wall theater, but when an older lady piped up and stated, "I used to go courting around South of the Mountain, and I always hoped the car would break down on a lonely mountain road so I could smooch in the back seat," the Roadside project manager noticed the students stirred in their seats.[10] In the ensuing months, the company held story circles with the youths and elders, and from these the students created plays combining their own and the senior citizens' stories, which they performed around the county to full houses and standing ovations.

As this example in Virginia attests, Roadside's CCD theory and methodology are shaped by the goal of helping the host community become more inclusively and deeply aware of itself, and the story circle has proven itself effective in this regard. CCD projects can take many forms—the celebration of a local population's diverse traditions and histories through a cultural festival or the self-identification of a particular issue to address. How a community uses Roadside's CCD process is up to those from it to decide, with the caveat that whatever the project's purpose(s) and goals, a cross-section of the entire citizenry be continuously encouraged to participate as equals in it. Roadside does not solicit work in communities outside its region, believing to do so would be presumptuous. Nevertheless, when invited into a community for a CCD effort, the company begins the process of working itself out of a job, with the goal of leaving behind an inclusive group of citizens carrying on cultural projects in their own ways toward collectively identified ends.

Cultural development work is ever exciting as the residents of each community realize they have something important to say to one another and to offer to anyone who will listen. As one Western rancher said to the author in 1992 over a beer, "We're tired of everything coming in on us. We want to send something out." CCD work is as complex as the individuals and communities that practice it and typically has many moving parts occurring simultaneously. To guide its practice, Roadside has developed a philosophy of change and an accompanying methodology. Both have proven useful for keeping a project on track toward its (community-defined) goals.

## Theory of Change

Effective development seeks a dynamic relationship between the individual and the group, each discovering through experience and reflection their relationship to the intellectual, emotional, spiritual, and material traditions and features of their community. As those with direct knowledge of the culture interact, individuals and therefore their communities (however defined) become more aware of themselves and more self-confident. They gain voice and agency.

Development can be sustained only when this bottom-up process of individual and collective exploration and learning continues to inspire and shape awareness and action. Conversely, when individuals, their groups, and their organizations lose touch with such broad-based cultural knowledge as the shaping force of change, development will begin to collapse. This bottom-up theory constitutes a critique of some accepted forms of progressive art making. For example, suppose an artist with a formidable reputation has an exciting idea for a performance that addresses some aspect of social justice. Funders then agree to support that individual and his or her "cutting-edge" conception, and the artist begins working with the community to realize his or her performance. The problem, from the perspective of Roadside's philosophy of change, is that if the performer's conception is not iteratively tested and reconceived by people in the community based on their individual and group knowledge, it will be launched some distance off the ground. Roadside's members believe such efforts eventually float away without affecting the problems they seek to address. They fail because those most involved, those with the most knowledge, are not the generative base for devising and enacting strategies to confront the perceived challenges.

## *Practice*

Roadside begins its multiple-year community cultural development projects with as many of the stakeholders as are known present as possible. If a project is receiving resource support from private foundations and public agencies, they, too, must be active partners in an initiative rather than play a more typical role of stepping back until the project's conclusion, thereafter to pass judgment on its successes and failures. Instead, all stakeholders share some of the responsibility for the process, the products, and the outcomes of a cultural development effort.

As the partners get to know one another, Roadside's members emphasize a willingness to reexamine basic assumptions and test hypotheses through repeated cycles of posing questions and trying to answer them. A humble curiosity, openness to direct questions, and a willingness not to know the answers—these are the qualities the Roadside CCD approach seeks to cultivate among all involved stakeholders. In an important sense, the company strives to work with all concerned to facilitate a process not only of consciousness raising concerning often-latent assumptions but of active discernment and learning concerning how the community might wish to act on those once identified.

In particular, Roadside seeks to establish collective governance and consensual practice among engaged stakeholders in the pursuit of three questions linked to a process of intentional learning:

- What aspect of our community life are we trying to celebrate or transform, and why is that important?
- How are we trying to achieve this, and why is that the best strategy?
- How will we know we are succeeding; what data will provide us evidence, so we can improve the work and demonstrate its accomplishment to others?

The commonly derived answers to these concerns create shared overarching project objectives and goals. In addition, Roadside asks each partner to offer individual goals for an initiative. For example, by knowing that a public agency hopes to build its reputation among local legislators by supporting an initiative, project partners can better understand certain aspects of that organization's behavior and look for ways to help its representatives achieve their individual goal. In a word, Roadside asks that all stakeholders involved in a CCD initiative be transparent with their collaborators about all the aims of their engagement— to lay their cards on the table and trust the group to respect their intentions.

Program design is determined by a project's focus, separating what is known from what is unknown and discerning the difference between causes and effects, root and branch. Having agreed on a point of departure, the partners can proceed thereafter in an orderly fashion, relying on manageable cycles of action and assessment to learn together. At that point, too, the participating stakeholders can agree on their individual roles and responsibilities along with various common and individual goals and yet-to-be-addressed concerns. Such documentation is updated as the project unfolds and is made available to all partners for guidance as efforts proceed.

If the cycles of action and assessment are producing learning among those engaged (generating knowledge, developing skills, altering attitudes, changing behaviors), the stakeholders can expect that their plan of work will evolve as the work proceeds. Flexibility is an important value. This willingness to rethink and reconfigure action plans does not absolve the partners of accountability to outside stakeholders or of the important need to develop and follow strategic roadmaps. Nonetheless, those engaged should demonstrate a readiness, indeed a desire, to revisit and reorient the strategies they are following, as new evidence is uncovered and fresh ideas are generated. As a CCD project gains momentum, Roadside's members pay greater attention to when they should lead and when they should follow community members' lead.

Overall, Roadside's community cultural development method rests on five broad principles:

* active participation;
* partnerships and collaborations involving an inclusive range of community organizations;
* local leadership;
* knowing when to lead and when to follow; and
* engagement during the course of at least two years.

The community engagement process can be represented as a diagram. Activity, Partnership, and Principles continuously inform one another, and it is this flow between and among them that creates the "sweet spot" of community cultural development. The major activities in the Roadside method do not necessarily occur as discrete events but can be mixed and matched when warranted by stakeholder insight. Likewise, project design and partnership agreements are modified as stakeholders learn together through periodic reflection and analysis. Nonetheless, the five underpinning principles outlined above are constant throughout a project. The typical steps in which Roadside engages in its community cultural development work follow.

### The First Activity Point

The company selects one of its plays appropriate to a CCD residency's goals so local residents can witness and evaluate what the theater group does. In interactive workshops after the performance, Roadside's members explain their company's history and share its artistic process with community members.

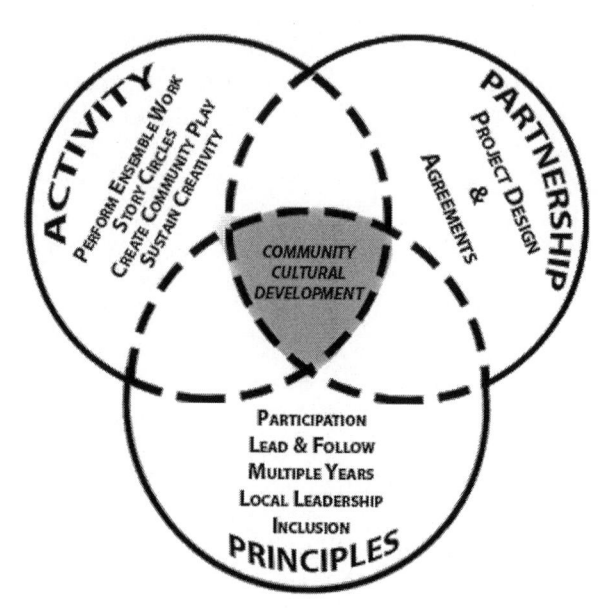

**FIGURE 7.5**   Roadside Theater's Community Cultural Development Methodology (graphic courtesy of author)

## The Second Activity Point

Roadside's principals themselves conduct and thereafter train others to facilitate community story circles so local residents can begin to hear and appreciate the way their narratives speak to the purpose and theme of the residency. This step often becomes compelling because participants often hear new information about a common experience. From the circles, a complex sense of a particular place begins to emerge. These stories (and songs), which are often recorded, become the basic ingredients for community celebrations that end the second phase. These events usually include potluck suppers at which participants play music, sing, and share the stories they have now begun to craft. Through such open yet structured programs, the community voice begins to proclaim itself. All such celebrations are composed of many voices and Roadside asks all of those engaged to welcome new stakeholders to the process at all times.

## The Third Activity Point

The community stories and songs (and sometimes dances) become the resources for creating drama relevant to a particular CCD residency's goals. Drama, by its nature, gives permission for conflict, so, for example, a play's theme might be as contentious as the effects of racism and economic inequality on the identified goal of developing a better public school system in the jurisdiction. Nascent and experienced community playwrights, producers, directors, actors, and designers use an expanding body of local expression to develop performances with residents. Roadside's members help as necessary, filling the gaps of inexperience. The focus, however, is on community assets and on citizens' finding strategies to use the arts to address compelling local claims. Roadside does not direct these efforts but instead seeks to catalyze local artists in their shared efforts to address them themselves.

## The Fourth Activity Point

After a drama is up and running, Roadside's principals suggest ways for those involved to recognize and honor the community's efforts in bringing it to fruition. The company's members also help broker creation of an infrastructure to establish a community-based theater or other development organization. Roadside's principals introduce their colleagues to the national network of artists and communities engaged in similar explorations. Now the population that has hosted the CCD residency for several years or longer creates its own means to continue exploring its story in public. Meanwhile, the community cultural development field gains a new peer organization.[11]

## Choteau, Montana

As previously mentioned, each Roadside community development project is guided by a partnership agreement drawn up in the early stages of the effort and modified by consensus as the initiative develops. How this process occurs was exemplified in the company's collaboration with members of the ranching and farming community of Choteau, Montana from 1992 to 1995. The project was sparked by the community's concern for the loss of its young people to the cities. State economic development money provided initial funding for the effort. Here is the "Mountaineers–Cowfolks" agreement that served as a touchstone for the three years of collaboration between Roadside and the town.

> We agree:
> - Economic development and cultural development go hand in hand.
> - The project's process and products will witness a commitment to place. They will be grounded in the local and specific, which, when rendered faithfully and creatively, can affect people anywhere.
> - The new plays will be given their voice by the community from which they arise. The artists will be part of the culture from which the work is drawn. The people who are the subjects of the work will be part of its development from inception through presentation. Their stories and histories will inform the work; their feedback during the creation process will shape it. The audience will not be consumers of, but participants in the performance.

- The traditional and indigenous are integral to rural life and valued for their ability to help us maintain continuity with the past, respond to the present, and prepare for the future. Thus, the relationship to the traditional and indigenous will be dynamic, not fixed.
- The project will strive to be inclusive in its producing practices. The work will be made in partnership with community organizations. Activities will be held in meeting places where the entire community feels welcome. Any tickets will be affordable.
- The collaboration and exchange will recognize that management structures and business practices are value-laden, affecting the mission, goals, and creative process. Through its structures and practices, the project will endeavor to support broad participation, self-reliance, and collective responsibility.
- The project will be consciously linked to the struggles for cultural, social, economic, and political equity for all people in the community. Although the project offers hope and joy, it also recognizes that advocating for equity often meets resistance and that such resistance, when articulated, is an opportunity for positive community change.

(Cocke, Newman, and Salmons-Rue, 1993, pp. 80–81)

Living up to such agreements is part of the challenge of this form of art-based community development. For example, it might at first appear to be relatively simple to address the stipulation in the above agreement that "Activities will be held in meeting places where the entire community feels welcome," but, in fact, most localities do not have a public performance space where everyone feels welcome. This can lead directly into the aesthetic nightmare of the "caf-a-gym-a-torium," which is where the Choteau project was headed once several community leaders reported that the areas' churches were contested spaces. Then someone suggested the town's small public park with its amphitheater as a suitable "neutral" venue, and everyone quickly agreed. About two weeks before the performances, however, the project's Blackfoot tribe's Native American partners informed everyone that the facility the production was to use had been built on their ancestral burial ground. There was only one thing to do: ask for their permission to perform there, which they formally gave with a traditional blessing ceremony after the audience had gathered and before the performances began.

Reflecting on the four-year Choteau project, farmer (and participant) Ralph Paulus concluded,

You have to feel good about yourself to stand up for what you believe in. The problem with democracy is that there's a risk, you have to stand up and shoot your mouth off once in a while. … You have to have guts to make democracy work.

(Montana American Festival Project, 1992–1995, p. 5)

## Arizona State University

As part of its Arizona State University's (ASU) three-year (1997–1999) CCD project, "Untold Stories," Roadside created a performance (1998) that brought those involved together with two groups of Native American dancers (Zuni and Pima) and a popular Chicano solo artist.[12] The production occurred in Scottsdale's Kerr Cultural Center, which had been built as a private concert hall for Mrs. Kerr and was now owned by ASU. An issue with complimentary tickets was the first warning sign that the center's leadership was feeling uncomfortable about hosting the event. About an hour before the performance, Roadside's artistic director noticed that there were ten or so people waiting outside in the cold, and when he tried to invite them into the lobby, Kerr's management said that such was strictly forbidden for another thirty minutes. The Roadside company member recognized that the majority of those in the queue had earlier been cast members in the popular play the troupe had developed with ASU's "classified" employees—maintenance personnel, kitchen staff, secretaries, and receptionists—entitled, *Highly Classified*. The production had been supported by the workers' union, which arranged with the university's administration for compensatory time for its members to participate in its creation and performances. Unsure of Kerr etiquette, cast members of the *Highly Classified* production had arrived more than an hour early in case "adjustments" needed to be made. Even as the time arrived to open the doors, management refused to do so until one of the performers tuning his banjo cleared the stage. Unconcerned with a fourth wall, Roadside cast members often choose to tune instruments and to banter with the audience before a performance begins.

Serving as the event's producer and director, the Roadside member next noticed that the foster-care children from the Boys and Girls Club, who had been part of the "Untold Stories" project from its inception and who arrived excited and all dressed up, were being directed to bleachers in the back of the auditorium, farthest from the stage. Kerr staff members said this was a strategy aimed at being able to eject them quickly should they act up. In direct contradistinction, however, in Appalachian, Native American, and Chicano cultures, the elderly and the children are given places of honor in the front. At Kerr, the best seats were reserved for patrons with season tickets. They were down on floor level in an odd reversal of what would have been the lowly social pit in Shakespearean times. No other audience members were allowed in that section.

As the hour arrived for the performance to begin, the theater was alive as the approximately 100 Latino, Native American, and other newcomers to the Kerr Cultural Arts Center hugged one another and exchanged news. It was indeed a happening. Five minutes after the appointed performance hour, a Kerr staff member ordered the play to begin immediately, and when the Roadside director replied that it already had, the staffer suggested that he was making fun of her. And so the evening played itself out as a contest between the accepted protocols of behavior of the majority of the audience in league with the performers and those of the venue's regular patrons, which were consonant with those of Kerr's management.

The evening ended with a traditional southwestern Native American "Split Circle" dance. As the boys and girls from the bleachers rushed down to participate and were joined by almost everyone else, the Kerr's regular patrons remained seated. The joyous dance swirled around them. With their refusal to join the fun, these audience members did not appear to comprehend that they were in a public university's community-oriented space and that the central purpose of the "Untold Stories Festival" was to bring different people together to share their common humanity.

## Conclusion

As the Arizona State University story illustrates, CCD work can provoke a clash of values, and its practitioners must address the many ways that those holding power will seek to preserve their hold on it while also grappling with how community members relate to those efforts. The Kenyan writer Ngugi wa Thiong'o has observed that in post-colonial Africa, the censorship of his plays was not aimed at his text but at how he wanted those dramas produced. He encountered an insistence on maintaining colonial production protocols: "The struggle may take the form of the state's intervention in the content of the artist's work—what goes on by the name of censorship—but the main arena of struggle is the performance space: its definition, delimitation and regulation" (Thiong'o, 1997, pp. 11–30).

Though cultural development practice requires focus and a willingness to confront issues as they arise, its secret weapon is the joy of individual and community expression. Because CCD locates itself in a specific population's intellectual, emotional, spiritual, and material traditions and features, the stakes of identity could not be higher. Again, as Ngugi wa Thiong'o has observed,

> The effect of the cultural bomb is to annihilate a people's belief in their names, in their languages, in their environment, in their heritage of struggle, in their unity, in their capacities, and ultimately in themselves. It makes them see their past as one wasteland of non-achievement and it makes them want to distance themselves from that wasteland. It makes them want to identify with that which is furthest removed from themselves; for instance, with other peoples' languages rather than their own. It makes them identify with that which is decadent and reactionary, all those forces which would stop their own springs of life. It even plants serious doubts about the moral rightness of struggle. Possibilities of triumph or victory are seen as remote, ridiculous dreams. The intended results are despair, despondency, and a collective death wish.

(Thiong'o, 1986, p. 3)

The Universal Declaration of Human Rights (1948) affirmed a simple and profound concept: "Everyone has the right freely to participate in the cultural life of the community, to enjoy the arts and to share in scientific advancement and its benefits" (United Nations, 1948). This principle of cultural equity has always animated Roadside's activity in community, whether at home in Appalachia, on tour, or in extended residence.

Often described as the theater wing of the civil rights movement, the Free Southern Theater (FST) was founded in 1963 at Tougaloo College in Mississippi by Student Nonviolent Coordinating Committee members, including Roadside's steadfast collaborator, John O'Neal. In 1985, O'Neal held a funeral, "a valediction without mourning," in New Orleans for the FST. Snaking from Congo Square down Dumaine Street into Treme, the relic-filled FST coffin, its pall bearers, and its gathering of followers shimmied and shook to the syncopated beat of a traditional brass marching band. People came to the funeral from struggling communities in different regions of the United States to perform and witness theater's power to address human rights—and to think critically about social justice. At the weeklong "valediction without mourning," Roadside offered *South of the Mountain*, which tells the story of the time in an Appalachian family when hillside farming and barter gave way to coal mining and the company store. *South of the Mountain* is the fourth play in Roadside's Appalachian history cycle. Here is part of one of its songs:

Winter time in the mountains,
And the snow is falling down.
Daddy's loading the pickup truck,
Hauling bakker into town.
There'll be new shoes for me and Carrie,
And for Momma, a new gown.
Peppermint sticks and orange slices
When Christmas rolls around.
(Chorus)
We believed in the family,
And the Old Regular Baptist Church.
We believed in John L. for a while
'Till things couldn't get much worse.
They tell me times was harder then,
And I remember that for a while.
But I remember the way my Daddy laughed
And the way my Mamma smiled.
Daddy would come home from work in the mines
With his shirt froze to his arms.
And every time my Momma would cry,
He'd say, "It ain't gonna do me no harm."
You know a man's got to work for a living today

And come spring I want to build a new barn.
But a man can't raise a family no more
On a rocky hillside farm.
(Chorus).

(Short, 1982)

The year 2013 marked the fiftieth anniversary of the FST and was the occasion for another FST reunion in New Orleans. Artists and activists of different ages and backgrounds joined with civil rights veterans who often had put their lives on the line for freedom in the 1960s. The commemoration, again organized by O'Neal and FST's organizational successor Junebug Productions, made the author think about what a twenty-first-century democratic theater might look like and the role community cultural development could play in such a movement. Those who understand power understand the influence of culture and its devised expression, art. They understand that those who control the means of cultural production control the story a community or nation tells itself.[13] Roadside's CCD practice seeks to unmask power so that it may be shared in service to the ideal of a cultural democracy in which all individuals, their communities, and their cultures have an equal opportunity to develop—and inevitably to cross-pollinate.

FIGURE 7.6 Roadside Theater performs *South of the Mountain* (photo by Judy Ehrlich)

Are there any present signs of a new populist democratic movement, akin to the labor and civil rights movements of the last century, in which the practice of CCD can be an actor? One can be sure that resistance to such a movement by those relatively few currently holding inordinate amounts of political and economic power will be swift, unilateral, and, if necessary, brutal. Those in power will be counting on unwitting allies—those who can be riled up by the red herring of some enemy out to destroy them and those within progressive ranks who can be co-opted by being told that it is about them as exceptional individuals rather than about collective struggle. As the Kentucky writer and farmer Wendell Berry has observed, "… individual genius of the modern kind never has courage equal to its essential loneliness, and so it commits itself passionately to clichés of individualism and a uniformity of innovation, ignorant of what precedes it, destructive of what it ignores" (Berry, 1987, p. 45).

We know that even movements originating from good intentions can become problematic as unintended consequences mount, and that power—even when used with the best of intentions—can corrupt. The antidote to such occurring or to co-option by those in power is vigorous critical discourse in which citizens agree to build and sharpen one another's perspectives, even as they hold one another accountable for their collective decisions. Presently, this iterative discourse is almost nonexistent in the nonprofit arts sector and in communities across the United States, so plenty continues to go wrong. Struggle, however, is an alternative to despair, and cultural development can energize communities, making them more conscious of their capacity to transform themselves on the basis of their own people.

## Notes

1 There is an abundance of documentation including multimedia and writing on Roadside Theater's Website: http://roadside.org. All unattributed quotations are from the author's memory.
   Cecil James Sharp (1859–1924), the founding father of the folklore revival in England in the early twentieth century, recorded and published England's traditional dances and music. A quotation from Cecil James Sharp's diary entry of August 27, 1916, when he was collecting in the Appalachian Mountains:
   > Last week I went to Hot Springs, where I got thirty beautiful songs from a single woman. The collecting goes on apace, and I have now noted 160 songs and ballads. Indeed, this field is a far more fertile one upon which to collect English folk songs than England itself. The cult of singing traditional songs is far more alive than it is in England or has been for fifty years or more.
2 Roadside Theater received grants from the National Endowment for the Arts, Folk Arts Program in 1979, 1981, 1983, 1990, and 1997 (Heritage and Preservation).
3 The five plays in the cycle are *Mountain Tales and Music* (1974); *Red Fox/Second Hangin'* (1976); *Pretty Polly* (1979); *South of the Mountain* (1982); and *Leaving Egypt* (1987).
4 The Wallace Foundation (then the Lila Wallace-Reader's Digest Fund), a national United States philanthropy funding education and audience development for the arts, commissioned the firm AMS Planning and Research to conduct a six-year (1991–1996) independent study of Wallace's performing arts grantees' audience

demographics. According to the study, Roadside Theater's audience was an anomaly: 68% of its national audiences were comprised of those with incomes under $50,000, and 27% of those had incomes of $20,000 of less.

5  Script ad-lib was excerpted from video of a 1986 *Pretty Polly* (Baker and Short, 1979) performance at Cleveland Technical College, Shelby, North Carolina. The video in VHF format has not been digitized.

6  "A nouveau riche hillbilly family moves to Beverly Hills and shakes up the privileged society with their hayseed ways." The Beverly Hillbillies is an American sitcom originally broadcast for nine seasons on CBS 1962–1971, starring Buddy Ebsen, Irene Ryan, Donna Douglas, Max Baer, Jr., Raymond Bailey, and Nancy Kulp. (http://www.imdb.com/title/tt0055662/).

7  Conversation noted on the 1988 performance producing sheet by the tour manager, Donna Porterfield, and confirmed orally 2013 by Porterfield.

8  Story noted on the 1995 producing sheet of the tour manager, Donna Porterfield, and confirmed orally in 2013 by Porterfield.

9  A digitized copy is available on Roadside Theater's Website: http://roadside.org/asset/book-ground-grassroots-theater-historical-contemporary-perspective?unit=245

10  Story noted on the 1989 producing sheet of the project manager, Donna Porterfield, and confirmed orally in 2014 by Porterfield.

11  Idiwanan An Chawe, the first Zuni language theater, was born of this process (1995). The first seventeen years of the Roadside Theater—Idiwanan An Chawe collaboration is documented in *Journeys Home: Revealing a Zuni—Appalachia Collaboration* (2002), D. Cocke, D. Porterfield, and E. Wemytewa, editors. Zuni, NM: Zuni A:shiwi Publishing. A digital copy is available on Roadside Theater's website(http://roadside.org/asset/book-journeys-home-revealing-zuni-appalachia-collaboration?unit=73).

12  Arizona State University's Public Events' 1998–1999 season featured the "Untold Stories Festival: Celebrating Campus and Community," which was dedicated to stories that connected communities by helping them see one another and themselves from new perspectives. The undertaking was a joint project of ASU and the American Festival Project, a multicultural alliance of a dozen artists and performing arts companies from across the United States, of which Roadside was a founding member. Roadside worked with: ASU's classified staff (secretaries, grounds keepers, cleaning crews, maintenance engineers) and an ASU Communications class to create a performance script, "Highly Classified," from the life stories of the staff, which was performed by classified staff in fall 1998; State Police Officers assigned to work at the ASU campus to create a play, "Police Stories," that was performed by Police Officers in April 1998; and the Metropolitan Boys and Girls Club and the Phoenix Theater's Cookie Company to create a script that was performed energetically by Club members in April 1998. Roadside also performed in collaborations with Idiwanan An Chawe of Zuni New Mexico, Junebug Productions, local artist Zarco Guerrero, and student dancers from the Gila River Reservation.

13  The author wrote more about this topic in "What is America? What is an American Theater?" In Todd, L., Ed. (2013). *An Ideal Theater: Founding Visions for a New American Art*. New York: Theatre Communications Group. It is an underlying theme in many of the author's articles (http://roadside.org/program/articles).

## References

Anderson, V. and deNobriga, K. (1994). *Alternate ROOTS plays from the Southern Theater*. Portsmouth, NH: Heinemann.

Auden, W. H. (1991). *Collected poems*. New York, NY: Vintage International.

Baker, D. and Short, R. (1979) *Pretty Polly* (play). Whitesburg, KY, Roadside Theater/ Appalshop, Inc.

Beaufort, J. (1978). Appalachian spring wafts into New York. *The Christian Science Monitor*, May 1, p. 26.

Berry, W. (1987). *Home economics: Fourteen essays by Wendell Berry*. San Francisco, CA, Norton Point Press.

Caudill, H. (1963). *Night comes to the Cumberlands: A biography of a depressed area*. Boston, MA, Little, Brown and Co.

Cocke, D., McGarvey, C., Kohl, E., Burnham, L., and Quay, J. (1999). *Connecting Californians: Finding the art of community change*. Retrieved July 15, 2014, from http://www.roadside.org/asset/booklet-connecting-californians-inquiry-role-story-strengthening-communities?unit=248

Cocke, D., Newman, H., and Salmons-Rue, H. (1993). *From the ground up: Grassroots theater in historical and contemporary perspective*. Ithaca, NY: Cornell University.

Franklin, B. (1977, May 12). An Appalachian drama captures Washington audience. *The New York Times*, p. 17.

Montana American Festival Project (1992–1995). Roadside Theater, Whitesburg, KY (Booklet). Retrieved April 13, 2015 from http://roadside.org/asset/booklet-montana-american-festival-project-1992-1995?unit=246

Mootz, W. (1978, April 10). Mountain tale beguiles New Yorkers. *The Louisville Courier-Journal*, p. 21.

Prine, J. (1971). "Paradise." Retrieved November 20, 2014 from http://www.azlyrics.com/lyrics/johnprine/paradise.html

Sainer, A. (1977, May 30). Foxy folks. *The Village Voice*, p. 89.

Short, R. (1982) *South of the mountain* (play). Whitesburg, KY, Roadside Theater/Appalshop, Inc.

Sidford, H. (2011). *Fusing arts, culture and social change: High impact strategies for philanthropy* (p. 1). National Committee for Responsible Philanthropy. Retrieved July 15, 2014, from http://www.ncrp.org/files/publications/Fusing_Arts_Culture_Social_Change.pdf

Thiong'o, N. (1986). *Decolonising the mind: The politics of language in African literature*. Portsmouth, NH, Heinemann.

Thiong'o, N. (1997). Enactments of power: The politics of performance space. *The Drama Review*, Autumn, 41(4): 11–30.

United Nations. (1948). *The Universal Declaration of Human Rights*. Retrieved on July 15, 2014, from http://www.un.org/en/documents/udhr/

Yates, M. (1999). *Cecil Sharp in America: Collecting in the Appalachians*. Retrieved July 15, 2014, from http://www.mustrad.org.uk/articles/sharp.htm

# 8

# A DIALOGUE ON DANCE AND COMMUNITY PRACTICE

*Liz Lerman and Jawole Willa Jo Zollar*

Liz Lerman and Jawole Willa Jo Zollar began their friendship one evening in 1985 when they shared the program at an event at a Harlem theatre. The two choreographers have carried on a lively dialogue about life, cultural aesthetics, and community practice since. They have shared and compared their modes of artistic research and have supported each other in the challenges of running their respective dance companies, Dance Exchange and Urban Bush Women.

While they had occasionally co-taught and made joint appearances at conferences as the years passed, it was not until 2011, after Lerman had left the Dance Exchange, that they began a full-scale collaboration, *Blood, Muscle, Bone: the anatomy of wealth and poverty*. Multi-disciplinary in its process and its outcomes, the project examines how wealth and poverty affect the body while asking new questions about how these opposed conditions are defined and imagined. Seeking to move beyond "compassion fatigue," the work addresses economic inequality and animates the seemingly intractable crisis of poverty. With a development arc of several years, the public offerings of *Blood, Muscle, Bone* have included stage performance, prayer breakfasts, lecture tours, workshops, teach-ins, panels, and cabarets. These community-engaged events are part of the creative process and product of this work.

In the following conversation, Zollar (JZ) and Lerman (LL) discuss the most recent versions of *Blood, Muscle, Bone*, reflect on their origins as community-engaged artists, and share insights on various dimensions of their professional work.[1]

Q:   May we start by having you describe your current collaboration, *Blood, Muscle, Bone: the anatomy of poverty and wealth*?

JZ:   The project is drawing on some of the tools, techniques, and methods that each of us has accumulated, embodied, thought about, and worked with throughout our careers. It employs those strategies in the form of a performative teach-in, which encourages people not to turn off to ideas that are challenging or issues that might have become somewhat numbing over time. I think Liz and I were starting to feel that there is a kind of uprising against the wealthiest one percent that is reactive, and not necessarily as powerful as it could be, because it is just gut emotional response based on information that the wealthy are getting richer and everyone else's income is either stagnant or declining. The teach-in allows people to think bigger than just being mad at those who have accumulated wealth.

Q: Could you say a bit about the legacy of the teach-in and how you are using it as point of departure?

JZ: My own awareness of the teach-in arose during the Vietnam War, which is when the format first manifested. Much later, I heard from my friend Steve Kent that his theater company, Provisional Theatre, had started doing performative teach-ins that used theatre techniques to engage audiences in different ways that went beyond the original idea of sit-down lecture, question-and-answer sessions, or let-me-tell-you-what-the-facts-are experiences.

LL: As artists, Jawole and I are interested in investigating many formats for performance that extend beyond the stage, much as we both love that. The teach-in idea really captured our imaginations during our early conversations about the project, and we developed our first attempt at one at Wesleyan University in November 2013. There, we worked with several scholars who gave lectures. In one case, we collaborated closely with a speaker to insert performance interruptions into her talk. In another case, we worked with an individual who was a last-minute substitute, to develop a beautiful improvisational structure that accompanied her lecture, rather than interrupting it.

We worked intensively with a group of students, ten days in a class format during three consecutive weekends. I am excited about what we were able to do in terms of embodying the lecture information and statistics and also about how we were able to channel a moment of intense emotion that came up during the class. Jawole was magnificent in guiding the students through a way of exploring their own personal relationships to the subject matter, which resulted in each of them having a solo piece. So the teach-in included a moment when audience members left their seats and could wander around to find monologues all over the performance space. The participating students were able to have a voice at a most personal level.

Q: Will the performers in these teach-ins always be students?

JZ: I think it will depend on the model of the performance and where we do it. I think if it is at a university, there will be both students and professional performers, and we are also excited about the potential of doing it with all

FIGURE 8.1 Jowale Willa Jo Zollar and Liz Lerman at the Performative Teach-In Event of *Blood, Muscle and Bone*

professional performers, with the event having a different kind of time frame and the audience being even more mobile.

Q:   Can you describe the makeup of the group at Wesleyan?

LL:   It was primarily undergraduates; we had about fifteen students, eleven were women, four of them men, and four or five of those participating were people of color. A few of them identified as dance people or theatre people, but many of them did not.

Q:   You mentioned a moment of intense emotion that led to the creation of solo material. Please say more about that.

JZ:   I think it was toward the end of a day. We were checking out in a final circle.

An African American woman—in an emotional, profound way that was a little unexpected in that moment—brought up the deep wounds that she was feeling around the subject of wealth and poverty. She spoke to the feeling that others were not understanding how deep those injuries were, that it was not just a matter of academic study but something that she was living. It came out in a way that others perceived as "us-versus-them," the good guys are the ones who have suffered, and the bad guys are the ones with the wealth. It created an unexpected flashpoint in the moment, but it also revealed what we knew was beneath the surface. It was the end of the day; she'd told us that she was going to be leaving early, so she basically laid this big powerful turd in the middle of the room, which was necessary, and then left. We did not have the time in that moment to really deal with what had happened. And it was when we came back the next weekend that we knew we had to address it.

LL: Jawole, I think you even dealt with it immediately. It reminded me of the moment when we were at Harvard University, where we were watching some work at the end of a workshop, and a student twisted her ankle pretty seriously. After she left to deal with it, I said, "Does anyone need to say anything? It's kind of scary when something like this happens. …" Nobody said anything, and I would have been content to move on, but you said, "Okay, everybody, let's get into our bodies for a minute," and you led us through a way of contacting what we were all feeling but wouldn't speak to. That's when I first got the hang of the fact that you could jump into this at an emotional level. My intellectual structuring, although it signaled me to acknowledge the incident, was insufficient. Having observed that at Harvard a year earlier, here comes this moment at Wesleyan, not a twisted ankle now but something much more emotional, and you have us on our feet, asking us to embody what we are feeling. So everyone there had acknowledged the student's deep concern personally before we ended the class. We had something to build on when we came back together.

One of the challenges at certain universities is that the progressive white students have a lot of language related to white guilt and even a set of historical associations, but it is not the same thing as living it, or dealing with it, or understanding it, or getting through it. That language becomes a code that substitutes for really addressing the issue: Here is the language, we will put it here, and we will go around it. The more it happened, the more I wanted to elucidate ways we could get at the essence, because just naming it is only a beginning.

Q: What happened when the class came back together?

LL: We gave people some writing assignments, asking them to respond to the moment in a variety of ways. That became the raw material for each student to develop a short monologue that had to be under a minute in length. We had the students add movement to them and set them site-specifically.

Q: As your first major collaboration, *Blood, Muscle, Bone* is the convergence of two important lines of work. What are the antecedents for the project, particularly the performative teach-in, in your past bodies of work?

JZ: We annually conduct a ten-day process during Urban Bush Women's Summer Leadership Institute. At the end of each one, we do a culminating performance, which is an embodiment of all the information and learning that has come up within the Institute. Topics include the People's Institute for Survival and Beyond "Understanding and Undoing Racism" and the UBW "Entering, Building, and Exiting Community." At the culmination, the audience has a chance to hear information and statistics and experience them as performance. When we moved the institute to New York in 2004, the title was "Are We Democracy?" We had Demos, a public policy organization, come in and give a talk on voter rights and voter repression;

it was quite a revelation how much voter repression was being perpetrated by both political parties and how the electoral system gets manipulated. We teased all that apart in a performance that synthesized the information from the Demos talk. *Blood, Muscle, Bone* is similar but with an opportunity for more depth than we get in the ten-day time frame of the leadership institutes.

Q:   What introduces the opportunity for more depth?

JZ:   In the Wesleyan model, it was a course, so that people had time between classes to do research and more time to filter that inquiry through their own experience. I think the students could invest more time in learning and gain more ownership of the knowledge they had gained. I also think depth comes from a group of professional performers along with Liz and me sharing their insights and learning about the subject matter. This increases the range and character of their responses to the research while helping to hone their creative responses and artistic direction.

LL:   I have sometimes talked about my ongoing interest in placing information and feeling side by side in performance as opposed to treating them separately, which I have often felt is the standard in our culture. It is as though we're supposed to get our information from the news and our feeling from fiction, or other forms. When you look at the subject matter of an awful lot of dance and contemporary songs, for example, it's primarily about love, but we have just as much feeling about money or wealth or disrespect, so I made it my calling to spend time in those places. My strongest antecedents for the performative teach-in work are probably in my series of *Docudances*, which began in 1980, where I explored contemporary political subject matter using concrete data and documentary sources.

More recently, working with theater companies, I have been challenged by one of the classic ideas of theater, the requirement for a narrative that builds to a crisis, and I'm realizing that I don't love crisis but am actually more interested in discovery. The audience's experience of uncovering something is what gets me excited, and I think that is why my work has sometimes been called didactic or educational. The teach-in format offers an opportunity to explore a continuum from a declaration of facts all the way to a personal interpretive score. It puts the cards on the table. You do not have to hide the elements of discovery and didacticism, and I like that.

Q:   There is also a way in which the teach-in seems to function as a site-specific or place-based event. What are the antecedents for that?

JZ:   It's funny, I didn't think of myself as having a focus on site-specific work because that seems like its own genre in some ways, but people have reminded me of how Urban Bush Women has worked in different environments. We *would* talk about alternative settings and have explored what it means to create performance in those environments that are not traditional theatres. "Site-specific," however, suggests an approach where you go in and you study a site and you transform it somehow choreographically, and that is a little different from how we worked.

LL:   What I think is at play here is a broader vision that both you and I have had for most of our lives, which is a deep interest in the people we are with, the actual participants and their evolution. I know that in my work, you start to see them choreographically in these big projects, in communities that maybe did not have theatres, so we were by necessity out and about and gathering in alternative settings. That is where the dancers I work with have to step up, and suddenly we start devising entirely different ways of performing by paying attention to the needs of the participants. Very early on, when I was teaching at Sandy Spring Friends School in Maryland, I just didn't want my students in the theatre right away, so I gave them site-based assignments so they would have other experiences, and suddenly I discovered a whole way of working that surprised me. With Dance Exchange there were the actual commissions from places that wanted us to come in, such as the Music Hall in Portsmouth, New Hampshire, where it was illuminating to work in contexts like the Naval Shipyard in which participants lived their lives. There were all these pressures—in a good way—to expand our practice. It looks like site-specific work because it is not on a stage.

JZ:   There are works that I make that are fundamentally for the audience to sit and to see in the theatre, with lights and costumes and stage design and the beauty of what that particular environment can give. And I am also interested in what happens in community settings and immersive environments. All of them hold great curiosity for me. A new piece we are working on now, *Hep-Hep Sweet Sweet*, began its life in the theatre, but as we got into the rehearsals, we quickly recognized that this was a work that was begging to be located in a setting in which the audience is less passive. It is set in a club, so why not actually produce it in one?

At one point when Liz was with our Summer Leadership Institute, we had three different sites, and one of them was an amazing church. What the choreographers and performers did in that space … I mean, the pastor was just blown away by seeing his church in a new kind of way, with new potential. So I think there is something that happens when you are in a community space, an ownership that leads to excitement when people see the environment utilized in ways they might not have imagined, because the performance is generated out of their own commitment. I mean, look, "community" as it is often used is such a low word, such a coded word, but for me, when I say community, I'm talking about a group of people committed to something together, or working toward an intentional idea; it's not haphazard.

Q:   What are your origin stories? Can each of you take us back and talk about the roots of the community component in your practices?

**FIGURE 8.2** Urban Bush Women's *Hep Hep Sweet Sweet*

JZ: Let's see … how to be concise? I grew up in a community dancing school, and my first dance teacher, Mr. Stevenson, always talked about "dancing from the inside out," about developing your own style. He would tell us that we were entertainers, dancing *for* people, but also dancing *from* the inside. I think that set up something about how I viewed the dancing experience.

Later, in college, I started to read a lot about the Black Arts Movement, which emphasizes the idea that art should come out of community culture and serve the people. I was very much immersed in that idea and became confused about what my response should be when I went to things that were aesthetically beautiful but not necessarily connected to anything other than an artist's own yearning and expression. If I saw a ballet, I wondered whether I should give myself permission to like it, if it wasn't art coming from the people. All of that bubbled around with the idea that in some African societies there is no such word as art: It is all part of how a community lives, all part of the integral aesthetics of a society, whether you are making an urn or a feather headdress. And even within that kind of tradition, the how matters, and things get made because someone says, "I want to express something."

I was living with these tensions in my creative practice when I enrolled at Florida State University and studied under Nancy Smith Fichter and read Susan Sontag and Antonin Artaud. That is when the postmodern movement and the Black Arts Movement somehow all came together for me. This occurred partly through Artaud's Theatre of Cruelty, the idea that theatre can expose a reality that is not abstracted or made into something pretty, just raw emotional form that through artistic rigor is brought to life. His conception aligned very closely with the philosophy of the Black Arts Movement. After Florida State, I went to New York, where I trained with Dianne McIntyre, when I decided to throw out all my past education to the degree that I could, including Merce Cunningham and Martha Graham. I started training with a woman, Kei Takei, who was working with natural movement, and I began to see through my study with McIntyre and Takei the connections among Post-Modernism, Africanist dance forms, and naturalism/realism. I told my dancers, "Don't point your feet, I don't want to see you pulled up." We also started learning vocal production, which forced us to rethink how we were holding our bodies, sometimes working against the standards of what people call *dance technique*.

So I was interested in working from a really visceral place and allowing emotion to determine how the form was defined. I worked that way for a long time, but at some point I started thinking, "All of these dancers have strong ballet and modern dance training, how could I use this? Is there a way to bring these two things together?" It became the idea of, okay, I have established a voice that came from undoing the training, now, how I can bring those particular skills back in? There was a kind of funky period where it didn't work. I was putting things together that didn't quite fit yet, and it took a long time to really make them connect. I eventually came out on the other side of it. I think that working in communities is what kept me cohesive in the practice because whatever was happening in the studio was steady and steadying. We were developing concrete skills for community facilitation. I could count on how that was working, on what I was learning in that setting, even if I had not entirely figured out how to combine the visceral and skilled on the stage. I remember saying in one post-performance discussion, "I'm traveling right now. I'm not in the old place and I'm not in the new place and I'm just traveling. And I don't know where I'm going." That kind of middle period is why I am so passionate about wanting to support choreographers. I think you've got to go through transitional periods like that; it's awkward; and it's ugly; and I think it's where a lot of artists lose faith and presenters and funders.

Having recently come back after a hiatus from Urban Bush Women, I have found a place that makes sense to me on so many levels. And the undergirding of the whole trajectory has been community practice. That is the element that has been the most steady, the most consistent. I continue to grow and be challenged in it but, because it was under the radar, it really was not in the critical eye. I think that was the difference for me. The work I did in community was not reviewed in the papers, it was not up for judgment from outside critics, though we were held accountable by local allies. So it was a safe haven, a place of experimenting and trying things and learning. I think that was my saving grace.

LL:    That was beautiful, Jawole. Maybe I can try a parallel construction: I grew up in a political household with a father who was an organizer and a mother who was just an extremely aesthetic person, so the two poles of community and artistic thinking were very present from the beginning. I am not going to talk about my first dance teacher, but my second dance teacher was pretty extraordinary, and I think she set in motion the thinking body. She yelled a lot, too, in ways that seemed arbitrary, so she also set in motion my terror of teachers who scream and the beginning of my attempts to try to understand what kind of environment I wanted to build as a teacher and choreographer and what I came to believe brings out the best in people.

When I arrived at Bennington to start college, all I knew how to do was "dance from the inside," as your teacher put it. Of course, I was ridiculed because it was a Cunningham-based department; I had to strip myself of what I called my Midwestern lyricism as fast as I possibly could. Like you, I also read. So, as you were getting the Black Arts Movement influence, I think I was filling myself up with things like Dada, the early twentieth-century artists in Russia who were doing huge pageants, and the German artist Kurt Schwitters, with his entire house built up into a collage. So I was filling myself up with a lot of support, but it was not coming from the performing arts. Instead, it arose from the visual arts and extreme situations, like revolutionary Russia. Some of these readings were suggesting the sort of society where-there-is-no-word-for-art that you noted, Jawole, but the practice I encountered at Bennington was just the opposite. I was terribly confused. I was perplexed enough to consider quitting, many times, during that period.

Jawole, you talked about the connection and disconnection between an emotional foundation and a skill base. For me, my mom's death when I was twenty-seven and the dance I made about the experience were the beginning of my march away from feeling as the only place to work. I was sad, and I would spend a period rehearsing all these sad phrases, and then one day I came in the studio, and suddenly I wasn't feeling sad anymore. I didn't know what to do. I didn't know how to dance. That was the beginning of an idea: Well, wait a minute, if you're sad, your back is curved, your fingers are spread, your focus is down, so I'll make a phrase with curved backs, spread fingers, and focus down. I didn't have to dance direct from the emotion, and I didn't have to dance an abstraction that had nothing to do with feelings, either. That was probably the earliest tool I developed.

I think that both of us have experienced a spiraling period where we got our tools together and then were ambitious, and we moved our practices to a new place and stopped doing some of the things for which we were known. My perception is that I wasn't always rewarded by the presenting world for those practices. Not everyone will stand by you through that kind of change, and I do think you see some artists whose growth has stopped in response, but I think that with every single piece in which I over-extended myself, I was able to achieve a breakthrough in the next.

Q:  Now you have come to a point in your lives and arrived at a collaboration. What are you learning from observing each other, and how would you compare yourselves?

JW:  The learning is happening on so many levels and layers. Liz is just a brilliant mind, and seeing the way that she processes and how she builds structure is really incredible for me. I think that I probably give more room and allow more space before I go in with directorial ideas than Liz does. A big difference that I notice is that I probably let the performers, you know, *goo around* for a longer period of time before I go in to shape it, where Liz sees structures and interventions that are really powerful and moves in with them more quickly.

LL:  I think it should be said that Jawole and I have been in conversation for a really long time, and it has been collaborative in the sense that our exchanges were like a guidepost, a gentle guiding spirit in relation to issues of how you manage a company and how you oversee a rehearsal and how you supervise personnel, all of those things, but then *Blood, Muscle, Bone* comes along, and it is really a change. Among the things I am noticing is that we both have a great sense of humor, but they are really different. I do not know whether it is cultural or individual. I can crack a joke, and it can break the tension in the room, but Jawole is funnier than I am, she just opens up a big guffaw, I mean it's just fantastic, so I love that. I think on the deepest level, though, this difference between us has something to do with the way you trust your emotional self, and I have come to rely strongly on my intellectual self. Since making the discovery after my mother died, I have built structures that approach material from other directions and trusted in allowing the emotion to emerge: I'm not going to go after it, it's going to develop but, to me, Jawole, you harness it early and deeply. That's a huge reminder to me. I don't know what it's going to mean for my own work, but I know it's really different.

JZ:  I do think that approach to feeling comes from working in the communities that we have worked in, and through this collaboration I have come to realize that you and I have worked with very different populations. Urban Bush Women usually works in economically poor black communities. We have rarely been brought in to work with white working-class or affluent communities. So the methods that we have honed are about working with those populations in particular, groups in crisis that are facing racism and other heavy burdens. Everything is right on the surface, so if you don't go in and tap into that quickly, it's going to explode as it did with the student at Wesleyan. What I've learned is that we need go in there right away and address it, otherwise it's going to bleed all over the room and explode.

I do think we go right into the impact of racism, because that's always sitting in the room with us. And so, working with our partner, The People's Institute, we have learned to go in there and see where that is sitting with us. What we are learning better—and when I say "we" I mean the collective that is Urban Bush Women—is about flashpoints. When we do our community-based work, there is always a flashpoint of conflict or the perception that someone has done something particularly egregious or wants to press a specific agenda. We used to see such situations as an obstacle, but now we are seeking to learn from them so as to be able to improve our leadership and our art making. We have come to a point of welcoming flashpoints as a creative departure, as a way to understand that something is unfolding to which we need to pay attention. And it is the same in the company. It used to be that when conflict came up I would personalize it. Now I'm coming to understand that disagreement represents an opportunity to uncover something creative. For me, it is a spiritual place, believing that every experience you have represents an opportunity for you to learn something.

LL: Well, I would agree, Jawole, that flashpoints are incredible moments of learning. Thinking on the company level, when I ran the Dance Exchange, I used to say that we would get a major one about every five years. The image in my mind was that the gears were shifting and people got caught in them, sometimes it was just a sleeve, but sometimes the whole person would get caught. I always learned a lot from the flashpoints; I think people around me did, too.

It's also worth paying attention to what pushes your buttons and why, which led us for a while to an insistence on integrated teams working in communities. For example, we had a company member who grew up going to under-resourced public schools in Harlem. His buttons would get so pushed by being in a poor black school where there was trash that had not been picked up or was not tidy, that he would just go crazy. Similarly, I would go crazy in Jewish communities where there was too much display of wealth, too much gold. I would just react, "I can't love these people, I'm too mad." And we felt that by integrating the team we had a chance at loving the people we were with, working through the fact that individuals in the team might be struggling with the situation in which they found themselves. Our approach contradicted the kind of community creed that dictates that you should send gay people to gay people and black people to black people and Jewish individuals to Jewish individuals. I did not agree with this view, and that stand led to an awareness of how we could function as catalysts and the power we could have as outsiders.

JZ: Returning to the comparisons between Liz and me, I think for me structure is the thing that often comes later and with which I struggle. I usually get there, but it takes me longer to get to structure. I will go to structure via emotion: What is the emotional arc of this work, of the performer, of what they're searching for? Liz, however, goes to the internal structures of the piece, and she defines those very quickly in a way where things overall become clearer. I think the two approaches are a really powerful combination in our work together. That is an exciting aspect of this collaboration.

LL: I consider structure such a friend, but it is also very changeable. It's always there from the get-go. It's like a kind of poetry in my brain for most of the trip of the piece or even of any given rehearsal.

Q: When we talk about accessing emotion or structure, we could be talking about a performance piece or about a community process. With that in mind, I wonder if you could discuss the relationship of your stage works to your community projects.

JZ: I talk about this in this particular way. For me, they're both art-making processes. I like to think of a sculptor who sculpts in both wood and marble. You have to use different logics to do each one. So, if you use the mode to work with wood on marble or vice versa, you are going to have a mess. Nonetheless, you are still the same artist, you still have the same vision, but you are working in two different artistic media, with different materials that require discrete ways of working. I started articulating this because even the dancers in the company were getting confused about what the differences were between working in a community and in a theater. When we work in community, it is important to obtain as broad a scope as possible, as comprehensive a coalition of participation as possible, to get as many ideas from that population on the table and in the performance as possible. Some of that holds true for concert practice, too, but there I allow my directorial vision to have more power and focus.

LL: Yes, there's something about the calls of concert dance where the protocol of self-expression and individual vision plays out more. We used to joke at Dance Exchange, "Dance is for everyone ... and that includes Liz Lerman." I was more likely to carve that place out for myself in relation to the concert work. I think for me that there is a lot of overlap in methods, there is a lot of difference, but usually the choice goes back to questions like who is this for, what is this about, and who is the audience?

Questions like these allow me to change up some of what I am doing in a positive way. One of the benefits for me as an artist—and maybe you are suggesting this by your sculptor analogy, Jawole—is that my own methods changed, grew, and enlarged because of these multiple urgencies and audiences. I would never have developed the tools I did if I had only worked with one set of people. It was the opportunity to test and retest on different audiences that allowed me to see that the strategies could be employed in different ways.

I have been thinking about this in relation to *Healing Wars*, a project I am currently developing with veterans, in which I am still working to evolve my approach. I was remembering my early work I did with old people and how simple and elegant it was. Partly it was because I was only twenty-seven, partly because it was all brand new, partly because my mom died,

**FIGURE 8.3** The company of Liz Lerman's *Healing Wars*

**FIGURE 8.4** Paul Hurley and Keth A. Thompson in *Healing Wars*

and I was hurting, but it was just such a potent meeting of purpose and need; I taught them to dance, and they taught me how to make it all work and make it meaningful; and it was just an amazing thing. This is so hard with the veterans. The layers of complexity that are going on in their lives, the machinations of exploitation, of giving and taking, make working with them very complicated. I still completely believe that making art together with a group of people will lead to something amazing, but it is a new challenge each time.

Q:   Was community practice a choice for you? Did you consciously make a choice to head in this direction?

LL:  It was pretty conscious, but it was conscious with some defiance and with the assertion that I'm never going to feel less for making this decision. I've felt lessened by others, but I never personally felt less. One of the comments I have made over the years is, "I'm not fragmented; the world is." In order for me to be my full self, it looks like I have to step out into these odd regions. And it fulfills not just me but my whole art form. What was so weird about it was why would anybody think the art form was less for it when it, to me, just seemed like a big, grand plan of how you could use movement, dance, and art in a variety of ways.

JZ:  Yes, I was always amazed that writers are still writers, whether they are writing about events in the real world or fantasy fiction. Either way, they still get to be called a writer, but the moment that you, as a dance artist, want to bring in community voices or have some point of view about the world based in politics or social justice, suddenly you are no longer a choreographer—you are a social worker or therapist. I was always confused by why that standard was applied to choreographers in a way that it was not to other genres.

LL:  I still feel that the relationship between what happens in the studio and what happens out in the world is compelling and has an impact on audiences. I think there's a third element, as well, Jawole, that I realized through our work together at Wesleyan. There's our concert work and our community-based practice, and there's the additional fact that we are both narrative artists.

JZ:  Yes.

LL:  The more you spend time in the world, the more compelled you are by the stories you hear, and you say, "Wait a minute, I want that to be part of things," but bringing narrative into the foreground also creates dilemmas in how we are perceived as artists.

JZ:  It's so interesting because I think that I am story-driven. Even if it is abstract, for me story is always a driver. And that has continued to be something that is threatening to the greater, elitist part of the dance world. I get it time and time again: The work would have just been better if there were no story, if there were no text. I have started really to push back at that and say, "Well listen, I think our field is not singular, that it can hold those of you who are attracted to the movement only as the embodiment of what you think of as pure dance, and those who want to tell stories where the movement is a part of how they are told." I am getting really feisty about it. We are as much an art-making movement as postmodernism. We just have not received a blessing from the particular powers that be.

Q: You say they are threatened by story. Why do you think that is so?

JZ: Oh, for heaven's sake, that you might connect emotionally, or spiritually, or intellectually to what I am actually talking about. That's what I think; I don't know, Liz, what do you think that threat is?

LL: You know, I would like to take a really hard look at Merce Cunningham and George Balanchine. Because I think there's something in the way in which these two men were embraced at a particular time in our culture that was extremely powerful and important. I am grateful, particularly in Cunningham's case, for some of the liberation that came with it. However, I think there is some deeply masked, disguised animosity to emotion, to psychology, to expression, to women, to any number of things that modernism was reacting to at that time. What I don't understand is why there's a whole establishment that persists around it. Academic and concert dance are so firmly entrenched around those two figures that many people would have to change their entire perspective to embrace other possibilities.

JZ: Well, I have a kind of a provocative thought …

LL: Good! Go!

JZ: I went to see one of the Cunningham Company's last performances. I think I saw the next-to-last performance at Park Armory. It was stunningly beautiful and amazing, and as I watched it, I thought, "Okay, this is the end of whiteness as embodied as a value in dance." The work is *white personified*. This is it: There's no use of the torso, there's no emotion, there's no story. It is about privileged space. I think one must recognize, even though it's not named, that African and African American culture has deeply influenced the later generation of white ballet and formalist choreographers, such as William Forsythe and others. After that, I don't know that we're going back to the deliberate white formalism that Cunningham brought to twentieth-century choreography.

I don't know if this phenomenon has been studied or written about. I just remember the first time I saw Lucinda Childs's work in performance; it was beautiful: *Available Light*,[2] with the dancers all in white, and I sat there thinking, "Well, if I'm black, this is definitely white; if you're going to call my work black, then this is definitely whiteness," but there's no articulation of that.

LL: That's brilliant, Jawole. I've mostly seen it as feminist thing; that is to say, I saw Cunningham erasing Graham. …

JZ: … Yes, yes …

LL:   … and all of her deeply emotional things that women do. So I'm with you on the next step you've taken. I'm trained in those white methods, and to this day I can't move my center.

Q:    This suggests another provocation for you both: dance technique. To what degree does it underpin your work, to what degree do you push against the concept, to what degree is the notion of dance technique as a singular either limiting or liberating?

JZ:   Well, as a singular idea, it is very limiting. Because then it is measured in how much turnout you have or how your feet point. One of the things I have learned from working with one of our dance scientists at Florida State University is that the so-called beautiful hypermobile feet that everyone covets are actually fairly weak and actually do not function well in my choreography. Dancers with such feet are more likely to incur ankle injuries from the kind of athleticism we use. So, I actually look for people who do not have hypermobile feet. Technique is relative to the thing you want to accomplish, but it has been defined as monolithically singular in relation to the ballet aesthetic, and that is unfortunate.

LL:   Singularity is a problem when applied to most things, including the label of technique. I'm happy to be a female artist, I'm happy to be a Jewish artist, I'm happy to be postmodern, I'm happy to be a narrative artist, but I'm not happy to be singularly any one of those things.

      And, Jawole, I am compelled by this idea that technique depends on what you want to accomplish, that the wrong technique for the job can be an impediment. A scholar interviewed me recently at a public event at Hebrew Union College. We were discussing art, orthodoxy, and ritual. At one point, he said to me "But, you must love your classical training, because it set you up," and I *shocked* the room when I said, "Are you kidding? I wish I didn't have it! Because when I get up to be myself, I instantly assume classical forms, and that's not me." I suppose the benefit was the thirty years of pushing back that led me to all the tools that emerged from efforts to trick myself out of patterns that were set when I was six years old.

JZ:   And yet at the same time, I love classical form. I love the training. There is this thing going on in the modern dance world now where people teach symmetrically up to a point, and then they will do a long combination that is only on one side, but some of us who are old school, we want to train symmetrically. That is the beauty of ballet; it is absolutely training the right side and the left side equally, and they are not given preference. I think in some ways that is one gift of European-inspired classical form.

LL:   But it's right, left, up, down, not middle.

JZ:   No, not middle. [Laughter.]

LL:   Back during your origin story, Jawole, you talked about your effort to throw out the training before you re-integrated it. That suggests the notion that the art form itself has something to gain from the participation of people who might not be trained. That idea has long been critical to my work, but it wasn't until 2011 that I learned a term for it from Harvard professor Robin Kelsey: de-skilling. Kelsey teaches the history of photography, where "de-skilling" describes how certain photographers intentionally pulled back from hyper-exacting technique to seek another aesthetic. I got excited when I heard him use the word, and I said, "Oh, there's an actual term for that! Oh, look, we have a parallel!" In my earlier work, I definitely felt that the presence of the older people was absolutely signaling to an audience that this is not merely going to be about technique, because how could it be? We significantly don't have any. The way the older people upended the audience's expectations about technique was one of the compelling forces that kept me at it for so long.

JZ:    And I would offer that there is a technique that people who are not professionally trained are able to bring the stage, and that is simply based on their life experience, because it has not been trained away. It hasn't been put on the back burner. Their technique arises from living life and not having to filter it through ideas of correct or incorrect movement; their technique is embedded in their ability to be present as a living human being. That practice of being able to bring the authentic self to movement is something the non-professional more naturally brings in a profound way but that trained dancers have to seek through somatic practice.

Q:     In talking about community encounters, aesthetics, and technique, we are touching on a topic that, for want of a better word, I would call *diversity*. So, let me just throw that word out to you and ask you to respond to it because, from the outside, people might look at Dance Exchange and call it diverse and Urban Bush Women and say culturally specific, though surely these descriptors are limiting. Can you respond to that?

JZ:    All work is culturally specific. Culture is a way of life, and all artistic work comes from that. So, why is an African American company culturally specific while a white company is not? Because what we're talking about, but not naming, is racism. The fact that Urban Bush Women is not seen as diverse is really interesting because that is using a limited idea of what "blackness" is. Right now, there is a woman who is perceived to be white in the company: she's blonde-haired, blue-eyed. And the comments I have been hearing about her are really interesting, either [*enthusiastic*] "Oh, you got a white woman in the company!" or [*skeptical*] "You got a *white woman* in the company?" Now, when you go into her background, she is Cuban American. I met her parents. They are dark, so the complexity of this dancer's background is removed by the black-and-white construct that we live in that results from racism. The complexity of identity is removed, and so a dance company is either black or, if it has one Asian or African American, it is diverse. It is unfortunate that we are still uncomfortable dealing with the fundamental racism that underpins these categories. We would like to wish it away and then code it with words like *diversity*, *community*, *culturally specific*, but until we can address it, I think we will just be—excuse my metaphor—dancing around the thing that we're talking about.

There is so much deep mythology that we have not dealt with as a society. When Urban Bush Women went to South America on a State Department tour in 2010, I think one of the most powerful things we noticed, in Colombia, Venezuela, and Brazil, was how people talked about their history, which was roughly: "Our country is built primarily on three cultures: the indigenous people who were here, the Europeans who came in and who colonized, and the Africans they brought over as slaves; those are the three primary cultural influences." We heard something like this in every country we visited, and of course we have a similar history here in the U.S., but we never speak of it so matter-of-factly. It doesn't mean that racism does not exist in those countries, but they have not denied history the way we have. There's a deep psychosis in the American attitude to history.

Q:   Would you like to offer any closing thoughts about community-based work?

JZ:   Thinking back to the entire question of narrative and narrative structures: This concern has been the subject of an ongoing tension within the dance world. One fundamentalist camp says that if you have narrative, you are putting dance in the service of something else, which diminishes the art form. The other fundamentalist camp believes that any "art for art's sake" is irrelevant because it is not of service to a community, but neither extreme is very helpful in my view. Instead, I think that each artist must discover what excites them about making work. Returning after a hiatus from Urban Bush Women, I realized that what animates me is having a sense of community, having a sense of purpose with people who are together, who are in relationship to one another. I mean, we do company class together, we train together—there is something about that sense of community that I really enjoy and that defines my art making, but it is not a fundamentalist position. It is what works for me. If we can come to a world where we understand that you go to the things that are most compelling, the subjects and the ways of making, you will create your highest and most powerful choreography. For me that comes from being in a community of art makers dedicated to a common goal but without all having the same perspectives.

LL:   For a long time, I thought that I was developing things in the studio and "taking them into community," but it became clear to me after a while it was the other way around, too.

JZ:   Absolutely, absolutely.

**FIGURE 8.5** Urban Bush Women's *Walking with 'Trane, Chapter 2*

LL: ... And I started to notice how audiences experienced things when I took my work into synagogues. Within the course of an hour at a synagogue, they were sitting and praying, sitting and watching, sitting and listening, sitting and talking, sitting then standing. They went through far more than a typical audience would go through if they came to see a show. I began to wonder about that. How could we get a theatre audience to engage at that level? That idea became instrumental in how I have reframed my work during the last ten years.

JW: In *Group Genius*, Keith Sawyer argued that "collaboration is the secret to breakthrough innovation" (Sawyer, 2007). I think that's what's exciting to me about working in communities. You are working in collaboration, and you are working with intention. As you have just articulated, Liz, it teaches you something, and the expansion of your vision, if you are open, is inevitable.

## Notes

1  This dialogue contains material from two separate interviews, the first conducted by Jennifer Calienes at Florida State University on November 21, 2013, and the second facilitated by John Borstel through an online video chat on February 19, 2014. John Borstel sequenced and edited the composite offered here.
2  *Available Light,* 1983. Choreographed by Lucinda Childs, musical score by John Adams, set design by Frank Gehry, lighting by Beverly Emmons, costumes by Ronaldus Shamask.

## References

Sawyer, R. K. (2007). *Group Genius: The Creative Power of Collaboration.* New York, NY: Basic Books.

# 9

# ASSESSING ARTS-BASED SOCIAL CHANGE ENDEAVORS

## Controversies and Complexities

*Kate Preston Keeney and Pam Korza*

For arts practitioners who work to address civic and social concerns, it is imperative that they have ways to gauge the impacts of their efforts. These artists and their partners and stakeholders want to know whether they have contributed to a desired change. As culture workers, they want to understand how arts strategies work and what factors yield success. They seek to improve practices to be more effective in their efforts. Yet, arts practitioners are challenged by the use of traditional evaluation tools to assess and share the effects of their work adequately. As such, contemporary arts and social change work requires a "shift in evaluation from a means to *proving* value and impact to *improving* practice and efficacy" (Schaffer Bacon and Korza, 2013, p. 3).

This chapter examines the complexities of understanding the social impact of nonprofit organizations employing arts and cultural practices in efforts to contribute to positive community, civic, and social change. We use the term *impact* to describe the full range of social effects that may arise from arts-based endeavors including short- to intermediate- to long-term outcomes, acknowledging that many evaluation professionals would reserve the term for longer-range effects or results. The three organizations we highlight operate in unique geographical and social contexts, including Portland, Maine, which is working to address the morale of its employees and public perceptions of its efforts; the city of Tucson, Arizona, which is culturally rich and home to two Native American tribal nations but also faces significant economic and social challenges; and the historically significant yet environmentally challenged communities neighboring major oil refineries in southeastern Louisiana. Working in these contexts, each entity we profile is attempting to make space for citizens to participate in and take ownership of positive community change. They are applying the unique capacity of the arts and culture to engage people in such initiatives in the places where they live and work.

Although each case is distinct, taken together, these organizations—a creative program led by an artist embedded in municipal government, a local arts council, and a social justice action group using cultural strategies—offer important lessons to scholars and practitioners struggling with the complexities inherent in evaluating social change. Though their on-the-ground assessments draw upon some conventional evaluation practices, these institutions also challenge notions of predetermined outcomes at the core of standard evaluation approaches. These organizations demonstrate that the process of understanding impacts must be fluid, reflexive, context-appropriate, inclusive, and culturally competent.

Stern and Seifert (2009a) have argued that "Community engagement and social change can occur as an unintended consequence of collective arts and cultural activity" (p. 13). Their Social Impact of the Arts Project at the University of Pennsylvania has contributed substantially to understanding the effects of the larger ecosystem of arts and cultural agents on neighborhoods and communities. Indeed, their research is seminal in understanding the influence of arts and culture on place. To add to this literature, we investigate arts-based projects and programs that *intentionally* work to influence community, civic, or social outcomes.

We address the complexities inherent in assessing the impacts of arts-based social-change work through six research questions:

1   Why is it important to understand social impact?
2   What motivates organizations employing arts and cultural strategies to understand social impact?
3   How do such institutions involve multiple stakeholders in defining meaningful outcomes and in assessing and communicating desired social changes?
4   How do entities engaging in arts- and culture-based work use data to make the case for employing the arts as a social-change strategy?
5   How does place influence the way these organizations approach their work and evaluation practices?
6   In what ways do social-change institutions learn and develop from evaluations of their work?

In examining these questions, we first offer a portrait of the general landscape of arts and culture-based social-change work and the challenges associated with evaluating such initiatives. We then explore the efforts of three organizations actively working in this landscape, including descriptions of their programmatic foci, desired social-change outcomes, and evaluation approaches and methods. We conclude by offering a synthesis of findings that underscores challenges from the field and offers new issues to consider when evaluating arts and culture-based social-change work.

## Key Dimensions of Arts and Culture-Based Social-Change Work and Their Implications for Evaluation

Artists and cultural workers have consciously deployed creative practices and products and cultural experiences in many ways to contribute to community, civic, or social change (Jackson, 2009; Stern and Seifert, 2009a; Schaffer Bacon and Korza, 2012). The intended outcomes of these initiatives vary as widely as arts-based approaches to social change because arts- and culture-based work can inform, provoke, inspire, connect, engage, improve, and empower and may also shape social discourse concerning public issues of consequence (Korza, Schaffer Bacon, and Assaf, 2005, p. 3).

The Shipyard Project, mounted by the Music Hall in Portsmouth, New Hampshire in the mid-1990s, provides one example of an arts-based social-change project intended to affect civic capacity (Putnam and Feldstein, 2003). The initiative sought to engage residents in dance-based activities and dialogue through an extended artist residency by the Liz Lerman Dance Exchange and to provide them an opportunity to understand differing perspectives regarding the possible closing of the U.S. Naval shipyard in their community. Choreographer Liz Lerman used dance practices to collect stories from community members in an effort to find "common ground, a meeting place, while recognizing and respecting differences" (Putnam and Feldstein, 2003, p. 64). Scholars have shown that narrative and storytelling can "express the complex realities of particular people and places and their possible unique ability to express thought and feeling simultaneously" (Putnam and Feldstein 2003, p. 6; Ganz, 2010; VanDeCarr, 2013). The Shipyard Project showcased the capacity of art to foster dialogue about shared experiences that can promote understanding across difference and subsequently build social capital in communities (Putnam and Feldstein, 2003).

Arts practitioners engaged in social-change work use various tools to define the intended outcomes of their practice. Based on research concerning numerous projects, Animating Democracy (2011) developed a continuum of social outcomes that arts practitioners and their partners most commonly aspire to achieve. Outcomes fall into six "families:" enhanced awareness and knowledge of social concerns; improved public discourse; clarified values and confirmed or shifted attitudes; increased capacity—skills, resources, social capital—to engage in civic issues; increased and more effective participation in public action and choice processes; and better-quality systems (such as prison reform), policies (such as for fair treatment of the homeless), and conditions (including improved public safety) (Korza and Schaffer Bacon, 2012). These outcomes do not necessarily play out sequentially, nor is there a hierarchy of importance among them. For example, relationship building among fragmented and uninvolved residents may be a singular desired outcome of a neighborhood arts project intended to build civic engagement capacity. A different effort may aspire to policy change as its ultimate outcome, but require sustained dialogue and action to secure it (Korza and Schaffer Bacon, 2012).

Who is undertaking arts and social-change work? Many arts and culture-based efforts are driven by individual artists or by small to mid-sized organizations that operate at the neighborhood or local community level. They may be guided by a mission oriented to the public good, prompted by a desire to address a pressing concern that affects local residents' well-being, or see the potential for a particular art production or project to have greater public value. Putnam and Feldstein (2003) have noted the importance of intimate settings to foster civic participation and stated, "Listening and trusting are easier in smaller settings. One-on-one, face-to-face communication is more effective at building relationships and creating empathy and understanding than remote, impersonal communication" (p. 276). Indeed, the organizations included in this research aim to create such opportunities through arts and culture processes and products. Not only are they able to effect change with limited resources, but also they recognize the importance of including and learning from participants as they also define their work and desired outcomes.

How do place and community factor into arts and culture-based work, and how are its effects understood? Place can be defined as what binds people geographically—neighborhood, city, or region. Beyond physical space, communities are distinguished by social connections. Borrup (2006) has suggested that community includes "social, civic, and economic bonds, in addition to the physical bonds, among people who reside, work, or otherwise consider themselves a part of a geographic place" (p. 4). The Tucson Pima Arts Council (TPAC), for example, has considered all of these elements, and Roberto Bedoya (2013), TPAC's executive director, has suggested the notion of belonging as a cornerstone of effective place-based arts and social-change work with the building of relationships and human capital—both individual and collective—as a key indicator of success (p. 7).

How one understands community context has significant bearing on interpreting the effects of arts-based social-change work. For example, comprehending the traditional cultural forms of Louisiana will influence the assessment of the use of parades and music employed in cultural organizing strategies. Similarly, knowing that a community has participated in previous initiatives addressing morale issues in municipal government is an important factor in interpreting the effects of any subsequent project addressing the concern.

## Problems in Evaluating the Effects of Arts-Based Social-Change Work

Although there is literature on how the arts have been applied to contribute to community betterment, challenges remain in defining the range of social goods the arts may address. Arts-based change approaches draw upon humans' desire to belong to a group, participate, connect, and contribute to society. These behaviors also strengthen democracies (Inglehart, 2000) and may be catalyzed through the creative self-expression inherent to the production and practice of art. Yet, these goals are often not clearly defined, nor easily measured (Murray, 2010; Weiss, 1995).

A common argument against evaluating arts-based social-change work is that "artistic activities, which are based fundamentally on aesthetic principles and subjective judgment, are not amenable to traditional forms of evaluation" (Schuster, 1997, p. 259). In a similar vein, cultural chronicler and theorist Arlene Goldbard (2008) has vigorously challenged the urge to apply quantifiable metrics borrowed from science or industry to highly complex human endeavors and social systems: "In the quest for metrics, feelings, ideas, relationships, beliefs and other such important dimensions of experience are dismissed or devalued precisely because they can't be adequately demonstrated by quantitative measurement" (p. 2). Arts-based social-change projects often unfold in unpredictable non-linear ways, and outcomes may be defined or revised through the creative process, making predetermining results not only difficult, but also counterproductive. Artist Lerman has discussed her willingness to trust in "an unknown outcome as 'an incredible life skill' not just an artistic strategy" (Putnam and Feldstein, 2003, p. 72). Given these arguments, we conclude that arts-based initiatives and related evaluation processes should be rooted in a theory of change but simultaneously receptive to changing assumptions as new information is created and knowledge attained.

Adverse reactions to evaluating arts-based strategies to social change have as much or perhaps more to do with the narrow concepts of change too often adopted and a lack of awareness of alternatives to conventional linear and metrics-based theories of change (Reeler, 2007). A theory of change is a guiding frame and set of assumptions that describes why the strategies one chooses should produce the results one intends (Weiss, 1995; Stern and Seifert, 2009a; Fiennes, 2013). A clear theory of change requires would-be change agents to be explicit about what they are trying to do and why and influences the vigor of programs. Operating with strong ideals and passion, artists and those who support them may set unrealistic social-change goals, especially at the project or program level (Jackson, 2009). Adopting a clear description of what precisely artists aim to change and how and why can help to mitigate this possibility.

Evaluation professionals urge a more honest and realistic look at what change can occur, cautioning practitioners against the temptation to "prove" that an arts intervention "caused" a particular outcome. Jackson has commented on this concern:

> The arts field, perhaps more so than any other policy area in which I have worked, is particularly concerned with establishing causality to confirm its value. Perhaps this approach stems from the art sector's positioning against issues deemed more important by other fields—housing, health, education, etc. It can also be due to a lack of formal knowledge about what an evaluation strategy can reasonably accomplish.
>
> (Jackson, 2009, p. 6)

Many factors contribute to change. The mere establishment of correlation with an intended outcome is enough, in many fields, to command attention and make a case about effects (Jackson, 2009).

Partnerships between arts and non-arts agencies may result in differing frameworks for evaluation, with divergent assumptions about success and measurement (MacDowell et al., 2013). This can lead to the choice of only a few specific outcome measures that "often cannot begin to capture the full range and complexity of the effects caused by the program, organization or system interventions" (Cutt and Murray, 2000, p. 38). To address limited outcome measures, practitioners and funders alike are seeking to elevate qualitative data and story as legitimate, broadly acceptable, and potent evidence of change (VanDeCarr, 2013) and to couple such narratives with additional quantitative metrics.

Most organizations undertaking arts- and culture-based work have limited capacity to undertake evaluations, let alone the resources necessary to implement programs. One aspect of the ideal evaluation process, as defined by Cutt and Murray (2000), is that the choice of methods for producing data must be "timely and feasible to use in terms of cost and effort" (p. 36). With limited capacity, organizations seek methods that fit their existing knowledge and technical resource base. When external funding is available, entities may temporarily expand their capacity for evaluation, yet continued follow-through remains a challenge.

Documenting effects and the impact of arts-based social-change initiatives in a way that generalizes beyond a specific community context presents a challenge to most organizations engaged in such efforts (Dwyer and Animating Democracy, 2008). For this reason, it is important to understand the role that context and place play in the success of particular efforts. Important contextual variables include community demographics; economic conditions; community cohesion/polarization; history and prevailing norms; and position/history of sponsoring unit(s). Similarly, information about contextual variables should help guide the choice of evaluation approaches (Dwyer and Animating Democracy, 2008).

Given various external demands and internal motivating factors that prompt a need for evaluation, the field cannot avoid the call to assess its efforts, even if its participants wished to do so. They instead can work to adapt and perhaps redefine conventional approaches through a more nuanced understanding of the complexities facing organizations in this landscape and a values-based approach to program evaluation. Fortunately, practitioners and scholars have called for flexibility in evaluation techniques and understanding.

Combining practice, scholarship, and advocacy, organizations such as Animating Democracy; Imagining America; and the Arts, Culture, and Social Justice Network (ACSJN) are engaging artists, scholars, and practitioners in discussions that have led to a better understanding of approaches to assessment that are useful, equitable, and meaningful in arts-based contexts.[1] The Social Impact of the Arts Project at the University of Pennsylvania School of Social

Policy and Practice and the Urban Institute's Arts and Culture Indicators in Communities Project are simultaneously producing important and related research about the impact of arts and culture on communities.[2] Together, these thought leaders are working to examine and adapt traditional approaches to evaluating social change so that they are better suited to the unique complexities of arts-based work.

Practitioners are testing the understanding of evaluation and its purposes. Specifically, this reorientation seeks to make sense of extremely complex social environments and promotes ethical, meaningful, and learning-oriented approaches to understanding impact and improving practice. As Mark, Henry, and Julnes (2000) have noted, "The primary role of evaluation is to enhance and supplement the natural sensemaking efforts of democratic actors as they seek social betterment" (p. vii). These practitioners and thought leaders are actively shaping dialogue in the field about appropriate approaches, frameworks, and tools for making sense of and assessing the impact of arts-and culture-based social-change efforts.

Contemporary scholarship suggests that

> Evaluation can occur in a formal, systematic way through the application of a professionally designed evaluation program, or it can be carried out with varying degrees of informality ranging from gathering a few reports to completely impressionistic estimates about how things have been going.
> (Murray, 2010, p. 433)

As such, assessment may be understood on a continuum from impressionistic to systematic, allowing organizations to apply techniques that best capture their intended impact(s).

Guided by this understanding of the challenges in evaluating arts-based social-change work, we seek to expand on the evolving practice and notions of evaluation by highlighting those that are participatory, reflexive, and practicable. By operating within varying ranges of established evaluation processes and challenging norms, organizations are aiming for greater flexibility to assess their work in meaningful ways that are program- and context-specific. In-depth interviews with representatives of three organizations in the field help to illuminate how arts-based social-change agents are working to understand and communicate the outcomes of their efforts internally and externally.

## Arts and Social-Change Organizations: Art at Work, Tucson Pima Arts Council, Louisiana Bucket Brigade

Wildavsky (1972) defined self-evaluating organizations as those that continuously monitor their own activities: "The spirit of the self-evaluating organization suggests that, in some meaningful way, the entire organization is infused with the evaluative ethic" (p. 511). We selected the three organizations profiled in this chapter because they have demonstrated reflexive and adaptive approaches to evaluation and a willingness to share lessons learned, even as they have encountered challenges and dilemmas in their efforts to do so. We intentionally included entities that employ arts- and culture-based strategies but vary in mission and intended outcomes. We also selected our cases on the basis of our knowledge of existing work and documented evaluation efforts. We conducted in-depth interviews with the organizational leader responsible for evaluation in each organization. After transcribing the interviews, we interpreted the data by establishing categories and themes (Marshall and Rossman, 2011). We collected additional information concerning each organization's programs and evaluation methods from existing documents, such as research and evaluation reports, to corroborate our interpretation of interview data. We then sought to relate our case findings to a broader set of challenges related to evaluating arts- and culture-based work.

This section provides a brief background for each organization we analyzed, including its programmatic focus, theory of change, and evaluation practices. The subsequent section synthesizes these three groups' evaluative efforts as they relate to challenges common to the assessment of all arts-based social-change work.

## Art At Work and Artist Marty Pottenger

Art At Work is a national initiative to improve municipal government through art-making projects with city employees and public officials.[3] Created in 2007 by artist Marty Pottenger in Portland, Maine, the project is based on the theory that art making can "advance public understanding of what government workers contribute to society, foster reflection that improves municipal operations, and strengthen awareness of their significance to the community" (Animating Democracy, 2014a). Pottenger has outlined the following questions as foundational to her work: What if police wrote poetry to improve morale? What if city councilors sang to practice listening? What if sanitation workers carved prints to combat racism (Art At Work, 2013)? These questions suggest that art making might address deeply held misconceptions about municipal employees while also affecting their own attitudes to their life and work.

One of multiple Art At Work projects, the Police Poetry Project, engaged law enforcement officers in writing poetry and taking photographs to reflect experiences, challenges, and emotions related to their work, home lives, and relationship to community members. Pottenger undertook this effort to improve department morale and public perception of the police in Portland. Officers' artwork was assembled into a calendar widely distributed, and public readings of their poetry by the officers themselves engaged community members in dialogue about the issues embedded in the poems.

In 2009, evaluator Chris Dwyer, of RMC Research, coached Pottenger on practicable ways that she, as a one-person program, could assess the impact of Art At Work projects (Dwyer and Animating Democracy, 2009; Korza and Schaffer

Bacon, 2012). For the Police Poetry Project, the two worked for twelve months with targeted stakeholders and opinion leaders using an evaluation framework Dwyer had developed to define outcomes and indicators of concern to them as well as strategies for data collection and communication of results (Dwyer and Animating Democracy, 2009). By collecting data concerning participation and relationships through interviews, surveys, documentation of internal meetings and external exchanges with citizens, and personal observation, Pottenger has shown that her work influenced the administrative systems and decision processes of municipal government while also enabling more open relationships and robust communications among stakeholders. On the whole, Art At Work has demonstrated that the arts are "a valuable, cost-effective, sustainable tool to both address intransigent municipal problems and deepen the public's awareness and appreciation of local government's role in creating healthy, educated, engaged, economically vibrant communities" (Art At Work, 2014).

Pottenger has used the evaluation process and findings from the Police Poetry Project to make the case for Art At Work within Portland city government to attract and educate new stakeholders, to increase participant engagement as contributors to the evaluation process, and to inform her decisions as an artist and project director (Dwyer and Animating Democracy, 2009; M. Pottenger, personal communication, April 4, 2014). Today, Pottenger includes evaluation as a component of every project she undertakes. Assessment efforts encourage reflection that helps her and program participants make meaning of their creative experience and public engagements around a project while also providing a shared language to communicate their work and experiences to others (M. Pottenger, personal communication, April 4, 2014).

## Tucson Pima Arts Council

The Tucson Pima Arts Council, a 501(c)(3) organization and arts agency for Tucson and Pima County, Arizona, fosters artistic expression, civic participation, and the economic growth of its diverse community by supporting, promoting, and advocating for the arts and culture. The city of Tucson and Pima County are located in the Sonoran Desert and are home to two Native American tribes. Cultural practices related to survival in the desert help to define residents' connection to the county and the landscape. Between 2010 and 2013, TPAC implemented a community-based arts funding initiative, called the PLACE Initiative (People, Land, Arts, Culture, and Engagement).[4] The project was based on the belief that "arts and cultural activities are essential to making meaningful places and can help transform shared spaces into vibrant and nurturing communities" (TPAC, 2013, p. 4). TPAC funded fifty-three PLACE projects during a three-year period, addressing issues such as racial profiling, ethnic intolerance, and concerns related to new immigrants. Part of the Art Council's intent in supporting such efforts was to engage artists and residents in dialogue and action (L. Maahs, personal communication, April 29, 2014).

Two years into the PLACE Initiative, TPAC undertook a comprehensive evaluation "to assess how and to what degree the PLACE-funded projects were helping to transform communities" (TPAC, 2013, p. 5). The evaluation occurred in part at the request of the Kresge Foundation, which provided the funds for assessment that the arts council then granted to local organizations. Irrespective of the Foundation's encouragement and funding, TPAC was already motivated to evaluate its activities. As an agency serving the public and committed to the region, the Council operates with a sense of responsibility to its community, symbolized by a recent strategic plan that articulated advancing arts-based civic engagement and increasing social capital of the population it serves as desired outcomes of its work. In addition, TPAC staff had already invested significantly by learning ethnographic evaluation methods to improve qualitative data collection and analysis (Alvarez, 2009) and by seeking consultation from the Social Impact of the Arts Project (2014; Stern and Seifert, 2009b) to develop a plan to collect and analyze data on civic engagement systematically (L. Maahs, personal communication, April 29, 2014).

TPAC focused its evaluation of the PLACE Initiative on the program's main impacts, including residents' engagement through the arts, TPAC's role as a creative place-making intermediary, and artists creating opportunities for new discovery, growth, and affirmation among participating residents. Social scientist, James Roebuck, of the Evaluation Research and Development office of the Department of Nutritional Sciences of the University of Arizona, led staff members through the assessment process. Roebuck used discussions with numerous stakeholders (working group members, grantees, community partners, civic and cultural leaders, etc.) and both qualitative and quantitative data collection, including focus groups, personal interviews, and a survey distributed to grantees, to gather information concerning the program (TPAC, 2013). Specifically, TPAC collected data such as participation rates, engagement by geographic region, and changes in relationships among project stakeholders (TPAC, 2013).

At the project level, the Council convened PLACE grantees to help them develop their individual project goals and create a pre- and post-logic model (a hybrid theory of change logic model the organization named "a Strategy of Action"). These efforts helped artists to define and refine their projects and impact expectations. Grantees were then asked to respond to seven plausible interrelated impacts of the PLACE Initiative: civic engagement, empowerment, stewardship of place, cultural self-determination, bridging differences, aesthetic accomplishment, and community health and well-being. The grantees' perceptions revealed that these impacts were collective and could not be separated from one another (TPAC, 2013). In some instances, individual programs contributed to these areas and in others "multiple projects, especially if co-located in a place or tied to other larger efforts" led to collective impact (TPAC, 2013, p. 8).

## Louisiana Bucket Brigade

The Louisiana Bucket Brigade (LABB) is an environmental health and justice organization that "uses grassroots action to create an informed, healthy society with a culture that holds the petrochemical industry and government accountable for the true costs of pollution" (LABB, 2014a). Founded in New Orleans, Louisiana in 2000, LABB works with communities located near oil refineries and chemical plants in the southeastern region of the state. LABB employs a variety of change programs and strategies, including cultural organizing. Yet, with a focus on environmental justice, the leader we interviewed underscored that the organization's focus is "not to generate art, but to generate change" (K. Evans, personal communication, May 13, 2014).

LABB's theory of change is to transform the way people think and talk about the industry to alter the future trajectory of the state. Organizational leaders contend that the petroleum industry has long controlled politics and promoted oil as providing jobs and economic benefits. However, truths about low pay, dangerous working conditions, environmental effects, and threats to fishing and tourism industries are not consistently part of the public story of the oil industry's effects. As a consequence, the people of Louisiana have "become boxed into a mindset of [seeing] no other options apart from oil" (K. Evans, personal communication, May 13, 2014). LABB's staff believes that until this perspective shifts, necessary larger changes related to industry policies and actions will not occur (K. Evans, personal communication, May 13, 2014).

A second important outcome toward which the Bucket Brigade works is to mobilize and sustain public participation so as to hold the oil industry accountable. One of LABB's trademark initiatives is to provide easy-to-use air sampling devices, or "buckets," to community members living in affected neighborhoods. Residents collect air samples that are thereafter professionally analyzed, paid for by LABB. The Bucket Brigade is concerned over the long term to secure change in the industry, so the nonprofit uses a number of programs and strategies to maintain public participation and momentum to pursue its goals.

LABB employs arts- and culture-based approaches in its Art-to-Action program as an avenue to effect environmental and social change. The organization's strategy is based on the notion that art can get people involved, make people think, and garner public attention through events and subsequent media attention (LABB, 2014b). LABB builds on Louisiana's rich cultural history and forms of expression—parades, costuming, music, street performance, and storytelling—and integrates these into its organizing and activism tactics. For example, LABB staged an event using costumes and puppets to protest certain politicians and oil executives promoting the economic impact of the petrochemical industry in the state. The event drew the attention of media members already present to cover the news of high-profile elected leaders who had traveled to the area. As a result, LABB was able to influence the news content that day, changing it from the usual supporting contention that "oil exploration and production means economic progress" to ethical development within the context of safe and healthy communities. As a result of such cultural approaches and others previously mentioned, LABB leaders believe that they have influenced the public narrative surrounding the oil industry in Louisiana and have been instrumental in creating post-program synergies between other interested stakeholders and organizations.

LABB's small staff includes a full-time VISTA person who works to collect data for all of the organization's programs and is responsible for analyzing and reporting quantifiable evidence such as event participation rates and media coverage and hits. Staff members also make a strong effort to analyze the tenor and content of press, radio, Internet, and television stories to document how they have contributed to changing the conversation and public discourse concerning oil in Louisiana (K. Evans, personal communication, May 13, 2014).

LABB personnel have begun to utilize qualitative data of this type more effectively, including narratives, case studies, and oral histories, but have found that these methods are time-consuming and require creative and technical expertise that the organization lacks. To this point, Evans remarked in an interview with us, "It's not so much about collection. It's about taking the info collected and putting it to good use" (personal communication, May 13, 2014). Capacity and funding are barriers to using this type of information to its fullest potential. LABB continues to seek ways to demonstrate its impact on public perception and understanding of the state's petroleum industry.

## Challenges from the Field

The following section identifies five complexities in evaluating arts-based social-change work as they were defined and illuminated by in-depth discussions with leaders of the three organizations we examined. Although there is extant literature on *how* to evaluate nonprofit organizations and arts-based work, this body of knowledge is limited by a lack of understanding of the tensions and hurdles implicit in measuring the community, civic, and social outcomes of these efforts.[5] Our interviews shed light on the unique character of arts-based social-change work and the complexities it creates for evaluation approaches, processes, and organizational learning.

### *Divergent Stakeholder Interests Concerning Success and Measurement*

Social-change organizations, their partners, and stakeholders often come to arts-based projects with different assumptions about their intentions and goals. Art At Work's police participants, for instance, valued improvement in morale while law enforcement department heads placed priority on outcomes, such as reduced number of filed grievances. Social justice workers also must acknowledge that the stakes are high for those directly affected by existing injustices. For example, Louisiana residents whose health is at risk due to exposure to pollutants ultimately want the oil industry to change that situation. For these citizens, shifting the public narrative is less important than solving the pollution problem. Finally, artists' and cultural workers aim to effect change through their arts-based practice yet often reference outcomes unrelated to the arts when making the case for such efforts to civic leaders and funders. Clearly, defining common outcomes and determining which of these will be the focus of programs and evaluation and when can be a complicated proposition.

There are many reasons why organizations want to understand the impacts of their efforts, often influenced by multiple stakeholders involved in programmatic processes (Behn, 2003; Thomas, 2010). These constituencies affect the initiatives that civil society organizations pursue and their capacity to pursue them. Scholars have described the purposes sought by various stakeholders and their influences as the political complexity of measuring performance (Wildavsky, 1972; Cutt and Murray, 2000; Ospina, Diaz, and O'Sullivan, 2002; Behn, 2003; Murray, 2010). All three of the organizations analyzed here were actively engaged in negotiating the political intricacies of evaluating social impact.

To build city support for her program, Marty Pottenger knew that evaluation of Art At Work would have to measure what mattered to key government leaders. Indeed, she has suggested that artists should "Start with these outcomes; don't start with the arts" to capture and enlist community leaders' buy-in from the outset (M. Pottenger, personal communication, April 4, 2014). To do so, she identified the various audiences for evaluation results, including their highest-priority desired project outcomes from their particular perspectives. She also sought to identify the likely thresholds of evidence that key stakeholders would find convincing. Pottenger used these identified desired outcomes to keep her accountable to Art At Work's overarching goal "to improve municipal government" and focused on collecting and analyzing evidence that helped her frame the case for the program's continuation (M. Pottenger, personal communication, April 4, 2014). By foregrounding outcomes in day-to-day relationship building and informal dialogue with partners and stakeholders, she has effectively fostered a culture of evaluative thinking within many parts of the municipal government. Engaging stakeholders continuously in this way has increased their investment and ownership in the program's success.

Additionally, holding herself accountable to constituent interests has garnered Pottenger respect and influence. When, for example, she was asked to produce a city-themed song based on the notion of happiness, she used evidence from her previous work to suggest that that particular approach would be potentially damaging to the trust being built between city leaders and citizens, not all of whom could claim happiness amid economic and social challenges (M. Pottenger, personal communication, April 4, 2014). In another instance, when asked by the chief of police to create a theater piece that would promote dialogue between police and immigrant youths after an altercation, Pottenger insisted on the participation by those police officers most likely to cross existing behavioral norms and boundaries. She exercised her capacities as an informed artist to negotiate expectations, values, and mores to raise the potential to effect change within the department and the community.

Both the Art At Work and the Tucson Pima Arts Council evaluation efforts are guided by the same democratic values that are at the heart of their arts-based social-change programs. Each in various ways employs participatory evaluation approaches. Participatory evaluation is a collaborative process in which staff members, program participants, residents, and/or evaluators work together to understand data (Patton, 2002). By involving others, participants take ownership of the evaluation process and related findings (Thomas, 2010). For example, TPAC's participatory program development and evaluation processes are rooted in a cultural awareness of place and community. As Maahs noted in an interview, "We consistently cast a broad net and invite cultural stakeholders to give us really candid feedback about our own assumptions" (personal communication, April 29, 2014).

In consideration of artists and their interests, Maahs stated, "The challenge for us is to provide evaluation methods that meet artists' specific intentions for their own social-change work and provide a bigger picture, connecting artists to a broad overarching civic agenda" (personal communication, April 29, 2014). Though most grantees saw the benefit of finding common language to describe impacts, some artists argued that such broader frames had the potential to water down their intent and potential project outcomes and did not validate their work as originally conceived. TPAC addressed this tension by supporting grantees in implementing story and ethnographic approaches to evaluation and funding small reflective case studies so that the public and officials would have access to particular and "intimate" accounts of arts-related work and its documented effects (L. Maahs, personal communication, April 29, 2014).

These examples speak to these organizations' abilities to communicate their impact to different stakeholders and other sectoral actors while also sharing the value added by art and cultural strategies. Their evaluation practices strengthen findings in terms of meaning, application, and use by various stakeholders. As Murray (2010) has observed, "Effectiveness is thought of as a 'social construction.' It exists in the minds of the organization's diverse internal and external stakeholders" (p. 433). Thus, a thorough understanding of results is possible when multiple stakeholders contribute to defining outcomes that matter to them as well as analyzing data. TPAC built evidence of the role of the arts in increasing cultural vitality and healthy communities by developing a qualitative evaluation approach and a common outcomes framework with its grantees. As a result, TPAC was able to make the case for the arts beyond the standard economic development argument to one that resonated with others' such as local public housing and behavioral health agencies (L. Maahs, personal communication, April 29, 2014). Additionally, Pottenger found that involving participants in the evaluation process reinforces the programmatic impact of such efforts: "The listening component in an evaluation process not only reveals impacts and outcomes to the participants and evaluators, but also on occasion it can drive them" (M. Pottenger, personal communication, April 4, 2014).

## Contextual Factors That Influence Projects and Evaluation of Outcomes

Many arts-based social-change initiatives, because of their grounding in a particular place, contest the idea of singular, narrowly defined ideas of value (MacDowell et al., 2013). Organizations with well-designed initiatives are conscious of historical, cultural, political, and social context and the ever-shifting dynamics of place that influence their programs and assessment of change.

Practitioners are asserting the need for evaluation that embodies values and practices congruent with arts and social justice work—equity, inclusion, and understanding of context. The Arts, Culture and Social Justice Network—a loose group of arts practitioners, funders, and organizers who work to advocate, build knowledge, and increase resources for arts-based social change—is one of the organizations leading the charge for appropriate evaluation of such efforts. ACSJN member and TPAC executive director, Roberto Bedoya (2013) has written that interested analysts should view social impacts "through a frame of a social movement, one that weaves ethics and aesthetics into engagement projects (p. 7). This means disrupting mainstream evaluation practices that "undermine or distort the connections among art, culture, and social justice" (Bedoya, 2013, p. 7). Evaluating the social efficacy of arts-related community work will require identifying and adapting evaluation practices from social justice and other fields; equalizing power relationships; ensuring cultural competence in evaluation; elevating qualitative evidence and narrative discussion to the same status as quantitative measures; and articulating criteria for artistic and civic and social efficacy.

Cultural competence in evaluation requires an understanding of social context, including the norms of partners, stakeholders, and participants. Reeler (2007) has suggested that misapplied interventions reduce the relevance of existing social-change processes, and when the conditions for such projects "are not favorable [they] can be profoundly counter-developmental and destructive for people and their relationships" (p. 6). Reeler (2007) has argued further that as Western notions of knowledge based in professional expertise have prevailed, indigenous knowledge and experience are often disregarded or even considered unimportant. This scholarship underscores the importance of context and of truly listening and honoring non-dominant cultural understanding and dignity in effective program implementation and evaluation.

A context of "dis-belonging" experienced by marginalized populations motivated the PLACE Initiative in Tucson to expand the often-singular notion of creative placemaking focused on improvement to the built environment to embrace the idea of "belonging" as fundamental to a healthy place. As Bedoya has remarked:

> To acknowledge the importance of belonging, of course, is to acknowledge the discomfort—and even violence—of dis-belonging. Dis-belonging occurs through acts of gentrification, racism, and speculation culture, which often occur under the name of 'civic revitalization,' but in reality betray the democratic ideals of a just, civil society.
>
> (Bedoya, 2013, p. 7)

The Arts Council considered how grantees understood and addressed "dis-belonging" in making grants and as a frame for understanding the effects of the PLACE Initiative. Several of the "plausible effects" that the Arts Council tracked for both individual projects and the entire PLACE Initiative related to increasing and enhancing belonging as an indicator of a just, democratic, and healthy community, including individual and/or collective empowerment, residents' acceptance of responsibility for the stewardship of place, cultural self-determination and affirmation, and bridging differences.[6]

Social-change agents included in this study have also noted how power imbalances rooted in historical and contemporary contexts may affect evaluation practice. Core to the intentions behind evaluation must be engagement with stakeholders that invites questions about an initiative's theory of change, its definition of outcomes, and its analysis of existing power imbalances. For example, the Arts Council recognized the need to work with tribal communities in the region. To this point, Maahs stated,

> When invited to engage in dialogue with tribal communities I have to be aware of the cultural norms associated with each specific community. I may be invited to a discussion, however it may take months or years of respectful listening for tribal leaders to invite me to speak.
>
> (personal communication, April 29, 2014)

Exercising patience and empathy and respecting cultural norms and processes has been key to TPAC's success. Working with respected bridge builders from targeted communities has also been critical to understanding the impact of TPAC's PLACE Initiative.

LABB has also been attentive to context as it aims to influence public and media narratives concerning the oil industry. LABB continually assesses political and media conditions and discourses to ensure that its defined outcomes and messaging are relevant. In one instance, the nonprofit succeeded in reorienting the media's message from economic development to improving safety as a way to stimulate the economy: "You have to shape the message based on what's going to work in that context," explained Evans. "We couldn't have come and talked about shutting down the oil industry. The narrative can't be too extreme"

(K. Evans, personal communication, May 13, 2014). With this understanding, LABB was able to promote a public safety message when local television covered its Parade for Big Oil event linked to a congressional tour of offshore rigs. In this and other cases, LABB compares media coverage before and after such events to track its contribution to shifting public discourse. The nonprofit's programmatic and evaluation activities are linked closely to the changing context in which it works; it routinely gathers data related to planned programs but remains open to a range of possible initiatives and outcomes as dictated by shifting conditions and opportunities. In doing so, LABB is able to experiment with strategies and processes, be opportunistic and responsive, and learn from its efforts through evaluation (K. Evans, personal communication, May 13, 2014).

## Revisiting Norms and Assumptions to Adapt and Expand Evaluation Practice

Prevailing conventions in evaluation premised on cause-and-effect thinking and linear logic model approaches are predicated on assumptions that largely do not hold true for most arts-based social-change work. For example, in arts-based projects, outcomes often remain deliberately undetermined so that creative planning and implementation processes can reveal the most meaningful outcomes to stakeholders. Reeler (2007) has suggested that logic-based models assume that problems are discernible to the practitioner up front and that solutions can be posed as predetermined outcomes; project interventions themselves are the vehicles that actually deliver change; participatory process during planning can get all stakeholders on board; unpredicted factors are inconveniences to be dealt with; and desired outcomes can be coded in advance as detailed action plans and pursued in a logical and linear way.

The three organizations highlighted in this chapter have challenged many of these assumptions and instead emphasized employing evaluation practices that can clarify and sharpen intent and improve planning; serve in an iterative process that informs action and decisions during the unfolding of projects; identify success factors that advance practice; and help communicate impact(s). Such a reflexive approach to evaluation allows for experimentation and supports risk taking and learning from both successes and failures. It also promotes ethical accountability to program findings and encourages co-learning with others involved in the evaluation process.

This expanded approach to evaluation is more complex and context-specific than traditional evaluation techniques. As Thomas (2010) has claimed, "Outcomes assessment planners should be prepared for the possibility that discussion of measures may rekindle debate about goals. ... When that happens, planners should be open to a possible need to reformulate goals" (p. 412). Fortunately for the TPAC, its strong process orientation allowed for a continual reassessment of values, assumptions, and ideological perspectives. To this point, Maahs has argued that the challenge of evaluation is

> ... re-visiting assumptions about what it is that you want to know and why. Even in this broad process we engaged in, eight months into the work ... we were still questioning why we wanted to know certain things and still coming up against our own assumptions and challenges around wanting to find one neat definition that all projects could fit within.
>
> (personal communication, April 29, 2014)

Another way in which evaluation practice is being expanded by arts-based work is through experimentation. Experimentation and the potential for failure are acknowledged as realities of arts-based social-change work and therefore an appropriate topic for the evaluation conversation (Wildavsky, 1972; Schaffer Bacon and Korza, 2013). Senge (2006) has offered a similar argument suggesting, "Failure is an opportunity for learning—about inaccurate pictures of current reality, about strategies that didn't work as expected, about the clarity of the vision" (p. 154). For example, LABB deliberately employs different cultural strategies: "Through experimenting and looking at opportunities that present themselves we just go for it. ... Sometimes it doesn't work and sometimes it works great, sometimes in surprising ways" (K. Evans, personal communication, May 13, 2014).

Despite the benefits of experimenting to achieve robust change, case making and the need to secure resources make practitioners reluctant to report failure or less than desired results. According to one funder, for evaluation to enable deeper understanding of the complexity of arts and social-change work it will require "radical truthful relationships" between funders and grantees, ties that encourage honesty and transparency, and "the authentic telling of our work without claiming excellence at all times" (Schaffer Bacon and Korza, 2013, p. 12). Funders have to understand their own level of risk tolerance and replace an oversimplified paradigm of success and failure with a more realistic view that acknowledges the iterative and long-term nature of movement building and social change and includes incremental and cumulative measures of success (Schaffer Bacon and Korza, 2013).

Of course, the most important reasons organizations evaluate are to learn and improve practice. Senge (2006) has defined a learning organization as one in which "people continually expand their capacity to create the results they truly desire, where new and expansive patterns of thinking are nurtured, where collective aspiration is set free, and where people are continually learning how to learn together" (p. 3). Increasingly, as the three organizations in this chapter demonstrate, evaluation must be linked to such learning to be deemed *useful* to arts agents, their community partners, and stakeholders in order for evaluative thinking and practice to become truly internalized.

## Common Methodological Challenges in Evaluating Social Impact

There are many methodological challenges to evaluation practice—most commonly operational issues associated with causality, measurement validity, and unit of analysis. Social-change organizations "should bear in mind the sober reality often faced by social scientists: what you can measure easily isn't important, and what is important, you can't measure easily" (Stern and Seifert, 2009a, p. 36). This statement suggests that well-executed assessments require methods that are often difficult for organizations to implement in practice.

The evaluation literature and practitioners interviewed for this research each have underscored the significance of this "causality problem." Cutt and Murray (2000) have contended, for example, "When it comes to analyzing almost any aspect of human behavior, there are too many variables and there is too little control over those variables to permit solid conclusions about causal connections" (p. 40). Instead of indicating causality, cultural programs such as those highlighted in this chapter seek to show evidence of *correlation* between, *contribution* to, or *influence* toward change. For example, although Pottenger believes that Art At Work has resulted in cost savings for the municipal departments with which she has worked, she can only correlate her program's activities to such positive change rather than claim causal effects. After working with a social scientist, TPAC had to come to terms with "the broad claims about the work we are supporting and what it's doing" (L. Maahs, personal communication, April 29, 2014). To address this concern, TPAC framed the impacts of the PLACE Initiative on the plausible collective outcomes of its aggregated grant making, acknowledging that no arts project alone could change long-standing and entrenched ways of knowing (TPAC, 2013).

The challenge with presenting evidence to support causality is partly tied to the inadequacy of existing tools to measure complex scenarios. Each of the leaders with whom we spoke collects quantitative data, such as attendance or media hits, because it is relatively easy to acquire such information through counting and simple surveys. At the same time, they recognize the limitations of such metrics, and each preferred qualitative techniques better suited to articulate detailed accounts of program outcomes.

Qualitative evidence is increasingly seen as a valid measure of social change. As Korza and Schaffer Bacon (2012) have noted, "It is now generally agreed that qualitative data, narratives, and storytelling combined with quantitative data can strengthen social impact assessment" (p. 14). Similarly, Reeler (2007) has argued that story is a strong alternative to simplistic analysis of cause and effect: "Without a sense of story, understanding becomes piecemeal, disconnected, ungrounded and misleading" (p. 19). Qualitative measures may not only be more meaningful but more practicable for non-researchers and creative work. Stern and Seifert (2009a) have observed that methods such as interviews, focus groups, and observation are accessible to non-researchers and complementary to participatory evaluation, "Qualitative methods support environments where creativity, spontaneity, and expression are valued" (p. 41).

Despite the increased application and support of qualitative evidence, collecting and analyzing such data require skill and capacity. For example, even though TPAC had previously worked with professional researchers to analyze qualitative data, it remained challenged to analyze the volume of information collected from PLACE Initiative grantees during a three-year period (L. Maahs, personal communication, April 29, 2014). In addition, the organizations we studied struggle to measure accurately post-program synergies, collaborations, and capacities such as "increasing the odds that people come up with new ideas, take action on those ideas, see each other in a new light, and engage in new ways" (M. Pottenger, personal communication, April 4, 2014). Such evidence is complex and time consuming to collect and analyze.

Another methodological challenge that surfaced in this research is translating program outcomes to different scales—from the individual to program to organization to system levels (Cutt and Murray, 2000; Stern and Seifert, 2009a; Murray, 2010). If, for example, an individual is affected by an intervention, one cannot assume that his or her community has experienced the same impacts by generalizing from one social level to another (Murray, 2010). Pottenger has described the challenge of making the leap from demonstrating Art At Work's outcomes on individual municipal workers to the program's influence on policy discourse and systemic change (personal communication, April 4, 2014). Stern and Seifert (2009a) have argued, "Only individuals can act upon or believe something—but the causes and effects of those actions are linked to higher levels of aggregation" (p. 24). LABB has sought to understand how its Art-to-Action efforts are shifting both individual and communal narratives. Thus far, it has not found methods to gauge and demonstrate their impact beyond the individual level confidently. Even if appropriate measure(s) could be identified, Evans questioned the feasibility of employing apt methods with limited human and financial resources (personal communication, May 13, 2014).

These examples highlight the methodological challenges that social-change organizations applying arts and cultural strategies encounter using traditional evaluation techniques. However, the leaders interviewed for this research have not allowed themselves to be limited by traditional strategies and instead sought continually to adapt existing methods to demonstrate the value and meaning of their work more effectively.

### Capacity Limitations

Social-change organizations interested in understanding the outcomes of their work soon discover that what is easy to measure is often less useful than what is more difficult to gauge. Many are aware of the statement attributed to Albert Einstein, "Not everything that can be counted counts, and not everything that counts can be counted."[7] In addition, Murray (2010) has noted that barriers to evaluation practice among nonprofit organizations include a "lack of internal capacity, such as staff or time" and a "lack of skills and knowledge in conducting evaluations" (p. 441). The demands on time, personnel, and funding cause many arts practitioners to feel overwhelmed when contemplating what it might take to complete credible evaluations (Korza and Schaffer Bacon, 2012). And, even though funding organizations generally recognize the time and resources needed to meet some of their evaluation requirements, most do not provide additional funds to support such costs (Korza and Schaffer Bacon, 2012).

Therefore, of concern to typically under-resourced cultural organizations and artists is the practicability of assessment approaches and methodologies; that is, evaluation that is proportional to the project and its associated resources (Imagining America, 2014). These organizations look for evaluation approaches and tools that are practical, useful, and robust enough to improve practice. Limited resources have challenged the entities investigated for this research, too, but despite these limitations, they have found ways to make evaluation a priority and to integrate it into their organizational goals, objectives, and operations.

Engaging outside specialists is one way in which organizations may increase their evaluation capacity. With the support of major funding agencies, TPAC and Art At Work completed evaluation efforts with such external evaluation specialists. As part of a larger national initiative supported by the Kresge Foundation, TPAC engaged both a social scientist and a national research advisor who worked collaboratively with its staff to frame the inquiry, design and implement methods, and assist with analysis and reporting. On the whole, the effort could be described as highly labor-intensive for staff and participants, but it resulted in significant learning. Similarly, Art At Work was able to engage an evaluation specialist after receiving support from Animating Democracy, a program of Americans for the Arts, and the Kellogg Foundation. The evaluator worked with Pottenger to develop an evaluation plan and to coach her, but Pottenger executed assessment activities largely herself, with the assistance of an intern.

Without continued external funding and professional expertise, however, TPAC and Art At Work will be challenged to continue to implement the same level of evaluation as the efforts described in this chapter. Consequently, they are seeking low-cost and practicable evaluation methods. For example, Pottenger has developed simple strategies to integrate evaluative thinking and methods effectively into her day-to-day work. She notes evidence of change she hears in meetings and conversations and organizes them into indicator folders; performs "evaluation go-rounds" at the end of creative activities with municipal workers to engage them in immediate feedback opportunities; and employs video and photo documentation and online surveys regularly. These, among other techniques, are low or no cost and have supplied valuable qualitative data to support the case for the Art At Work program. Still, Pottenger has begun to plan for evaluation costs when submitting grant proposals to reduce the impact of evaluation on her small program budget (M. Pottenger, personal communication, April 4, 2014).

Even when social-change organizations employ practicable assessment approaches, a challenge remains with following through to complete such efforts. As Behn (2003) has argued, "Converting performance data into an understanding of what is happening inside the black box is neither easy nor obvious" (p. 592). Collecting data is really a first step; analysis and communication require an even more refined level of expertise. As such, capacity limitations not only affect data collection but the understanding and communication of evaluation findings. Evans of the LABB described this concern:

> ... to take that data and transform it into something that other people can understand and share and learn from is another step that requires a lot of time, another level of creativity, and a level of technical expertise. It's not so much the collection; it's taking information and putting it to good use.
> (personal communication, May 13, 2014)

Considering the realities of limited capacity and resources, practitioners, funders, and evaluators are acknowledging gold-standard evaluation practices are often unrealistic. Instead, the field needs practicable, yet credible, approaches and methods that can be implemented with limited resources and staff capacity.

## Conclusions

In response to increased external demands for demonstrating the impacts of arts-based social-change endeavors and a desire among committed arts practitioners to understand their contributions to change, there have been advancements in discourse and practice in evaluating the social outcomes of such work. Arts practitioners, funders, and evaluation professionals are seeking to reconcile the tensions between what is expected concerning assessing impacts and what is possible, as evidenced by the scholarship and practice presented in this chapter. By referring to what is *possible*, we do not suggest that social impact assessment is impossible in arts and culture-based work but instead argue that representatives of these organizations should be given some latitude in how they conduct their efforts in light of the tensions and complexities involved in these initiatives. Fortunately, funders, artists, organizations, and thought leaders are working to move the dial in a direction that allows for the ethical and meaningful understanding of data in a way that is practicable and useful for those in the field.

This chapter has highlighted the centrality of people and context of place in the evaluation process of arts-based social-change projects. The experience of the organizations represented in this research suggests that the inclusion of disparate stakeholders in evaluation using participatory strategies enables a truer and more accountable meaning-making process for collecting and interpreting data and findings than do other frequently employed approaches. By engaging multiple points of view shaped by the personal experiences and settings of those affected, the organizations profiled here have positioned themselves to explore the rich meaning of their work and its effects.

External entities, such as funders and civic leaders, may have provided impetus for all three organizations to develop more systematic ways to understand their social outcomes. Two of the three organizations researched were fortunate to work with funding organizations and evaluators experienced in ethical and learning-oriented evaluation practices. They encouraged arts practitioners to integrate assessment in everyday practice and ongoing inquiry.

Our research also revealed a nuanced understanding of the value of reflexivity in practice. Organizations were challenged constantly to reexamine their assumptions about interventions, outcomes, and indicators. One participant likened this to addressing systemic racism, in which one has to "re-visit questions about ideological assumptions everyday" (L. Maahs, personal communication, April 29, 2014). This iterative process of learning is non-linear, messy, and time-consuming. We do not yet know whether the advantages of reflexivity outweigh the known shortcomings of standard linear and logic-oriented evaluation approaches. We are daily learning more, however, about the efficacy and drawbacks of these two approaches as more programs and organizations such as Art At Work, the Tuscon Pima Arts Council, and Louisiana Bucket Bridgade exert leadership by challenging existing evaluation practices and sharing their experiences in doing so.

## Notes

1  See the Web sites for Animating Democracy and Imagining America (2014b).
2  For more information on the Social Impact of the Arts Project, see Animating Democracy's website (2014b) for a description of the program. For an example of work published by the Urban Institute's Arts and Culture Indicators in Communities Project, see Walker, C (2002).
3  See "Art at Work: An Arts & Equity Initiative" (2013).
4  A year-long community-wide planning process and the resulting Pima Cultural Plan informed TPAC's PLACE Initiative. See TPAC's PLACE Initiative report (2013).
5  See Cutt and Murray (2000) for a thorough analysis of existing evaluation tools for nonprofit organizations. See Animating Democracy's website (2014b), Stern and Seifert (2009a), and Jackson (2009) for additional discussion of evaluating arts-based work.
6  See TPAC's PLACE Initiative report (2013) for a complete description of the plausible interrelated outcomes of the PLACE initiative.
7  Although this statement is often attributed to A. Einstein, evidence suggests that it is from W. B. Cameron's 1963 text, *Informal Sociology, A Casual Introduction to Sociological Thinking*, published by Random House.

## References

Alvarez, M. (2009). *Two way mirror: Ethnography as a way to assess civic impact of arts-based engagement in Tucson, Arizona*. Tucson, AZ: University of Tucson, The Southwest Center. Retrieved from http://animatingdemocracy.org/resource/two-way-mirror-ethnography-way-assess-civic-impact-arts-based-engagement-tucson-arizona

Animating Democracy. (2011). *Continuum of impact*. Washington, DC: Americans for the Arts. Retrieved from http://animatingdemocracy.org/social-impact-indicators/typical-social-civic-outcomes

Animating Democracy. (2014a). *Art at work: An arts and equity initiative*. Washington, DC: Americans for the Arts. Retrieved from http://animatingdemocracy.org/project/art-work-arts-equity-initiative

Animating Democracy. (2014b). Washington, DC: Americans for the Arts. Retrieved from http://animatingdemocracy.org

Art at Work. (2013). *Art at work: An arts and equity initiative*. Portland, ME. Retrieved June 3, 2014 from http://www.artatwork.us/about/aaw_booklet11-13.pdf

Art at Work. (2014). *Art at work initiative history*. Portland, ME. Retrieved June 3, 2014 from http://www.artatwork.us/about/index.php

Bedoya, R. (2013). Belonging: A cornerstone of the PLACE making in region. In the Tuscon Pima Arts Council, *People, land, arts, culture, and engagement: Taking stock of the PLACE initiative*. Tucson, AZ: Tucson Pima Arts Council. Retrieved May 23, 204from http://www.tucsonpimaartscouncil.org/wp-content/uploads/2011/08/PLACEreport-FINAL-web.pdf

Behn, R. (2003). Why measure performance? Different purposes require different measures. *Public Administration Review*, 64(5): 586–606.

Borrup, T. (2006). *The creative community builder's handbook: How to transform communities using local assets, art, and culture*. St. Paul, MN: Fieldstone Alliance.

Cutt, J. and Murray, V. (2000). *Accountability and effectiveness evaluation in non-profit organizations*. New York, NY: Routledge.

Dwyer, M. C. and Animating Democracy. (2008). *Reflections on the arts and civic engagement impact initiative briefing paper*. Washington, DC: Americans for the Arts. Retrieved June 4, 2014 from http://animatingdemocracy.org/resource/reflections-arts-and-civic-engagement-briefing-paper

Dwyer, M. C. and Animating Democracy. (2009). *Evaluation plan: Arts and equity initiative*. Washington, DC: Americans for the Arts. Retrieved June 4, 2014 from http://animatingdemocracy.org/sites/default/files/Portland_A%26EI%20EvalPlan.pdf

Fiennes, C. (2013). *Most charities shouldn't evaluate their work*. Stanford Social Innovation Review Blog, 29 May. Retrieved February 1, 2014from http://www.ssireview.org/blog/entry/most_charities_shouldnt_evaluate_their_work?utm_source=Enews&utm_medium=email&utm_campaign=Enews

Ganz, M. (2010). Leading change: Leadership, organization, and social movements. In N. Nohria and R. Khurana (Eds.) *Handbook of Leadership Theory and Practice* (pp. 527–568). Boston, MA: Harvard Business School Press.

Goldbard, A. (2008). *The metrics syndrome*. Retrieved May 5, 2014 from http://arlenegoldbard.com/wp-content/uploads/2005/12/Metrics-Syndrome-10-13-08.pdf

Imagining America. (2014. *Integrated assessment*. Retrieved April 1, 2014from http://imaginingamerica.org/research/assessment/

Inglehart, R. (2000). Culture and democracy. In L. E. Harrison and S. P. Huntington (Eds.) *Culture Matters: How Values Shape Human Progress* (pp. 80–97). New York, NY: Basic Books.

Jackson, M. R. (2009). *Shifting expectations: An urban planner's reflections on evaluation of community-based arts*. Washington, DC: Americans for the Arts. Retrieved May 5, 2014 from http://animatingdemocracy.org/resource/shifting-expectations-urban-planner%25E2%2580%2599s-reflections-evaluation-community-based-arts

Korza, P. and Schaffer Bacon, B. (2012). *Evaluating impact/Appreciating evaluation*. Washington, DC: Americans for the Arts. Retrieved May 23. 2014 from http://animatingdemocracy.org/resource/evaluating-impactappreciating-evaluation

Korza, P., Schaffer Bacon, B., and Assaf, A. (2005). *Civic dialogue, arts and culture: Findings from Animating Democracy*. Washington, DC: Americans for the Arts.

LABB (Louisiana Bucket Brigade). (2014a). *About us*. New Orleans, LA. Retrieved May 5, 2014 from http://www.labucketbrigade.org/article.php?list=type&type=136

LABB (Louisiana Bucket Brigade). (2014b). *Art-to-Action gallery*. New Orleans, LA: Internal unpublished document.

MacDowell, L., Mulligan, M., Panucci, F., and Badham, M. (2013). Spectres of evaluation. Retrieved from University of Melbourne, Center for Cultural Partnerships http://www.spectresofevaluation.com/uploads/2/0/3/2/20322601/spectres_of_evaluation_discussion_paper_feb_2013.pdf

Mark, M. M., Henry, G. T., and Julnes, G. (2000). *Evaluation: An Integrated Framework for Understanding, Guiding, and Improving Policies and Programs*. San Francisco, CA: Jossey-Bass.

Marshall, C. and Rossman, G. B. (2011). *Designing qualitative research* (5th ed.). Thousand Oaks, CA: SAGE.

Murray, V. (2010). Evaluating the effectiveness of nonprofit organizations. In R. O. Renz (Ed.) *The Jossey-Bass Handbook of Nonprofit Leadership and Management* (3rd ed., pp. 431–458). San Francisco, CA: John Wiley & Sons.

Ospina, S., Diaz, W., and O'Sullivan, J. F. (2002). Negotiating accountability: Managerial lessons from identity-based nonprofit organizations. *Nonprofit and Voluntary Sector Quarterly*, 31(1): 5–31.

Patton, M. Q. (2002). *Qualitative research and evaluation methods* (3rd ed.). Thousand Oaks, CA: Sage Publications.

Putnam, R. D. and Feldstein, L. M. (2003). *Better Together: Restoring the American community*. New York, NY: Simon & Schuster.

Reeler, D. (2007). A three-fold theory of social change and implications for practice, planning, monitoring, and evaluation. Community Development Resources Association. Retrieved June 2, 2014 from http://www.google.com/url?sa=t&rct=j&q=&esrc=s&source=web&cd=1&ved=0CCAQFjAA&url=http%3A%2F%2Fwww.hivos.nl%2Fcontent%2Fdownload%2F77421%2F673652%2Fversion%2F1%2Ffile%2F2007.Doug.Reeler.Theory.Of.Social.Change.pdf&ei=3Z76U7rwK42GyAT4g4KgCQ&usg=AFQjCNGZNpRZNS3Abt6Qg1vcleb77HqGXw&sig2=bEALRVnbzf3oiG3V-SJ0fw&bvm=bv.73612305,d.aWw.

Schaffer Bacon, B. and Korza, P. (2012). Evaluation: Evaluating impact, appreciating evaluation. In D. Borwick (Ed.) *Building Communities, not Audiences: The Future of the Arts in the United States* (pp. 110–129). Winston-Salem, NC: ArtsEngaged.

Schaffer Bacon, B. and Korza, P. (2013). *Cases and points: Funder exchange on evaluating arts and social impact*. Washington, DC: Americans for the Arts. Retrieved May 23, 2014 from http://animatingdemocracy.org/resource/cases-points-summary-funder-exchange- evaluating-arts-social-impact

Schuster, J. M. (1997). The performance of performance indicators in the arts. *Nonprofit Management and Leadership*, 7(3): 253–269.

Senge, P. M. (2006). *The Fifth Discipline: The Art and Practice of the Learning Organization*. New York, NY: Doubleday.

Social Impact of the Arts Project. (2014). Social Impact of the Arts Project, Philadelphia, PA: University of Pennsylvania Retrieved May 5, 2014 from Animating Democracy Web site: http://animatingdemocracy.org/organization/social-impact-arts-project

Stern, M. J. and Seifert, S. C. (2009a). *Civic engagement and the arts: Issues of conceptualization and measurement*. Washington, DC: Americans for the Arts. Retrieved May 5, 2014 from http://animatingdemocracy.org/resource/civic-engagement-and-arts-issues-conceptualization-and-measurement

Stern, M. J. and Seifert, S. C. (2009b). *Documenting civic engagement: A plan for the Tucson Pima Arts Council*. Retrieved May 23, 2014 from http://www.tucsonpimaartscouncil.org/wp-content/uploads/2011/08/TPAC-Social-Impact-of-the-Arts-Project.pdf

Thomas, J. C. (2010). Outcomes assessment and program evaluation. In R. O. Renz (Ed.), *The Jossey-Bass Handbook of Nonprofit Leadership and Management* (3rd ed., pp. 401–430). San Francisco, CA: Jossey-Bass Wiley

TPAC (Tucson Pima Arts Council). (2013). *People, land, arts, culture, and engagement: Taking stock of the PLACE Initiative*. Tucson, AZ. Retrieved May 30, 2014 from http://www.tucsonpimaartscouncil.org/wp-content/uploads/2011/08/PLACEreport-FINAL-web.pdf

VanDeCarr, P. (2013). *Storytelling and social change: A strategy guide for grantmakers*. Retrieved May 1, 2014 from http://workingnarratives.org/project/story-guide/

Walker, C. (2002). *Arts and culture: Community connections*. Washington, DC: Urban Institute. Retrieved June 2, 2014 from http://www.urban.org/publications/310512.html.

Weiss, C. (1995). Nothing as practical as good theory: Exploring theory-based evaluation for comprehensive community initiatives for children and families. In I. Connell, A. C. Kubisch, L. B. Schorr, and C. H. Weiss (Eds.) *New Approaches to Evaluating Community Initiatives* (pp. 65–92). Washington, DC: The Aspen Institute. Retrieved from http://www.seachangecop.org/sites/default/files/documents/1995%20Aspen%20New%20Approaches%20to%20Evaluating%20Community%20Initiatives.pdf

Wildavsky, A. (1972). The self-evaluating organization. *Public Administration Review*, 32(5): 509–520.

# 10

# THEATRE AS A TOOL FOR BUILDING PEACE AND JUSTICE

## DAH Teatar and Bond Street Theatre

*Lyusyena Kirakosyan and Max O. Stephenson, Jr.*

## Introduction

The use of arts-based approaches in peace building began only relatively recently, and research on the topic is still limited (Zelizer, 2004). As Craig Zelizer has suggested, the types and purposes of arts-based activities in peace building are quite diverse, ranging from protests against conflict to creative therapies aimed at addressing individual trauma. Likewise, as Harold Saunders (1999) has remarked, peace-building processes will be incomplete if they do not account for the human dimension of conflict: "Only governments can write peace treaties, but only human beings—citizens outside governments—can transform conflictual relationships between people into peaceful relationships" (p. xvii). Overall, research has suggested that the arts can be a powerful tool in affecting relational changes among individuals in society, including memories, attitudes, beliefs, and behaviors.

Some scholars (Blumberg, Hare, and Costin, 2006; Cohen, Varea, and Walker, 2011) have argued that peace should not be seen as an absence of conflict, but rather, as an absence of *violence* and the existence of conditions that allow communities to thrive. These insights suggest that peace building is "an enormously complex endeavor in unbelievably complex, dynamic, and more often than not destructive settings of violence," as Lederach (2005) has observed (p. 33). Lederach has compared peace builders to artists, contending that those involved in these delicate social undertakings should anticipate and seek to provide for the unexpected, a facility and aspiration more generally associated with the world of art and artists than with politics (p. 38). The value of theatre in particular, as a form of art, lies in its ability to expose complex and uneasy issues, to raise questions, and to formulate fresh ideas without imposing conclusions and judgments (Mroué, 2009, p. x).

Peace building and performance meet at the intersection of human suffering and potential, in efforts aimed at shaping the aspirations necessary for peace and justice. Because both have the power to affect epistemic-scale frames, peace building and artistic works each may unleash what Lederach (2005) has called the "moral imagination," a creative act of envisioning a better future while staying grounded in the troubled present. Lederach has suggested analysts must explore the creative process as "the wellspring that feeds the building of peace" (p. 5). Moreover, Hawes (2007) has argued that "Performance artists, like peace builders, can create a context that will assist disputing parties in seeing themselves, their beliefs about their adversaries, and their conflictual actions from a new perspective" (p. 68).

Both theatre groups discussed in this chapter, DAH[1] Teatar (DAH) and Bond Street Theatre (BST), have long sought to secure positive changes in relationships among groups within the conflict- and poverty-stricken societies in which they have worked. With a background in psychology, DAH's co-founder and artistic director, Dijana Milošević, has sought to use theatre as a space for collective mourning, for encouraging Serbs (and other national groups) to confront honestly what happened during the war in the Balkans in the 1990s, for grieving for what was lost, and for moving forward by developing new perspectives for the future. Since 1976, BST's theatre-based projects have been focused on "education, healing, and empowerment in critical areas,"[2] in a wide range of communities globally, from Haiti to Afghanistan to the Balkans and Burma.

After this brief introduction, this chapter is organized in three parts. It first presents a case study exploring DAH's trajectory and cultural and political environment, its productions, and its partnerships and investigates the fundaments and implications of the company's conceptions of peace and justice that have emerged in its work during the past two decades. The second section comprises a case analysis of BST's trajectory, productions, and partnerships that have explored violence, intolerance, poverty, and human rights violations around the world in an effort to discern the conceptions of peace and justice that have emerged in and guided its work during its history. Finally, the third part of the chapter examines the two companies' experiences comparatively, highlighting their approaches and contributions to cultivating peace, social healing, and forgiveness in post-conflict and poverty-stricken communities and discerning relevant lessons for practitioners and scholars interested in community change and development processes both in the United States and internationally.

## DAH Teatar

This section employs pertinent scholarly literature, analyses of published interviews with DAH Teatar's co-founder and artistic director, and pieces written by her (Milošević, 2011a; 2011b; 2012) and individual interviews with DAH's founders, to examine the conceptions of peace and justice that have underpinned the work of that Serbian artistic organization. This analysis is organized in three parts. We first provide a brief synopsis of the development of theatre in the former Yugoslavia with two goals in mind: to outline the conditions in which DAH was formed and to contextualize the group's peace-building efforts. Second, we discuss how the company's productions and partnerships have helped its members to explore the causes of recent widespread violence, intolerance, and destruction in Serbian society. Third, we investigate the foundations and implications of DAH's conceptions of peace and justice that have emerged in its work during the past two decades. The theatre group has self-consciously sought to create a space in which former Yugoslav citizens may reflect and share their understandings, grief, and memories of the nation's nearly decade-long war in the 1990s.

## Yugoslav Theatre

Yugoslavia has had a tradition of institutional theatre since the end of World War II. Most such entities were permanent state-supported and controlled groups (Milošević, 2011a, pp. 24–25). However, by the 1980s, as Knežević (1996) has recounted, a so-called political theatre emerged in Yugoslavia that "took responsibility for interrogating reality, unmasking prejudice, negating dogma, and slapping awake society's atrophied moral sense" (p. 408). These alternative companies emerged out of a history of civic resistance and a desire among some practitioners to experiment with new ideas not found in the country's more traditional theatres (Clemons, 2005, p. 110).

While the Yugoslav government did not formally prohibit alternative dramatic arts groups in the 1990s, they nonetheless were subject to periodic government harassment and oversight (Clemons, 2005, p. 108). The governing regime did not grant these unorthodox companies financial support. In consequence, they instead relied on their members' resources, aid from nongovernmental organizations and philanthropies such as the Soros Fund, private donations, and self-generated income (ibid, pp. 108–109).

Because this form of theatre was not state-supported, it became "the first and only opposition movement in the one-party system" in Yugoslavia in the 1980s (ibid). However, not all non-traditional dramatic troupes in the nation offered intentionally political content in the 1990s (Clemons, 2005, p. 115). Many of those who began this innovative theatre movement did not challenge the Milošević regime in the 1990s, which convinced DAH's artistic director, Dijana Milošević (no relation; 2011a, p. 25), that true political theatre did not really exist in Yugoslavia during that era. The institutional theatres in the country, meanwhile, continued to offer productions, but most of them remained silent from 1990 to 1995 in the face of the nation's grim political situation (ibid, p. 27).

Milošević's government tolerated performers and protesters in the streets because they did not consider them a threat (Stefanova, 2009, p. 150).

However, after the North Atlantic Treaty Organization (NATO) bombings in 1999, the government became more repressive and assumed control of Belgrade's independent Radio/TV B-92 and TV station Studio B (Clemons, 2005, p. 108). Thereafter, a clandestine B-92 operated as an Internet station from May until October 2000, when Slobodan Milošević left office after his defeat in the presidential election (Clemons, 2005, n. 10; B92, 2014). The opposition leader Vojislav Koštunica won the elections with slightly more than 50 percent of the votes. Initially unwilling to admit defeat, Milošević was forced to accept the popular outcome amid street protests.

## DAH's Productions and Partnerships

Three women formed DAH as the war began in Yugoslavia in 1991, out of a "personal necessity," as the company's founding director has argued (Milošević, 2012, p. 141). For Sanja Krsmanović Tasic, who joined the group in 1993, becoming part of DAH represented a "personal quest for peace" and, at the same time, a "personal quest for action" (Milošević, Mitić, and Krsmanović Tasic, 2013). Initially, the trio believed they needed "a place and space for healing [their] souls through the work," but later they came to a shared view that all of Yugoslav society needed healing, "through facing truths about themselves and the world" (Milošević, 2012, p. 141).

Since its foundation, the group has wrestled with such questions as "What is the role and the meaning of theatre? What is the responsibility and duty of artists in times of darkness, violence and human suffering? Can art, specifically theatre, be a tool for peace?" (Milošević, 2011a, p. 29). DAH has strongly opposed war and violence in its work for more than two decades. As one of the company's founders has commented, theatre was a way to oppose destruction and to celebrate life (Milošević, 2011a, pp. 28-29).

The still fledgling theatre company was very visible on the streets of Belgrade and in the alternative press, and it also toured internationally during its first decade, but, as we have noted, it lacked official acknowledgement and support from the Yugoslav government. That fact often effectively rendered the group politically invisible, irrespective of its popular and cultural salience (ibid). During the more than two decades of its existence, DAH not only has performed on every continent but has trained hundreds of performers from around the world in its International School for Actors and Directors, recently renamed The DAH Theatre Institute (Barnett, 2012, p. 264). To celebrate its twentieth anniversary in 2011, the company held a week-long festival it called Passing the Flame, with twenty-three performances by nineteen companies and solo performers from nine countries, to honor its lineage, legacy, and place in the national and international culture of performance (ibid, p. 265).

As a nongovernmental organization, DAH has sustained itself financially by means of grants and self-generated income (Milošević, 2011a, p. 29). In 2001, as the company celebrated its tenth anniversary, the group began to receive financial support from the Serbian Ministry of Culture for the first time in its history. DAH was the first alternative theatre in the nation to gain such standing (Clemons, 2005, p. 122).

The company's first public performance was *This Babylonian Confusion* in the summer of 1992, which brought the positive energy of Brecht's play against war and violence to the main street of Belgrade (Knežević, 1996, p. 415). As DAH's Web site has highlighted, "This performance was created from the need of the artists to place themselves in their duty as artists in 'dark times.' Four actors using the characters of Angels, say their share against war, nationalism and destruction."[3]

Knežević (1996) has described the courage and determination DAH's founders needed to speak out publicly against the Serbian government's war policy, which, at the time (1991–1992), viewed such efforts as "almost a crime, a form of disobedience typical of tiny civil and peace groups" (p. 415). When the theatre company began to perform in the street, one-third of its audience appeared in various kinds of uniforms, and many were armed but kept coming every day during the fifteen days the company performed *This Babylonian Confusion* to sing along with the actors, having learned the play's Kurt Weil melodies by heart (pp. 415–16). Dijana Milošević remembers the group felt it needed to take the risk and use the privilege of a public voice to tell the truth to people on the street, that they [the audience] were not alone in their pain and suffering (Milošević, 2011a, pp. 31–32). This period was deeply meaningful for the company as it created, "a healing experience for the audience," a possibility to oppose violence and destruction by creating, "a space for nurturing solidarity among people" (ibid, pp. 31–32). Nonetheless, many in Belgrade and the city's press perceived the production as highly political, and DAH group members received death threats from several supporters of the nation's regime (Clemons, 2005, p. 109).

After *This Babylonian Confusion*, the group refined its purpose and theatrical mission by founding the International Network of Young Research Theatres and by organizing a festival called "Art Saves Lives" in 1993. In June 1994, the company led the participants of a Belgrade meeting of the Network to the same location where its members had performed *This Babylonian Confusion*, so that visiting performers from Sweden, Denmark, Italy, Spain, Hungary, Norway, Greece, and DAH itself could commemorate that action and improvise scenes, each in his or her own language, on the theme of freedom and oppression (Knežević, 1996, pp. 416–417). The event gathered prominent independent, experimental theatre groups from Yugoslavia and abroad and allowed their members to exchange thoughts about their own experiences and the cultural situations in Europe, Israel, and the United States.[4] As Cleveland (2008) has described it, for both DAH and its audience, the festival's performances, which took place in the midst of harsh sanctions imposed on Serbia by the UN and the resulting isolation of the nation were, "a beacon of sanity" (p. 292).

The *Travelers*, first performed in 1999 when the city of Belgrade was under threat of NATO bombing, explored why people travel. Many Serbs could not tour at that time but, more deeply, many needed to decide whether they should leave the country or stay and resist their nation's repressive regime and try to foster change (Milošević, Randels, and D'Amour, 2003, p. 76). The play did not provide answers. Instead, it explored different possibilities for audience consideration (ibid). Later, when NATO indeed attacked Belgrade and its population had fallen into anger and despair, DAH created "something gentle that would search for the light within" (Milošević, 2011a, p. 34). *Documents of the Times* was a slow and peaceful performance that carried "the message of humanity and forgiveness" (ibid, p. 33).

In 2001, DAH's *The Maps of Forbidden Remembrance* sought to create a public space for mourning and to give voice to events when it was still taboo to speak publicly of the Serbian government's alleged complicity in war crimes, such as that at Srebrenica (Milošević, 2011a, p. 35). DAH's artistic director has argued that when the play was performed in Bosnia, it helped in the healing process, as Serbs themselves addressed the injustice the war had unleashed and "empathy was strengthened, losses were grieved, and bitterness was diminished" (Milošević, 2011a, pp. 35–36). In her view, the performance demonstrated that, "theatre can be a place to tell the truth, give testimony, and take responsibility. Through theatre, people can express mourning, bring memories to life, and give voice to the ones who cannot otherwise be heard" (Milošević, 2011a, p. 36). DAH actress Sanja Krsmanović Tasić's character in the performance was Plotnikov, an elderly Russian actor in exile. In an interview, she recalled a key phrase her character offered in the play, "The only way to heal the wound is to talk about how it was made," and explained:

> I deeply believe in this saying and for us it was very important because this is one of the first performances, actually I think the first performance where Srebrenica was mentioned, … Maja had a very powerful scene, naming all the people, men killed in Srebrenica, and putting loaves of bread on the floor.
>
> (Milošević, Mitić, and Krsmanović Tasic, 2013)

DAH created *Crossing the Line* in 2009, based on texts from the book *Women's Side of War* (2007), edited by the leaders of Women in Black-Serbia, a nongovernmental feminist peace organization with which DAH has cooperated for many years. The volume is a collection of Bosnian, Croatian, and Serbian women's testimonies of their personal losses arising from the Yugoslav war. The performance sought to establish a space for addressing the emotional and psychological wounds inflicted by the war and to encourage women who had lost loved ones in the conflicts to speak out so as to acknowledge their suffering while recognizing the pain experienced by others and to develop solidarity and gain insights into the essence of violence in war.[5] Actress Maja Mitić shared her experience in performing this play in an interview:

> When you give voice to the village woman on the stage, you hear this woman from Srebrenica sitting across from you, … giving her testimony about how she lost fifty members of her family, sons, daughters, husband, brothers, everyone. You give the space, you give the power, you give political context you really uncover something and after the performance you meet with that person and you make peace because she's Muslim and you are Serb and you were in the war and somebody from your side killed somebody from her family. Then on the human level, you make a bridge.
>
> (Milošević, Mitić, and Krsmanović Tasic, 2013)

One of DAH's recent projects, developed in partnership with the European Union in 2011–2012, is called *Networking Memories*. The effort seeks to produce multiple outcomes, including construction of a memory museum in each capital city of the former Yugoslav republics, a play, and a documentary. The galleries are intended to mount exhibitions in which the memories of common people from the whole of the former Yugoslavia will be displayed. The play, developed for the *Networking* initiative, was called *Borrowed Memories* and explores the dynamics that led to the disintegration of Yugoslavia, focusing on young people who did not experience it first-hand but whose lives have nonetheless been shaped by that socially rending period.[6]

### DAH's Conceptions of Peace and Justice

DAH's public performances often address issues that concern so-called memory politics, or the "politics of remembrance and forgetting," with the goal of stimulating dialogue with audience members (Stefanova, 2009, p. 146). These artistic efforts often merge with political activism (ibid, p. 147). DAH's activities and productions have conceptualized justice as a social process to attain truth and healing during a period often characterized by brutal injustice.

Different thinkers and activists have offered alternate views of what constitutes truth. For example, South Africa's Truth and Reconciliation Commission (TRC) has distinguished among four kinds of truth: factual, narrative/oral, social/dialogical, and restorative/healing (Boraine, 1999, pp. 9–10). The TRC leadership saw the process of acquiring and establishing truth as important to promoting social transparency, democracy, and participation as a basis for affirming human dignity and integrity in South Africa (ibid, p. 10). However, for healing to occur after large-scale violence, knowledge must be accompanied by public acknowledgement of truth (ibid), meaning, for Serbs (and other paramilitary and military groups involved in the conflict) at least, assuming responsibility for the war and the atrocities committed by their nation's regular and militia forces.

Since its founding, DAH has seen the healing process as closely associated with breaking silence and speaking truth. As one company member has noted,

> The power of the theatre lies in its power to cast light on dark truths and allow a process of mourning to occur in a society. Theatre can create a necessary space for collective mourning, for collective witnessing, for remembrance and action. It is important to ask the question: how to create space where we can meet and be together, [create] a place to mourn and not be in opposition with one another.
>
> (Milošević, 2012, p. 144)

Referring to DAH's work seeking to honor memory and to articulate truth, Knežević (1996) has suggested that the foundation for the potential healing power of the group's efforts lies in "the possibility of rearranging and reshaping reality according to human measure, replacing dead ideologies and their false eternal truths with the fundamental liberating spirit of human creativity" (p. 417). Dijana Milošević has linked this idea with a concept of the future:

> I feel that we definitely need to remind people what has been happening, because I think history proves that if we are not aware of what has been happening in the past, the future is only very brief. And on the other hand, of course we don't want to overpower, to stay only in that kind of very sad, gloomy place of remembering the atrocities and the guilt. So the question is about how to be aware of the past in order to really construct the future, not to repeat the bad deeds of the past. On the other hand, how to be able to go on to live the life fully, how to transform the experience. And this is what we are, is our aspiration.
>
> (Milošević, Mitić, and Krsmanović Tasic, 2013)

Becker (2006) has argued that an individual's (and more broadly, a society's) healing process cannot occur without "transforming the wound into a mourning process" (p. 233). He has drawn on an important study by Keilson that contended that traumatization continues even after active violence stops, challenging the notion of 'post' in trauma (p. 239), and likewise suggested that the wounds of war and atrocity need to be healed, both as individual trauma and as the destruction of the social fabric they represent, as human relations have been attacked and damaged in such situations (p. 240). Indeed, as Milošević (2011a) has explained, part of the population in Serbia continues to live in fear, afraid to search for the truth of the nation's war, feeling hopeless and helpless. This constant pain arises partly, she contends, from the fact that so many had friends and relatives in war zones and partly from the fact that some people suffer from guilt concerning their inability to do anything to address the situation as it unfolded. These individuals have, therefore, buried and denied those experiences while others have evidenced a great need to address them by creating a space of mourning. In any case, the regime sought officially to forbid grieving during the 1990s (p. 27).

Becker (2006) has also contended that healing after war and violence demands the reconstruction of memory and the establishment of shared social truth (p. 241). He has observed that such a process of public recognition is important for all victims (p. 242). DAH's involvement in the co-construction of truth by staging dramas that treat what happened in Srebrenica, for example, proved doubly meaningful for the families of the victims of that genocidal action in Bosnia, because it not only provided salience to the tragedy but demonstrated that Serbians were willing to acknowledge publicly their nation's complicity in it (Milošević, 2011a, p. 35). From the perspective of social healing, co-construction of truth is a complex process linked to grief processes, requiring that "the space for the co-construction of truth must become as much as possible a social space for mourning" (Becker, 2006, p. 253). While DAH seeks to help people express themselves, it never tries to tell individuals what to do or how to feel. DAH is concerned foremost with assisting Serbian society to confront what happened in the war and to grieve for what was lost and, at some point, to move forward by developing new perspectives for the future.

In their everyday work, DAH's members embrace conceptions of peace that appear to be underpinned by a call for coexistence. As Dijana Milošević has articulated this point,

> For me, peace [...] is people communicating in the same space together. In our region, we experienced the impossibility of people to communicate, to talk, and we create a space with a theatre performance where people can sit in silence and think together and listen together, and eventually after the performance, talk together. This is to me a possibility of peace.
> (Milošević, Mitić, and Krsmanović Tasic, 2013)

For DAH's principals, theatre is, "a tool for resistance, a tool for peace, a part of fulfilling their roles as human beings with regard to suffering" (Clemons, 2005, p. 122). DAH's artistic director believes it is possible for artists to play a vital role in creating a new social organization in the aftermath of a hatred-fueled war by offering a form of theatre that encourages individuals from a variety of ethnic communities to discuss the country's troubled history and build a common basis for exchange and possible collaboration (Milošević, 2011a, p. 42). As Dijana Milošević has expressed this aim, "Theatre can answer people's need to understand the moment they live in, and it can help them meet fear, anger, prejudice, pain, and suffering in safe surroundings. It can remind people of the suffering of others. ... It can make people smile together again" (p. 42).

## Bond Street Theatre

This brief analysis employs relevant scholarly literature, electronic and printed media, available video materials concerning BST's projects and partnerships, and interviews conducted in 2013 with the company's directors to explore the roles of theatre in building peace and advancing human rights through the lens of this New York–based artistic group's efforts during its more than thirty-five-year history. The questions that guided this inquiry included: What are the roles of theatre in conflict-and poverty-stricken communities? Can theatre be a tool for cultivating peace and human rights? We first outline how BST's productions and partnerships have explored violence, intolerance, poverty, and human rights violations and thereafter sketch the company's views of peace and justice that have emerged in and guided its work during its history.

### Bond Street Theatre's Background, Productions, and Partnerships

A small group of socially concerned actors founded Bond Street Theatre in 1976. The ensemble saw its mission as creating innovative, relevant, and accessible theatre works for diverse audiences that can translate social issues across lingual and cultural borders. Moreover, the group intended to further intercultural understanding by initiating community arts projects in a wide range of communities globally affected by conflict or poverty and in stimulating other artists toward these ends through collaborations, exchanges, and creative associations with artists and organizations around the world.

Bond Street Theatre's projects have promoted theatre's relevance as an instrument for healing and world peace in refugee camps, areas of conflict, and postwar environments and sought to build the capacities of local acting organizations to apply their art to social improvement. In 1984, Bond Street created and trained Jerusalem's first street theatre company that included both Arabs and Jews of all ages. In 1987, Montreal's International Youth for Peace and Justice Program invited BST to address sixty teenagers from forty-five war-torn nations on the power of theatre and to teach them practical popular drama techniques to promote peace. In 1990, the company gave workshops in Belfast for Catholic and Protestant children side by side and performed in East Berlin, the first legal political theatre to be presented there for nearly fifty years.

In 1999, responding to the Balkan war, BST members traveled to the Kosovar refugee camps in Macedonia, toured to theatres throughout the region with a nonverbal version of *Romeo and Juliet*, and worked with children in the rural villages. As a result, 75,000 Kosovar refugees (including more than 10,000 children) in seven refugee camps in Macedonia enjoyed a creative outlet through interactive performances. In collaboration with the Bulgarian puppet company, Theatre Tsvete, the company brought its Balkan Peace Project to Serbia, Bosnia, Albania, Romania, and Macedonia during the next five years and created the Performing Artists for Balkan Peace, an inter-ethnic network of artists.[7]

The group performed in Afghan refugee camps in Pakistan after the September 11, 2001 terrorist attack on the United States and continues to perform and teach across Afghanistan in collaboration with Exile Theatre of Kabul. Bond Street has been working in Afghanistan since 2003. Live performance theatre remains little known in that nation after years years of war and five years (1996–2001) of brutally repressive Taliban rule. As a result, for many Afghans, a visit by the company to their communities constitutes their first exposure to the live performing arts. And since Afghanistan today remains a socially restive, unsettled, and conflict-filled country, the BST's efforts often occur in environments characterized by ongoing violence and continued struggle. Bond Street has sought to develop ways it can help address that reality for the nation's citizens: "We do conflict resolution through theatre on a consistent basis, [...] offering workshops for children, to explore alternative ways to resolve conflict, without violence," Joanna Sherman observed in an interview (Sherman, personal interview, July 13, 2013).

BST has partnered with several local Afghan theatres, such as Nangarhar Provincial Theatre in Jalalabad, as part of an ongoing Theatre for Social Development project to bring much-needed creative programming to women isolated and stigmatized by incarceration as a means to give those women a voice and the confidence to speak out. BST company members have been deeply affected by the situations they encountered of women who had been imprisoned for alleged crimes, as they noted in a company newsletter,

> In the Juvenile Prison, most of the young women had fled forced marriages or abusive families. We came to understand that frequently the women face a situation far worse than jail if they were to return to the homes they fled. Many of the women have their children with them in the prison – infants and toddlers. It is sad to see children growing up in jail, and yet it clearly gave mother and child great joy to be together.
>
> (BST Newsletter, 2011)

Working with Bond Street, graduates of Kabul University's Theatre Program created White Star Company, the university's first two resident professional theatre groups (one men's entity and one women's group) in 2011. Not long after its creation, the company produced two original performances (for its male and female members, respectively) addressing corruption, inter-ethnic conflict, rule of law, family conflict, and conflict resolution. BST has also worked with Papyrus Theatre, the only female-led theatre group in Kabul, as part of the Theatre for Social Development project.[8]

Bond Street has likewise partnered with FAVILEK (Women Victims Get Up, Stand Up), a Haitian women's group founded by survivors of gender violence that uses theatre to mobilize public support and educate for justice. They turned to theatre a decade ago as their only way to reach out and be heard and requested BST's help to create a piece about the nation's 2010 earthquake and its tragic aftermath.[9] In 2011, Bond Street brought a three-week program to Haiti that focused on issues that women and girls in the camps faced while developing a supportive and constructive environment for the male population as well. The program included performances and workshops for the displaced population living in tent camps in Port-au-Prince, employing theatre-based methods to encourage post-crisis healing, empowerment, and improved life skills and as a means to promote community education and development. During the trip, Bond Street conducted research to determine appropriate future programming, focusing its attention on issues facing women and girls living in the camps. The BST team returned to Port-au-Prince in 2012 to teach theatrical skills to the women of FAVILEK; to develop a new show with that group about ongoing social violence and instability; and to perform in tent camps and other locations to raise popular awareness of the issue (Sherman, personal interview, July 13, 2013).

The diverse array of projects and partnerships in which Bond Street has been engaged for decades reveal its long-term emphasis on intercultural cooperation with other theatre companies and individual artists, and humanitarian outreach for individuals and communities stricken by war, natural disasters, or poverty. BST has extended its intercultural collaboration to design theatre-based programs to address the needs of particular groups, such as working street children, rural women and girls, and refugees (Sherman, personal interview, July 13, 2013). These foci have resulted in workshops and performances to build self-esteem, identify peaceful solutions to conflict, promote community action, share improved health practices, and educate concerning children's and women's rights. As Sherman explained this aspiration in our recent interview with her,

> We can't come in, as the foreigners, with the better way. ... Our strategy is always to collaborate with local artists and have our partnership on the ground and then we can work peer-to-peer and really discuss the issues and discuss their thinking and our thinking... Then and only then can you start at least to understand where each other is coming from. Then you could maybe create a play together that's addressing these issues from more of a fair point-of-view, or maybe a more culturally appropriate point of view...We're training organizations to use theatre in a certain kind of way ... to use theatre as a way to speak out about the issues that confront them.
> (Sherman, personal interview, July 13, 2013)

## BST's Views on Peace and Justice

BST promotes theatre as an instrument for healing and peace in areas of conflict. The company's principals view drama as a means to restore human dignity. In turn, that core attribute is foundational to peace and justice restoration in the communities in which BST works. Theatre can and should humanize those who have been dehumanized by "challenge[ing] the permission to look at others as subhuman" (Bogart, 2007, p. 119). For example, BST's *Theatre for Social Development* project brought theatre to women in prisons in three provinces of Afghanistan—Herat, Kabul, and Jalalabad. The company is now planning a project in women's prisons throughout the country to offer workshops designed to build self-confidence and encourage self-expression, critical thinking, and problem solving (Sherman, personal interview, July 13, 2013). Women in Afghanistan lack adequate access to justice and education and are often imprisoned for escaping abusive families or are falsely accused of crimes committed by others. BST has partnered in recent years with local Afghan artists to bring creative programming to women isolated and stigmatized by incarceration, as a means to provide a space for these women's voices, and to help them develop the confidence to speak out.

As Paul Rae (2009) has remarked, the relationship between theatre and human rights can be complementary: Theatre making is one way of fighting for human rights, and addressing such concerns in theatre performances can be a means of ensuring the art form's continuing social relevance (p. 1). By drawing attention to otherwise overlooked human rights abuses, grassroots theatre productions can contribute to processes of social understanding and reconciliation (Rae, 2009, p. 16). However, this relationship contains tensions as well, for theatre addresses the urgency of suffering and human rights abuses, while much of human rights theory is characterized by a reflective and measured tone (ibid, p. 4). BST addresses human rights violations in a reflective manner by engaging in community-based workshops that teach basic self-expression skills. By reflecting on human rights violations with those who suffer from them and finding ways to showcase those abuses in their performances, Bond Street has drawn on a variety of formats and techniques to highlight these important concerns.

Mroué (2009) has argued that theatre constitutes "a place for the struggle of ideas [...] a space for open discussion concerning an unresolved issue, in the presence of an alert audience, which is listening to the different voices and the conflicts between the characters" (p. xi). In addition, Schechner has similarly identified seven interrelated functions of theatre, which may overlap among themselves and in one performance:

- entertaining,
- producing something beautiful,
- marking or changing identity,
- making or fostering community,
- healing,
- teaching, and
- dealing with the sacred or the demonic.

(cited in Jackson, 2007, p. 14)

BST staged performances, whether undertaken alone or with its collaborators, typically exhibit many of these elements, particularly fostering community, healing, and teaching. While staged performances by many Afghan, Indian, or Guatemalan groups, for example, may lack artistic sophistication, every practice needs to be located within a series of cultural norms and expectations. For many such communities, theatrical experiments with BST have been their first contact with the performing arts, and they can build on what they learn and develop further thereafter. Jan Cohen-Cruz (1998) has contended that "change [is] brought on more by people making theatre than by watching it," reflecting on her own shift from performing in traveling street theatre to facilitating community-based workshops (p. 5).

BST performances and projects often address the everyday life issues of people in the communities in which the company is working with messages of hope and encouragement (Sherman and McGuigan, 2013). The testimonial form of addressing human rights concerns on which Bond Street and its partners draw privileges personal voice (Rae, 2009, p. 17). As we note earlier, BST seeks to create theatre that helps restore human dignity, which Sherman considers essential to peace and justice in the communities touched by the company's work:

> As long as women are kept under the conditions they are [in Afghanistan], there will not be peace. Women are definitely part of the peace quotient for sure. We end up working with the men separately from the women and it shapes the situation to a certain degree. My message to the men is: 'You can't be a country that just hops along on one foot. You really have to walk on two feet. And women are half of your country. And you will never be able to achieve peace alone and peace begins in the home, really.
> (Sherman, personal interview, July 13, 2013)

### *Comparative Analysis*

This section analyzes our two cases comparatively to highlight their twin subjects' approaches and contributions to cultivating peace, social healing, and forgiveness in post-conflict and poverty-stricken communities. Hawes (2007) has argued that performance arts can contribute positively to peace building in at least three ways:

- first, by focusing on emotions that may change viewers' perceptions;
- second, by engaging narrative and thereby influencing the agency of the narrators; and
- third, by affecting human relations when conflicting groups openly express their feelings and emotions (p. 136).

Drawing on Paulo Freire, Hawes (2007) has also observed that the act of questioning represents one of many contributions of artists to their communities:

"Questions help us discover and create stories that can lead to positive change" (p. 146).

Both BST and DAH ask just such questions as they work in communities to tap into the moral imagination, as conceived by Lederach (2005), to encourage residents to address ongoing on-the-ground realities, especially those where violence has dominated human relations. Both companies have sought to help those with whom they work to recognize the centrality of relationships, on which, according to Lederach, both peace building and moral imagination depend (pp. 34–35).

Seeking to respond to and transcend the patterns of animosity and violence that the Balkan war and its leaders unleashed, DAH Teatar embarked on a long journey of mobilizing its audiences' capacities to imagine themselves as part of a web of relationships interdependent with those perceived as "the other" while also avoiding dualistic polarity and believing in the power of the creative act as a mechanism of stepping "outside of the box," of transcending well-worn and destructive patterns of violence.

DAH's overall approach to building peace and justice can be framed as a genealogical search for truth, tracing the development of the ways of thinking that justified and perpetuated negative attitudes instead of accepting and legitimizing them. The company has adopted this stance to help Serb society understand itself better—how its citizens and leaders thought—to explore new possibilities for relationships that cross old boundaries of stereotypes and insecurities. DAH and its audiences live between memory and potentiality, "in a creative space ... [which is] the womb of constructive change, the continuous birthplace of the past that lies before us" (Lederach, 2005, p. 149).

In the spirit of Michel Foucault (1970), DAH has sought to highlight how prevailing views of truth are affected by power relations in society. The company's projects and performances have been a constant reminder of how power and privilege prevented Serb society from seeing and acknowledging the injustices committed against their neighbors. Championing nonviolent approaches by a humanizing rather than dehumanizing language, DAH Teatar has assertively promoted a search for peace and justice. By contributing to the healing of psychological wounds arising from past victimization and dehumanization, the company has sought not only to prevent future violence and recurrence of scapegoating ideologies but to encourage reflection and adoption of new views concerning security, tolerance, and coexistence. In so doing, DAH's members consistently have sought to inspire empathy and a sense of connectedness among members of groups previously in conflict. The theatre group's artistic director believes that through crafting programs for and with young people, drama can help to open the way for truth by giving voice to those who otherwise would not be heard, thus, "nurtur[ing] a foundation for the future that will enable people to live together" (Milošević, 2011a, p. 42). Similarly, Hawes (2007) has contended that the performance arts constitute "not only the means for changing negative attitudes toward individuals or groups, [...] [but] also offer[ing] a means to re-imagine our world so we can live together in it" (p. 148).

Adopting a human needs perspective, BST has worked in post-conflict communities in which political and economic actors and structures have systematically deprived citizens of interaction possibilities. Bond Street has developed an iterative and incremental approach to addressing human rights through the theatre, thus potentially reducing confrontations over intractable issues. BST strives to understand the practices of theatre and human rights in dynamic perspective, interrogating the basic conditions within which such rights are anchored and seeking to envision alternatives that can provide those circumstances in the communities in which they work (Rae, 2009, p. 41).

This approach requires a deep commitment to innovation and flexibility to adapt to ever-changing environmental conditions and to respond adroitly and sensitively to such context-based challenges. Even in the direst situations, such theatre-making can open up spaces for people to tell their stories and shape those narratives, aspirations, and beliefs in ways that other methods of engagement cannot. Rae (2009) has argued that theatre making represents one of many ways through which those interested may fight for human rights.

In sum, the experiences of both theatre groups in peace building through the arts suggest the following lessons:

- Peace negotiations and agreements do not by themselves ensure sustainable peace, because they do not address the psychological harm inflicted by past conflict(s) on the parties, such as memories, beliefs, and emotions. Artistic approaches may better deal with these realities than other peace-building strategies because they extend beyond the realm and expertise of diplomats and trained conflict professionals, by eliciting, acknowledging, and addressing emotions and uncovering the values threatened in conflict dynamics.
- Coexistence, rather than integration, per se is generally a more realistic goal for those seeking progress in previously deeply divided communities. Even after the Balkan war, ethnic intolerance was widespread but hidden, leaving a false impression of a relatively tolerant Serbian society (Milošević 2011a, p. 36). DAH offered its performances of *(In)Visible City* on public buses in a bid to tell the multiethnic history of Serbia's cities, aiming to contribute to the normalization of relationships among different ethnic communities and toward the development of a civil society based on tolerance.
- Restoring human dignity is foundational to sustainable peace and justice in any community. Theatre can and should seek to humanize those who have been dehumanized by the fundamentalist assumptions employed to justify conflict.

## Conclusions

Traditional methods of conflict resolution have been criticized for failing to consider the role of the "human dimension" or "subjective" factors in creating and sustaining social conflict. Conversely, as Beller (2009) has rightly suggested, arts-based peace building faces a number of challenges in demonstrating its effectiveness. The arts may promote different psycho-social and qualitative change processes compared to other approaches, but such shifts often occur in non-linear and unpredictable ways, which are difficult to capture via conventional evaluation frameworks (Beller, 2009, p. 2). Hambler (2006) has argued that dealing with the consequences of large-scale violence is a deeply contextual process, and it is therefore likely to be difficult to obtain clear evidence that at a certain date or time, the psychological impact of past violence has been ameliorated and individual or social closure achieved (p. 215).

As DAH has demonstrated throughout its twenty years of existence, peace building in the former Yugoslavia (and in other postwar nations) cannot be successful without rebuilding social relationships among previously warring individuals and groups. Reconstructing social ties will not occur without shared processes that permit social restoration of memory and establishment of common truths. DAH's principals have realized that co-construction of truth is a long and delicate process in which it is important to give voice to many conceptions existing in a society. While complete closure may never occur for some individuals, and indeed for Serb society at large, such healing as may occur will nevertheless involve co-constructing and sharing different truths present in the nation and in neighboring societies. Through addressing and acknowledging in its works the losses suffered by all of the ethnic groups involved and the injustices perpetrated by the Serbian government, DAH has expressed empathy with the suffering of all of those harmed by the conflict, thereby contributing to reducing bitterness while honoring the dignity of the victims and their families. The theatre company's efforts have also sought deliberately and, by such measures as are available, successfully to rebuild the Serb nation's sociocultural diversity, so badly damaged in the war.

Theatre that intends to address the complexity of human rights violations cannot be "easily subsumed into a conventional format," according to Rae (2009, p. 19), and this is particularly true for BST as it has promoted human rights by means of a variety of techniques and formats. Certain types of performance art interventions have the potential to create social change by stimulating public dialogue concerning dominant social, political, and ideological frameworks (Hawes, 2007, p. 147). Theatre can be a powerful alternative to passive spectatorship that is otherwise often encouraged in today's societies (Bogart, 2007, p. 75) by inviting the audience to play an active role by making room for their imaginations to construct narratives and associations that become a shared experience (ibid, p. 76–77). For example, in Afghanistan, where people did not have a culture of spectatorship owing to ubiquitous TV shows and lack of a tradition of live theatre, BST has found that audience members often express strong views about what should be done and have useful information that they cannot share in any other forum. Bond Street and its collaborators made wide use of talkbacks,[10] engaging audiences in problem solving concerning the issues presented in plays and allowing audience members to come on stage and address the characters in the play.[11] Bond's social theatre entertains while it teaches, heals, fosters community, and seeks to produce something beautiful.

In sum, in the aftermath of violence, "it is often the artist who penetrates the deeper essence of humanity's plight," helping expand people's capacity to imagine entirely new possibilities and insights, as Lederach (2005) has argued (p. 176). He called for elected officials and public leaders to imagine and enact politics as a field of human activity that is broader than merely cognitive understandings of complex realities, caring about the nature and quality of our relationships, and moving "from relationships defined by division and fear toward those characterized by respect and love" (ibid). In this chapter, we have examined how two theatre companies used their art form as a tool for building peace and justice, thus contributing to the work of building positive relationships in conflict-ridden and post-conflict communities both in the United States and internationally.

## Notes

1  "Dah" means "breath" in Serbo-Croatian. For the creators of DAH Theatre, "Breath" also means to breathe in, to gather strength, to persevere, to be spiritual, to honor the spirit of life—warmth, movement, creation (rereived September 19, 2014 from DAH's Web site, http://www.dahteatarcentar.com/aboutus.html). Spelled backward, DAH becomes HAD, or in Serbian, Hades, the ruler of the underworld in ancient Greek mythology. DAH's co-founder, Dijana Milosevic, has written, "through our work in DAH we can also explore dark, painful, or hidden sides of ourselves, our society, and the world" (2011a, p.29).

2  Retrieved August 21 2012 from the History page of Bond Street Theatre, http://www.bondst.org/history.html

3  Retrieved September 19, 2014 from http://www.dahteatarcentar.com/predstave/ovavavilonskapometnja_eng.html

4  Retrieved September 19, 2014 from http://www.dahteatarcentar.com/festivali/trajanjeitransformacija_eng.html

5  Retrieved September 19, 2014 from http://www.dahteatarcentar.com/predstave/prelazeci_liniju_eng.html

6  Retrieved September 19, 2014 from http://www.dahteatarcentar.com/Netmem/netmem_eng.html

7  Retrieved September 19, 2014 from Bond Street Theatre's Web page on the Balkan Peace project at http://www.bondst.org/balkan-peace-project.html

8  Retrieved September 19, 2014 from Bond Street Theatre's Web page on Afghanistan projects at http://www.bondst.org/afghanistan.html

9  Retrieved September 19, 2014 from Bond Street Theatre's Web page on Haiti projects at www.bondst.org/haiti.html

10  Talkbacks are after-performance opportunities that engage audiences in problem solving linked to issues presented in plays. Some of these encourage playgoers to come on stage and address the characters in the play to illustrate their points of view.

11  Retrieved September 19, 2014 from BST's Facebook page, http://www.facebook.com/photo.php?fbid=10151044002586637&set=pb.173939981636.-2207520000.1361652763&type=3& theatre

## References

B92. (2014). Information about B92. Retrieved September 19, 2012 from http://www. b92.net/about_us/history.php

Barnett, D. (2012). Passing the flame: DAH Theatre's 20th Anniversary Festival. *Theatre Journal*, 64(2): 264–267. doi:10.1353/tj.2012.0035. Retrieved September 19, 2012 from http://muse.jhu.edu/journals/theatre_journal/summary/v064/64.2.barnett.html

Becker, D. (2006). Confronting the truth of the Erinyes: The illusion of harmony in the healing of trauma. In T. A. Borer, *Telling the Truths: Truth Telling and Peace Building in Post-Conflict Societies* (pp. 231–258). Notre Dame, IN: University of Notre Dame Press.

Beller, S. (2009). *Sowing art, reaping peace: Toward a framework for evaluating arts-based peacebuilding.* Master's thesis, American University, Washington, DC. Retrieved August 21, 2012, from ProQuest Dissertations and Theses.

Blumberg, H. H., Hare, P. A., and Costin, A. (2006). *Peace Psychology: A Comprehensive Introduction*. New York, NY: Cambridge University Press.

Bogart, A. (2007). *And then, You Act: Making Art in an Unpredictable World*. New York, London: Routledge.

BST (Bond Street Theatre). (n.d.). Web site Retrieved August 21, 2912 http://www. bondst.org/historyarchives/3/a-brief-history-of-bond-street-theatre

BST (Bond Street Theatre). (2011) Newsletter: Fall 2011. Retrieved August 21, 2012 from http://www.bondst.org/uploads/1/4/5/7/14571600/newsletter_fall_2011_pg_12. pdf

Boraine, A. (1999). All truth is bitter: A report of the visit of Doctor Alex Boraine, Deputy Chairman of the South African Truth and Reconciliation Commission, to Northern Ireland. Retrieved October 17, 2012 from http://cain.ulst.ac.uk/issues/victims/docs/ alltruthisbitter99.pdf

Clemons, L. (2005). The winds of change: Alternative theatre practice and political transformation in the former FRY (Federal Republic of Yugoslavia). *Theatre History Studies*, 25: 107–124. Retrieved August 22, 2012, from http://connection.ebscohost. com/c/articles/17439789/winds-change-alternative-theatre-practice-political- transformation-former-fry-federal-republic-yugoslavia

Cleveland, W. (2008). *Art and Upheaval: Artists on the World's Frontlines*. Oakland, CA: New Village Press.

Cohen-Cruz, J. (1998). General introduction. In J. Cohen-Cruz (Ed.) *Radical Street Performance: An International Anthology* (pp. 1–6). London, New York: Routledge.

Cohen, C., Varea, R. G., and Walker, P. O. (Eds.) (2011). *Acting Together: Performance and the Creative Transformation of Conflict: Volume I: Resistance and Reconciliation in Regions of Violence.* Oakland, CA: New Village Press.

DAH Teatar. (n.d.). Web site Retrieved September 19, 2012 from http://www. dahteatarcentar.com/index_eng.html

Foucault, M. (1970). *The Order of Things: An Archaeology of the Human Sciences*. New York, NY: Pantheon Books.

Hamber, B. (2006). "Nunca Más" and the politics of the person: can truth telling prevent the recurrence of violence?" In T.A. Borer, *Telling the truths: truth telling and peace building in post-conflict societies* (pp. 207–230). Notre Dame, IN: University of Notre Dame Press.

Hawes, D. L. (2007). *Why art matters: How performance art interventions contribute to the field of conflict resolution*. Doctoral dissertation, George Mason University.

Jackson, A. (2007). *Theatre, Education and the Making of Meanings*. Manchester, New York: Manchester University Press.

Knežević, D. (1996). Marked with red ink. *Theatre Journal*, 48(4): 407–418.

Lederach, J. P. (2005). *The Moral Imagination: The Art and Soul of Building Peace*. New York: Oxford University Press.

Milošević, D. (2011a). Theatre as a way of creating sense: Performance and peacebuilding in the region of the former Yugoslavia. In C. Cohen, V. R. Gutierrez, and P. O.Walker (Eds.) *Acting Together: Performance and the Creative Transformation of Conflict: Volume I: Resistance and Reconciliation in Regions of Violence* (pp. 23–43). Oakland, CA: New Village Press.

Milošević, D. (2011b). *Talking to Mahmood. Conversation with Dijana Milošević*. Retrieved September 19, 2012 from http://www.youtube.com/watch?v=9_bNMeI3J80

Milošević, D. (2012). Some thoughts on the quality of attention. In C. Svich (Ed.) *Out of Silence: Censorship in Theatre and Performance* (pp. 140–144). Roskilde: Eyecorner Press.

Milošević, D., Randels, K., and D'Amour, L. (2003). Light in midst of darkness. In C. Svich, (Ed.) *Trans-Global Readings: Crossing Theatrical Boundaries* (pp. 73–76). Manchester, New York: Manchester University Press.

Milošević, D., Mitić, M., and Krsmanović Tasic, S. (2013). Skype interview conducted on July 17, 2013.

Mroué, R. (2009). Foreword. In P. Rae (Ed.) *Theatre and Human Rights* (pp. ix–xii). Hampshire, UK: Palgrave Macmillan.

Rae, P. (2009). *Theatre and Human Rights*. Hampshire, UK: Palgrave Macmillan.

Saunders, H. H. (1999). *A Public Peace Process: Sustained Dialogue to Transform Racial and Ethnic Conflicts*. New York, NY: St. Martin's Press.

Sherman, J. (2013). Telephone interview conducted on July 13, 2013.

Sherman, J. and McGuigan, M. (2013). Telephone interview conducted on August 23, 2013.

Stefanova, J. (2009). On public spaces and artistic interventions. *Kultura* no. 122–123, 141–157.

Zelizer, C. M. (2004). *The role of artistic processes in peacebuilding in Bosnia-Herzegovina*. Doctoral dissertation, George Mason University. ProQuest Dissertations and Theses. Retrieved November 11, 2012 from http://ezproxy.lib.vt.edu:8080/login?url=http://search.proquest.com/docview/305049788?accountid=14826. (305049788).

# INDEX

Bold page numbers indicate figures.

accessibility 29
Addams, J. 55, 56
Afghan refugee camps 222
Afghanistan 222, 228–9
agency, denial of 33
"AIR: Art in Roanoke" 119
Allen, M. 116, 121, 122, 126
alternative culture 78; community
    orientation 84–5; creative mess 93–
    4; differences 83–6; economics of
    85–90, 95; enabling 94–6; eviction
    92, 95; flexibility 83; interaction
    84; key features 79; legality 86;
    mixed-use neighborhoods 90–2,
    95–6; promotion and visibility
    84; survival 85–6; venues 84–5;
    vulnerability 83
American Festival Project (AFP) 64
Americans for the Arts 4
Anderson, M. 73
Anderson, V. 139–40
Animating Democracy 3–4, 188,
    193–4, 206
Anzaldua, G. 101
Appalachia 138–9
Appalachian Film Workshop 138–9
Appalshop 138–9
Arai, T. 60
Arizona State University (ASU),
    Roadside Theater 159–60
Art At Work 193–4, 197–9, 204, 206
art competitions, Quartier des
    Spectacles, Montreal 94

"Art for Everyone: Roanoke Public Art
    Plan" 119
Artaud, A. 172
ArtPlace America 73
arts: community roles 73; functions 3; as
    tool for planning 30
Arts and Cultural Plan, Roanoke 8
Arts and Democracy 56
Arts, Culture and Social Justice Network
    200
arts ecosystems 7; artists and
    neighborhoods 58; Chinatown
    History Project 72; context and
    overview 54; El Museo de Barrio
    58–9, 69–70; Fourth Arts Block
    (FAB) 56, 61–3, 73; framework 54–7;
    Museum of Chinese in America
    (MoCA) 72–3; New York Chinatown
    History Project (CHP) 59–60;
    "One New York, Rising Together"
    72–4; Staten Island Arts 65–6; Urban
    Bush Women (UBW) 63–5; see
    also Naturally Occurring Cultural
    Districts (NOCD)
arts initiatives, scope of 1–2
assimilationism 55
assumptions, social change assessment
    202–3
Atchely, D. 101
Atlas, C. 56, 68, 72
attraction 2
Auden, W.H. 142
autonomy 138–9

Bair, D. 114
Balanchine, G. 180
Balkan Peace Project, Bond Street
    Theatre (BST) 221
Bauman, M. 63–4
Beagle, B. 113
Bebelle, C. 70
Becker, D. 219–20
Bedoya, R. 29, 189, 200, 201
behavioral protocols 159–60
Behn, R. 207
Belfast workshops, Bond Street Theatre
    (BST) 221
Bell, D. 109
Beller, S. 228
Berry, W. 69, 163
Big Lick 111
Bilbao 128–9
Bingham, G. 115
Bishop, M. 112
Black Arts Movement 172
Blair, B. 39
*Blood, Muscle, Bone: The Anatomy of Wealth
    and Poverty* (Lerman and Zollar) 9;
    antecedents 169–70; overview 166–7;
    teach-ins 167–8; *see also* dance and
    community practice
Boal, A. 34–7
Bond Street Theatre (BST) 9, 213, 221–5;
    comparative analysis 225–7; evaluation
    of 227; founding 221; human
    rights 228; peace and justice 223–5;
    productions and partnerships 221–5
book: approaches taken 4–10; background
    and context 1–2; outline 6–10;
    questions asked 6; structure 5
boomtown syndrome 112
Boraine, A. 218
*Borrowed Memories* 218
Borrup, T. 189
boundary crossing 74
boundary locations 57
branding 108
Brooklyn Community Foundation 73
Bruguera, T. 66
Building Healthy Communities 56–7
Building Home project 7; activities 30;
    aha moment 33; audience interaction
    **31**; background 28; *Built NRV*
    game 47; closed-session events 44;
    collaborative working 43; community
    gatherings 41–2, 46; connecting
    with Livability Initiative 46; context
    and overview 28; contribution to
    Livability Initiative 43; data created

41–2, 48–9; development meetings
    39–40; engagement questions 37;
    facilitation 36–7; forms 41; Forum
    Theater 36; group sessions 41–2;
    identifying action steps 41; Image
    Theater 34–6; independent research
    38; initial meetings 30; *Livability
    in the New River Valley* Report
    42–3; mapping the region 37–9;
    moments-of-truth 49–50; *NRV
    Today* scene 44–6; obesity project
    44–5; opposition to 30–1; participant
    concerns 33; personal safety 44;
    perspective shift 33; remaining
    questions 48; report writing 48;
    Story Circle methodology 20–1,
    32–4; story corners 41–2; summary
    and conclusions 50–1; theater
    strategies 31–7; theory to practice
    41–6; trust-building 38–40
*Built NRV* game 47
Burton, P. 84–5, 86, 90

Cabral, A. 17
Calhoun, E. 126–7
California Endowment 71
Carlson, M. 57
Carroll, R. 119
Casa del Popolo 83, 84–5, 86
Casals, G. 58–9
case study research 110
Casey, D. 122–3
Caudill, H. 138
Center in the Square, Roanoke 114
champions 132
change: meaning and measurement 9;
    sources of 25
Childs, L. 180
Chinatown History Project 72
Choteau, Montana, Roadside Theater
    157–8
CHU Sainte-Justine 88
City of Philadelphia Mural Arts
    Program 22–3
civic dialogue 3–4
Civic Practice, performance-based 29
civil rights 17–18
Clemons, L. 214, 215, 216, 220
Cleveland, W. 216
co-construction of truth 220
Cocke, D. 147, 148
Cohen-Cruz, J. 3
Cohn, M. 65–6, 71
collaborative working 21–2; Building
    Home project 43; digital storytelling

100–1; and innovation 184; learning from 175–7; Quartier des Spectacles. Montreal 88; Roadside Theater 148–52; teach-ins 167–8
colonization 24
commercialism 24
commodification 19–20; Quartier des Spectacles. Montreal 82
communities: distinguishing 189; shaping 108
community character 61–3
community cohesion 65–6
community cultural development: activity points 155–7; Arizona State University (ASU) 159–60; Choteau, Montana 157–8; defining 3; expansion 4; meaning of 136; methodology **156**; and power 162; practice 154–7; principles 155; Roadside Theater 152–5; theory of change 153–4; value clashes 160
community development: arts' roles in 2–3, 4; Roanoke 109
community embeddedness 8
community engagement: Roadside Theater 155; Urban Bush Women (UBW) 64
community gardens, New York City 57
community gatherings, Building Home project 41–2
community involvement, Marginal Arts Festival (MAF) 127–8
community, meaning of 171
community orientation, alternative culture 84–5
community ownership and participation 144–6, 148–52
Community Voices Heard (CVH) 70
comparative analysis, DAH Theater and Bond Street Theatre (BST) 225–7
consultation, Roanoke 119–20
consumption 2
Cook, S. 100
Corona Studio 66, 67
corporatization 19
costs, Quartier des Spectacles, Montreal 87, 92, 95
creative class 2, 23–4
creative economy: policy support 68; theories 78
Creative Placemaking 29
creative placemaking 73
creative workers, policy support 78
creativity, messiness 93–4
*Crossing the Line* 217

Cultural Agents Initiative, Harvard University 34
cultural approach, power of 20
cultural assets 59
cultural competence 200
cultural democracy 14, 18–19
cultural development, aims 108
cultural development approaches, distinctions between 4
cultural economy 57
cultural embeddedness 66–7
cultural equity, and decolonization 17–18
cultural organization strategies 73
cultural policy 14–15
cultural policy debate 16
cultural roots 63–5
cultural specificity, dance and community practice 182–3
cultural strategies, Louisiana Bucket Brigade (LABB) 203
cultural vitality, promotion of 71
cultural wings of social movements 73
culture: as beliefs and understandings 54–5; as driver of development 11–12; functions 3; as inherent in community change 7; role of market 15–16
culture as development rhetoric 110
culture gap 16
Cummins-Russell, T. 78
Cunningham, M. 180
curators, Marginal Arts Festival (MAF) 125–7
Currid, E. 3, 78, 85, 92
Cutt, J. 191, 204, 205

DAH Teatar 9, 213–20; comparative analysis 225–7; concept of future 219; conceptions of peace and justice 218–20; evaluation of 226; funding 215–16; healing 219–20; memory politics 218; productions and partnerships 215–18; self-questioning 215
dance and community practice: closing thoughts 183–4; collaborative working 175–7; as conscious choice 179; context and overview 166; cultural specificity 182–3; dance technique 181–2; emotional expression 168–9; finding a place 173; flashpoints 176; innovation through collaboration 184; introducing depth 170; origin stories 171–2; power of outsiders 176; racism 175–6, 182–3; role of story 179–80; stage works and community projects 177–9; teach-ins **168**; *see also Blood,*

*Muscle, Bone: The Anatomy of Wealth and Poverty* (Lerman and Zollar)
Dance Exchange 9, 166, 188
dance technique 181–2
Davis, C. 46, 47–8, 49, 50
de Blasio, B. 54, 72–4
de-skilling 182
debates, continuing 13–14
decolonization, and cultural equity 17–18
democracy: and community-based art 3–4; majority tyranny 48–9; populist 163
democratic values, social change assessment 199
democratization, of elite culture 18–19
demographic change 2
Dennison, A. 113, 127
deNobriga, K. 139–40
development, culture as driver 11–12
digital storytelling 8; context and overview 99–100; knowing and being known 104–5; methodological framework 100–1; narrative praxis 100–2; process 101–2; public health 102–4; publicness and transportability 105; sharing expertise 105; summary and conclusions 105–6; youth agency 102–4
Dillon Rule 117
dis-belonging 200–1
discovery, theater as 170
Divan Orange 86
diversity 182–3
*Docudances* (Lerman) 170
*Documents of the Times* 217
Dotson, R. 111–12
Dwyer, C. 193–4
dynamic process 19–20
dynamized dialogue 34

economic change 2
economic impacts, as primary 12
Edinburgh Fringe Festival 124
effectiveness, as social construction 199
Einstein, A. 205
El Museo de Barrio 58–9, 69–70
elite culture, democratization of 18–19
embellishment, culture as 23
embodiment, of emotion 168–9
emergent arts: enabling 94–6; *see also* alternative culture
emotional expression: in dance 173; dance and community practice 168–9
empathy, learning 22
environmental sustainability 12

ethnographic case study research 110
ethnography 100
Evans, K. 196, 197, 201–2, 203, 207
event size 84
eviction 92, 95
Exile Theatre of Kabul 222
experience economy 2
experimentation, social change assessment 203
expert prescription, vs. self-determination 18

facilitation, Building Home project 36–7
failure, learning through 203
Fanon, F. 17
FAVILEK (Women Victims Get Up, Stand Up) 222–3
Feldstein, L.M. 188, 189
feminism, dance 180–1
Festival du Nouveau Cinema 83
Finkelpearl, T. 66, 74
flashpoints 176
Florida, R. 23, 68, 77, 78
Ford Foundation Animating Democracy Project *see* Animating Democracy
Forgotten New York 71
Forsythe, W. 180
Forum Theater 36, 42, 43
Foucault, M. 226
Fourth Arts Block (FAB) 56, 61–3, 73
Fragata, Y. 91
fragmentation, of artistic self 179
Free Southern Theater (FST) 161–2
Freire, P. 17, 225
fringe arts 124, 131–2; *see also* Marginal Arts Festival (MAF)
From the Neighborhood Up 69
Frost Kumpf, H. 78
Fuentes, D. 66
Fullilove, M. 71, 112
funding 24; alternative culture 85–6, 88, 89, 92–3; Appalshop 139; DAH Teatar 215–16; Roadside Theater 141; Roanoke 120–1
*Fusing Arts, Culture, and Social Change* (Sidford) 142
future, and peace building 219

Gadwa, A. 96
Geertz, C. 109
Gehry, F. 115, 128
gentrification 24, 57, 60, 61, 62–3
Gilliam, R. 62
Girard, A. 16, 19
Gish, T. and P. 138

Gladwell, M. 39
Glassberg, D. 55
globalization 18
Goldbard, A. 3, 190; development of interest 14; experiences 15
Graham, M. 180–1
grant programs 24
Greater Astoria Historical Society 72
Greenfield, T. 56, 61, 68
group sessions, Building Home project 41–2
guerrilla art 131
Guggenheim, Bilbao 128–9

*Hairstories* 63
Haiti 222–3
Hall, P. 78
Hamber, B. 228
Hart, M. 116–17, 118
Harvie, J. 57
Hawes, D.L. 213, 225–6
Head Start program, New River Valley (NRV) 45
healing 219–20
*Healing Wars* (Lerman) 177–9, **178**
healthy cities 68
Healthy New River Valley (Healthy NRV) initiative 102–4
Henry, G.T. 192
*Hep-Hep Sweet Sweet* (Zollar) 171, **172**
*Highly Classified* 159–60
Hinkes-Jones, L. 30
historical imagination 61–3
history, denial of 183
Holden Arts and Associates 143
Holmes, D.R. 105
hooks, b. 105–6
Horwitz, A. 66–7
housing rights activism, New York City 61
Howell, R. 63
Hull-House 55–6
human rights 16, 228
humor 175

ideas, histories of 13–14
identities, arts-based 109
Image Theater 34–6
imaginaries, concept of 5
immigrant cultural projects 55–6
Immigrant Movement International 66, 67
inclusion, Roadside Theater 145–6
inclusivity 4, 29
insight, acquiring 48–9

inter-organizational dynamics 7
interaction, alternative culture 84
interdependence: cultural organizations 69–70; social resources 55
International Conference of Indigenous Peoples on Self-Determination and Sustainable Development, 2012 13
international cultural policy discourse 13–14
International Network of Young Research Theatres 216
International School for Actors and Directors 215
International Youth for Peace and Justice Program, Montreal 221
internationalism 55–6
investment, effects of 110

Jackson, M.R. 56–7, 71, 190–1
Jackson, S. 55–6
Jacobs, J. 68, 90
Jayne, M. 109
Jerusalem street theatre, Bond Street Theatre (BST) 221
Johnson, L.B. 138
Julnes, G. 192
*Junebug/Jack* 148–52, **150**
Junebug Productions 148–50, 162

Kaas-Lentz, L. 47
Katacombes 92–3
Kelly, J.G. 106
Kelsey, R. 182
Kennedy, John F. 138
Kent, S. 167
Kentucky Arts Council (KAC) 141
Kerr Cultural Center 159–60
Kittredge, K. 115–16
Knežević, D. 214, 216, 219
Knox, P. 115
Korza, P. 3–4, 186, 188, 203, 204, 206
Koštunica, V. 215
Kotkin, J. 2
Kresge Foundation 195, 206
Krsmanović Tasic, S. 215, 217
Kundera, M. 25

Lai, C. 58, 59
Lambert, J. 101
Landry, C. 2–3, 78
language, as protective barrier 169
Lassiter, L.E. 100
Le Vivier 90
leadership 132
Lederach, J.P. 212, 213, 226, 228–9

Lee, D. 128
Lefebvre, E. 90
Lefebvre, H. 5
legality, alternative culture 86
Lerman, L. 64, 188, 190; in dialogue
    166ff; origin story 173–4
livability, criticism of 51
*Livability in the New River Valley: From
    Vision to Action* 42–3, 50–1
Livability Initiative 28, 30–1, 38, 42–3;
    civic process 48; connecting with
    46; opposition to 43–4; use of data
    49
logic-based models 202
Loman, N. 125, 127–8
Louisiana Bucket Brigade (LABB)
    196–7, 198, 201–2, 203, 205, 207
Lower East Side History Month 62
L'X venue 92–3

Maahs, L. 194, 195, 199, 201, 202–3,
    204, 205, 208
MacDowell, L. 191
Maheu, R. 16
majority tyranny 48–9
mapping the region, Building Home
    project 37–9
Marcus, G.E. 105
Marcuse, H. 3
Marginal Arts Festival (MAF) 123–8,
    130–1
marginality 127; dis-belonging 200–1
Mark, M. 192
market economy, logic of 19–20
market, role in culture 15–16
marketing 108
Markusen, A. 51, 96, 129
Martin, J. 120
mass media, effects of 152
mastery, meaning of 22
Mayer, H. 115
McIntyre, D. 172
memory politics 218
Mercer, C. 6
Milošević, D. 213–20, 226–7
Milošević S. 214–15
Mitić, M. 218
mixed-use neighborhoods 90–2, 95–6
moments-of-truth 49–50
Montanez Ortiz, R. 58
Montreal: arts scene 78–9; map **81**;
    overview 77–9; *see also* Quartier des
    Spectacles, Montreal
moral imagination 213
*Mountain Tales and Music* 152

"Mountaineers–Cowfolks" agreement
    157–8
Mroue, R. 212
municipal cultural policy 68
Murray, V. 191, 192, 199, 204, 205–6
Museum of Chinese in America
    (MoCA) 60, 72–3
Museum of Contemporary Art,
    Montreal 85

Nandy, A. 17
Nangarhar Provincial Theatre 222
narrative conventions 170, 183
narrative praxis 100–2
narratives: neighborhood-based arts and
    culture 71; Story Circles 32–3
National Endowments for the Arts
    (NEA) 16; Folk Arts Program 141
National Endowments for the
    Humanities (NEH) 16
natural cultural districts 56
Naturally Occurring Cultural
    Districts (NOCD) 7, 54; approach
    57; community concerns 69;
    creation of 56; goals, priorities
    and recommendations 70–1; as
    networks 56–7, 67–9; public forum
    69; researcher involvement 71–2;
    shared appreciations 58; support and
    encouragement 69–71; *see also* arts
    ecosystems
Neely, F. 126–7
neighborhood-based arts and culture,
    changing narrative 71
neighborhood-based networks, need for
    67–9
Nelson, J. 113, 114, 117, 119, 120, 121,
    122
neoliberalism 108
*Networking Memories* 218
*New Creative Community: The Art of
    Cultural Development* (Goldbard) 3
*New Cultural Policy for Sweden* 1972
    14–15
New River Valley (NRV), Virginia:
    community involvement initiative
    43; Head Start program 45; *Livability
    in the New River Valley* Report
    42–3; Planning District Commission
    (PDC) 28, 29–30, 37–8, 42–4, 48, 51,
    102; public health 102–4; tourism
    project 43; *see also* Building Home
    project; digital storytelling
New York Chinatown History Project
    (CHP) 7, 59–60

New York City: housing rights activism 61; mayoral leadership transition 69; tourism 71; *see also* arts ecosystems
Ngugi wa Thiong'o 160
*Night Comes to the Cumberlands: A Biography of a Depressed Area* (Caudill) 138
noise complaints 91
Norfolk and Western Railroad (N&W) 111
norms, social change assessment 202–3
nuisance 91
Nyseth, T. 108

Obama, B. 28–9
obesity 44–5
Occupy Wall Street 73
*Oedipus Rex* (Sophocles) 48–9
*On the Circuit* (Auden) 142
One New York Rising Together 54, 72–4
O'Neal, J. 32, 148, 161
oral history 60
oral tradition 146
organization building 132
Osborne- Lanthier, J. 84, 86, 93
Osman, A. 66
outsiders, power of 176
Owens, M. 70

pageantry movement 55
Parade for Big Oil 201–2
Parks & Arts 130
participation, as social good 19–20
participatory budgeting (PB) 70
participatory evaluation 199
participatory research 100–1
Partners in Performance! 120
Partnership for Sustainable Communities 28
Passing the Flame festival 215
Paulus, R. 158
peace building 9; Bond Street Theatre (BST) 221–7, 228; comparative analysis 225–7; concept of future 219; conceptions of truth 218; context and overview 212–13; contribution of performance arts 225–6; DAH Teatar 213–20, 228; evaluation of 227; healing 219–20; human rights 228; lessons 227; peace and justice 218–20, 223–5; recognition 220; research sites 213; reshaping reality 219; search for truth 226; social relationships 228; summary and conclusions 228; Yugoslav theatre 214–15

peace, meaning of 212
Performing Artists for Balkan Peace 222
Phillips, C. 118
place: definition and role 189; importance of 64, 65–6; meaning of 29
PLACE Initiative 194–5, 200–1, 204, 205
placemaking 29
Plenty! 44
pluralism 20
Poirier, G. 91
Police Poetry Project 193–4
policies, damaging 68
policy: Roanoke 122; supporting creative economy 78
politics of remembrance and forgetting 218
politics, polarized 32
Pop Montreal 83, 89, 91
populist democracy 163
Porterfield, D. 32
*Portraits of New York Chinatown* 60
Pottenger, M. 193–4, 198–200, 204, 205, 206
poverty: emotional expression 168–9; New River Valley (NRV), Virginia 42–3; Roanoke 113
power: community cultural development 162; of outsiders 176
power imbalances, and social change assessment 201
practice, community cultural development 153–4
Pratt, A.C. 99
Pregones Theatre 70
Prine, J. 138
produced space 5
Provisional Theatre 167
public art, as container for complexity 39
Public Art Policy, Roanoke 119
public health 8; New River Valley (NRV), Virginia 102–4
public involvement, methods and challenges 30
public participation 7
public support, Quartier des Spectacles, Montreal 96
Putnam, R. 188, 189

qualitative approaches, social change assessment 204–5
quantification 18
Quartier des Spectacles, Montreal 8, 90–2; alternative culture 83; art competitions 94; challenges 95;

context and overview 77–9; costs
87, 92, 95; creative mess 92–4;
cultural spaces 80–1; data issues 87;
development vision 81–2; *see also*
Montreal
Quartier des Spectacles. Montreal,
emergent arts 87–8
Quartier des Spectacles, Montreal:
enabling 94–6; enabling emergence
94–6; eviction 92, 95; funding
85–6, 88, 89, 92–3; history 80–3;
investment 82; map **81**; mixed-use
neighborhoods 90–2, 95–6; noise
complaints 91; nuisance 91; planning
88, 96; public support 96; real-estate
development 92–3; research method
79; space availability 95; space costs
89–90; tourism 94; underground
culture 88–9; urban renewal 80, 81–3,
92–3
Quartier des Spectacles Partnership
(QDSP) 81–2, 89, 94
Queens Museum (QM) 8, 66–7
questioning, and social change 226

Racine, C. 88
racism 73, 175–6, 182–3
Rae, P. 228
Rantisi, N. 78
Rappaport, J. 106
re-identification 8; aims of project 120;
arts and culture plan 117–23, 129–30,
132; Arts District 118; "big tent"
approach 131; choice of research
location 110–11; community focus
121; consultation 119–20; context
and overview 108–9; discussion and
evaluation 128–31; financial challenges
120–1; Marginal Arts Festival (MAF)
123–8, 130–1; methodology 110–11;
multiple strategies 131; Parks & Arts
130; planning 118; research approach
109–11; research location 111–14;
responses to 122–3; summary and
conclusions 131–3; Taubman Museum
of Art 114–17, **114**, 129, 131
real-estate costs 79
reality, reshaping 219
recognition: and peace building 220; of
role of culture 23
*Red Fox/Second Hangin'* 139–41; in
performance **140**
Reddy, P. 66–7
Reeler, D. 200, 202, 204
refugees, Philadelphia 22–3

regional mapping, Building Home project
37–9
regulation, of cultural spaces 86, 93–4
reinvention 132; *see also* re-identification
report writing, Building Home project 48
resources, and social change assessment
203
Richardson, B and J. 139
rights 16
Rio + 20 13
Roadside Theater 8–9; Appalachian
drama cycle 141; Arizona State
University (ASU) 159–60; call and
response 143–4; Choteau, Montana
157–8; collaborative working 148–52;
community cultural development 152–
5; community cultural development
methodology **156**; community
ownership and participation 144–6,
148–52; context and overview 136;
direction of development 142–6;
effects of touring 142; funding
141; guidelines 32; identity and
identification 142–3; inclusivity 145–6;
in New York 139–41; origins 137; in
performance **137**, **140**; performance
spaces 143; practice for change 153–4;
Story Circle methodology 20–1; story
circles 146–53, **148**; summary and
conclusions 160–3; theory of change
153–4; threats 151–2; traditional
stories 137–8
Roanoke 8; arts and cultural organizations
114; arts and culture plan 117–23,
129–30, 132; Arts District 118;
community development 109;
consultation 119–20; discussion and
evaluation 128–31; history 111–14;
Marginal Arts Festival (MAF) 123–8,
130–1; Parks & Arts 130; Public Art
Policy 119; summary and conclusions
131–3; Taubman Museum of Art
114–17, **114**, 129, 131; *see also* re-
identification
Roanoke Arts Commission (RAC)
118–20
Robert Wood Johnson Foundation
(RWJF) 102–4
Roebuck, J. 195
Rohd, M. 29–30, 47
Rolon, R. 70
*Romeo and Juliet* 221
Rosenstein, C. 67–8
Runnel, L. 126–7
Rwanda Healing Project 21

Sala Rosa 84–5
San Francisco Art Workers' Coalition 15
Sananman, A. 72
Saunders, H. 212
Sawyer, K. 184
Schaffer-Bacon, B. 186, 188, 203, 204, 206
Schuster, J.M. 190
segregation, socioeconomic 2
Seifert, S. 56, 71, 187, 204–5
self-determination 24; vs. expert
 prescription 18
self-evaluating organizations 192
self-knowing 104–5
self-reflection 104
Sen, A. 11
Senge, P.M. 203
Serbia *see* DAH Teatar
settings, importance of 189
settlement houses 55, 56
Sharp, C. 137
Sherman, J. 222, 223
Shields, R. 5
Shipyard Project 188
Sidford, H. 71, 73, 142, 149
singularity, problem of 181
site-specificity 170–1
Skeen, M. 130
Smit, J. 93
social capital 12
social change: aims 188; basis of 189–90;
 digital storytelling 105; importance
 of settings 189; practitioners 189; and
 questioning 226; tools for 188
social change assessment: approaches to
 191–2; Art At Work 193–4, 197–8,
 204, 206; capacity limitations 205–7;
 challenges 197–200; concepts of
 change 190; context and overview
 186–7; contextual influences 200–2;
 as continuum 192; costs 206; data
 production 191, 207; democratic
 values 199; evaluation frameworks
 191, 204; experimentation 203;
 key dimensions 188–9; logic-based
 models 202; Louisiana Bucket Brigade
 (LABB) 196–7, 198, 201–2, 203,
 205, 207; methodological challenges
 204–7; norms and assumptions
 202–3; participatory evaluation 199;
 power imbalances 201; problems
 of evaluation 189–92; qualitative
 approaches 191, 204–5; research
 questions 187; and resources 203; role
 of evaluation 192; roles of context and
 place 191; scales 205; self-evaluating

organizations 192; sites of study
 186–7, 192–3; social construction
 199; stakeholder interests 197–200;
 summary and conclusions 207–8;
 Tucson Pima Arts Council 194–5,
 199, 201, 202–3, 204, 205, 206; use of
 metrics 190
social class-rooted theater 145–6
social constructs, understanding space 5
social distancing 2
social equity 4
social imagination 22
Social Impact of the Arts Project (SIAP)
 56, 187, 191–2, 195
social justice 9
social practice 66–7, 73
social relationships, peace building 228
Society for Arts and Technology (SAT)
 88, 91
Sojourn Theatre 29, 47
Sommer, D. 34
South Africa Truth and Reconciliation
 Commission (TRC) 218
*South of the Mountain* 152, 161, **162**
"Southeast by Southeast" project 22–3
space: availability 95; costs 89–90, 95;
 non-neutrality 5; regulation 86, 91–2,
 93–4; subdivision 90
stakeholder interests, social change
 assessment 197–200
Staten Island Arts 65–6
Stefanova, J. 218
Stern, M. 56, 71, 187, 204–5
story, as threatening 179–80
Story Circle methodology 20–1, 32–4,
 46–7
story circles, Roadside Theater 146–53,
 **148**
story corners, Building Home project
 41–2
Stout, R. 114–15
Strom, E. 110
Stuart, A. 125
Suoni Per Il Popolo Festival 84
survival, alternative culture 85–6
Sustainable Communities Regional
 Planning Grant Program 28–9
sustainable development 12–13
Sze, L. 60

Takei, K. 173
Tate, S. 108
Taubman Museum of Art 8, 114–17, **114**,
 129, 131
taxation 117

Tchen, J. 59–60
Tea Party 30, 43, 49
teach-ins 167–8, 170–1
Tebtebba 13
teenagers, role in cultural development 23
*The Aesthetic Dimension* (Marcuse) 3
The Crooked Road 43
The DAH Theatre Institute 215
"The Great Struggle for Cheap Meat" 62
"The Hangzhou Declaration: Placing Culture at the Heart of Sustainable Development Policies" 24–5
*The Intimate Enemy: Loss and Recovery of Self Under Colonialism* (Nandy) 17
*The Joker* 36–7
*The Laramie Project* 73
*The Maps of Forbidden Remembrance* 217
*The New Jim Crow* 73
theater strategies, Building Home project 31–7
Theatre for Social Development project 222
Theatre of Cruelty 172
Theatre of the Oppressed (TO) 34
Theatre Tsvete 221
thematic universe 17
theory of change: community cultural development 153–4; features of 190
theory-practice gap 25
*This Babylonian Confusion* (Brecht/Weil) 216
Thomas, J.C. 202
Thompson, W. 113
tourism: benefits of emergent arts 94; concerns 65; New York City 71
tourism project, New River Valley (NRV), Virginia 43
traditional stories 137–8
*Travelers* 217
tribal communities, working with 201
trust-building: Building Home project 38–40; importance of settings 189
trust, in emotional/intellectual self 175
truth: co-construction 220; and peace building 218; search for 226
Tucson Pima Arts Council (TPAC) 189, 194–5, 199, 201, 202, 204, 205, 206

Ubisoft 78–9
UN Conference on Culture and Sustainability, 2013 24–5
UN Conference on Sustainable Development, 2012 13

underground culture, Quartier des Spectacles, Montreal 88–9
UNESCO portal on Culture for Sustainable Development 12–13
Unicorn Stables Project 126
United Nations Agenda 21 30
United Nations Educational, Scientific, and Cultural Organization (UNESCO) 12; "The Hangzhou Declaration: Placing Culture at the Heart of Sustainable Development Policies" 24–5
United Nations' Universal Declaration of Human Rights 16
United States, tacit cultural policy 16–17
Universal Declaration of Human Rights 161
Urban Bush Women (UBW) 63–5, 166; Summer Leadership Institute 169–70, 171
urban planning, comprehensive approach 56–7
urban renewal 92–3, 112
values, and cultural development 23–4

Vexilloid Project 127
Viken, A. 108

Wali, A. 71
*Walking with 'Trane, Chapter 2* (Zollar) **184**
Wallis, D. 129
Wangh, S. 73
War on Poverty 138–9
Watkins, D. 117
WB Games 82
wealth, polarization 18
Whisnant, D.E. 3
White Star Company 222
Wildavsky, A. 192
Williamson, J. 116
Women in Black-Serbia 217
*Women's Side of War* 217–18
working methods 21–2
Wright, P. 114

Yeh, L. 21
Yount 130
youth agency, digital storytelling 102–4
Yugoslav theatre 214–15

Zelizer, C. 212
Zollar, J.W.J. 63–5; in dialogue 166ff; origin story 172–3